THE MONTREAL MUSEUM OF FINE ARTS GUIDE

The Montreal Museum of Fine Arts would like to thank Quebec's Ministère de la Culture et des Communications and the Conseil des arts de Montréal for their ongoing support. Its gratitude goes also to the Volunteer Association of the Montreal Museum of Fine Arts as well as to all its Friends and the many corporations, foundations and individuals for their contribution.

THE MONTREAL MUSEUM OF FINE ARTS
Management
Nathalie Bondil, *Director*
Paul Lavallée, *Director of Administration*
Danielle Champagne, *Director of Communications*

P.O. Box 3000, Station H
Montreal, Quebec
Canada
H3G 2T9
www.mmfa.qc.ca

Authors

Stéphane Aquin	S.A.	Jean-Pierre Labiau	J.P.L.
Elizabeth P. Benson	E.P.B.	Hélène Lamarche	H.L.
Ken Bohac	K.B.	Robert Little	R.L.
Nathalie Bondil	N.B.	Jenifer Neils	J.N.
Diane Charbonneau	D.C.	Édith-Anne Pageot	E.A.P.
Guy Cogeval	G.C.	Rosalind Pepall	R.P.
Jacques DesRochers	J.D.R.	Hayat Salam-Liebich	H.S.L.
John M. Fossey	J.M.F.	Jenny F. So	J.F.S.
Hilliard T. Goldfarb	H.T.G.	Nelda Swinton	N.S.
George Kellaris	G.K.	Wendy Thomas	W.T.

Graphic design: Associés libres inc.
Pre-press and printing: Transcontinental Impression LithoAcme
Printed in Canada

© The Montreal Museum of Fine Arts, 2007
ISBN: 978-2-89192-313-2
Également publié en français
ISBN: 978-2-89192-312-5

Legal deposit, 2007
Bibliothèque et Archives nationales du Québec
Library and Archives Canada
All rights reserved.

TABLE OF CONTENTS

MESSAGE FROM THE DIRECTOR

For those who work in a museum, for those who visit our galleries or donate works to the institution – for most of us, that is – the collection brings us together, more so than a transient exhibition, and serves as a reflection of ourselves. It reveals who we were – Canada's first art museum, founded nearly 150 years ago by a small group of art lovers who quickly received the support of numerous collectors and donors. It tells the story of what we have become – one of the country's leading museums with a rich and diverse body of works, some 36,000 in number, that has been collected over the years. Finally, it speaks of what we want our future to be, what we aspire to become.

Our collection, a reflection of ourselves but also of others, is unique in Canada, and rare by any standard, in that it is encyclopedic. It is both a museum and an art gallery, containing collections of archeological objects and ancient cultures, the decorative arts and design, but also of painting, sculpture and other graphic arts associated with the fine arts of here and abroad, from the Old Masters to modern art, not to mention contemporary art, so vital to the art of tomorrow.

Dear reader, remember that most of these works of art have been generously donated by art lovers and friends of the Museum. Its fine collection – your fine collection, because it is always open to all, free of charge – has been established in the main from private funds, which remain essential.

On behalf of the Museum's staff, I would like to pay respect to the exemplary actions of collectors who enrich our shared heritage, our legacy, our monument to the future of our society. Thanks to them and, thanks to you, our collection will continue to grow.

Nathalie Bondil
Director, The Montreal Museum of Fine Arts

Robert Longo
Born in Brooklyn in 1953

Joe Test / Russian
2004
Charcoal
100.4 x 125.4 cm
Purchase, The Museum Campaign 1988-1993 Fund
2005.41

Raoul Dufy
Le Havre 1877 – Forcalquier 1953

L'Estaque
1913
Oil on canvas
46.2 x 55.4 cm
Purchase, gift of International Friends of the
Montreal Museum of Fine Arts and The Montreal
Museum of Fine Arts' Volunteer Association Fund
2005.37

Ferdinand Hodler
Bern 1853 – Geneva 1918

Halberdier
1895
Oil on canvas mounted
on plywood
308 x 107.5 cm
Gift of Mr. and Mrs.
Michal Hornstein
2005.175

Marcel Parizeau
Montreal 1898 – Montreal 1945

Coffee Table
About 1937
Rosewood, glass, brass
Produced by G. H. Randall
41 x 11.5 x 84 cm
Gift of Maurice and Giselle D. Corbeil
2006.143.1-2

César Isidore Henry Cros
Narbonne 1840 – Sèvres 1907

Feliciter or *The Scottish Girl*
1882
Painted terracotta
57.1 x 35.5 x 26 cm
Purchase, The Museum Campaign 1988-1993
Fund, the Marguerite and Cecil Buller Fund,
and gifts of Rachel Sachs, Raymond D. LeMoyne,
Guy Cogeval, Jean H. Picard, Betty Reitman,
Mr. and Mrs. Michal Hornstein, Mrs. Neil B.
Ivory, the St. Andrew's Society of Montreal,
Nathalie Bondil, Helgi Soutar and Ian Aitken
2005.36.1-2

Pierre Soulages
Born in Rodez, France, in 1919

Painting, 222 x 157 cm,
August 24, 1979
1979
Oil on canvas
243.84 x 154.94 cm
Anonymous gift
2006.115

Tiziano Vecellio, called Titian
Pieve di Cadore about 1488 – Venice 1576

Saint Jerome in the Wilderness
About 1530
Woodcut, only state
39 x 53.2 cm
Purchase, anonymous fund
2006.49

Jean-Baptiste Roy-Audy
Quebec City 1778 –
Trois-Rivières before 1848

Dr. Charles Paphnuce Anaclet
Boucher
Between 1831 and 1838
Oil on canvas
67 x 56.8 cm
Purchase, The Museum Campaign
1988-1993 Fund
2006.21

Jean-Paul Riopelle
Montreal 1923 –
L'Isle-aux-Grues 2002

Gravity
1956
Oil on canvas
300 x 200 cm
Gift of Yseult Riopelle
2005.134

Germaine Krull
Poznań, Poland, 1897 –
Wetzlar, Germany, 1985
*At the Sporting Club,
Monte Carlo*
Gelatin silver print
23.1 x 14.6 cm
Gift of Sir Neil and
Lady Elizabeth Shaw
2003.441

Jim Dine
Born in Cincinnati in 1935
Twin 6' Hearts
1999
Painted and patinated bronze, artist's proof 7/6
2.06 x 2.72 x 1.58 m
Purchase, gift of International Friends of the Montreal Museum of Fine Arts
2003.30

Jacques-Émile Ruhlmann
Paris 1879 – Paris 1933
Tripod Table
1928
Rosewood veneer over oak, brass
64.5 cm (h.); 50 cm (diam.)
Purchase, Société Générale/
Fimat Fund
2003.90

Pablo Picasso
Málaga 1881 – Mougins 1973
*Head of a Musketeer
(Cardinal Richelieu?)*
1969
Oil on canvas
81 x 64.8 cm
Gift of Stella and Adolf Ullman
2004.135

Jacques Stella
Lyons 1596 – Paris 1657
The Lamentation and Preparation for Burial of Christ
About 1655
Oil on canvas
50.5 x 61.2 cm
Purchase, The Montreal Museum of Fine Arts'
Volunteer Association Fund
2004.198

Hébert-Stevens workshop
Paris, founded in 1924
After a cartoon by Maurice Denis
(1870-1943)
To the War Dead – Pietà
Cartoon: 1920-1922; stained glass:
1924-1925
Polychrome glass, lead
171 x 109.5 x 2.5 cm
Purchase, Société Générale/
Fimat Fund
2006.83

Michael Snow
Born in Toronto in 1929
Four Grey Panels and Four Figures
From the series "Walking Woman"
1963
Oil on canvas
152.5 x 51 cm (each panel)
Purchase, The Montreal Museum of Fine Arts' Volunteer
Association Fund and Horsley and Annie Townsend
Bequest
2005.97.1-4

Alessandro Mendini
Born in Milan in 1931
La Poltrona di Proust
[Proust's Armchair], 1978 (2001)
Painted wood and fabric
Produced by Atelier Mendini
since 1989
106 x 102 x 92.5 cm
Purchase, The Museum Campaign
1988-1993 Fund
2005.88

Claudio Parmiggiani
Born in Lussara, Italy, in 1943
Venere di Montreal
[Venus of Montreal]
1999
Plaster, butterfly
71.5 x 27.5 x 32 cm
Purchase, The Museum
Campaign 1988-1993 Fund
2005.4.1-2

THE MONTREAL MUSEUM OF FINE ARTS

1860 Foundation of the Art Association of Montreal

In 1860, Montreal was the largest city in British North America and the economic centre of Canada. Yet despite its numerous collectors and art lovers, and its vibrant artistic traditions – some of them dating back to the period of French rule – the city had no art school or museum. It was in this context that a group of civic-minded, wealthy Montrealers founded the Art Association of Montreal, the forerunner of the Montreal Museum of Fine Arts. It was dedicated to the dissemination of the fine arts, and its founding president was Bishop Francis Fulford, the first Anglican bishop of Montreal.

1879-1912 The Museum on Phillips Square

The Art Association really took off with a bequest from a merchant named Benaiah Gibb. In 1877, he bequeathed land and a sum of money to build a museum, along with some paintings and sculptures, forming the nucleus of a collection that would become one of the largest in the country. Inaugurated in 1879 under the designation Art Gallery, the new building, which no longer exists, was the first in Canada specifically designed to house an art collection. It included a large exhibition gallery, a smaller gallery for works on paper, a reading room and an embryonic art school. This original building was the work of architect J. W. Hopkins and in 1893 it was enlarged by Andrew T. Taylor. The Art Association held annual exhibitions of works lent by members, and Spring Exhibitions of works by living Canadian artists.

The Art Association of Montreal, Phillips Square
Canadian Illustrated News, vol. XIX, no. 22, May 31, 1879

Classroom in the art school, Phillips Square, at the turn of the century

Left-hand page:

Michal and Renata Hornstein Pavilion
Sherbrooke Street, north side
Architects: Edward and W.S. Maxwell (1912)

Liliane and David M. Stewart Pavilion
Avenue du Musée
Architect: Fred Lebensold (1976)

Jean-Noël Desmarais Pavilion
Sherbrooke Street, south side
Architect: Moshe Safdie (1991)

James Wilson Morrice
The Old Holton House, Montreal
About 1908-1910
The Art Association's new
museum, inaugurated in 1912,
was erected on the site of the
Honourable L. H. Holton's house
on Sherbrooke Street, built in 1856

1912 The Museum on Sherbrooke Street

The growth of the collection made it necessary to build again. This time, the Council of the Art Association chose to move to Sherbrooke Street. The new museum, designed by architects Edward and William S. Maxwell, was sober and imposing with its white marble facade, tall colonnaded portico and monumental staircase. It included spacious exhibition galleries, a lecture hall, a library and studios for the art school. The new museum was inaugurated in December 1912, and over the following year it received fifty thousand visitors. However, the momentum of its development was slowed by the Great War and the economic decline of Montreal that ensued, spelling the end for the golden age of private collections. Some were scattered, while others were donated to the Museum, in whole or in part, by their inheritors.

1912-1939 A Comprehensive Collection

Since the construction of the new building, the Council of the Art Association had wanted to include the applied arts in its collection, along the lines of many American institutions. Entrusted to F. Cleveland Morgan, the decorative arts department opened in 1917, diversifying and enriching the Museum's collection so that by the 1930s, it offered an encyclopedic panorama of arts from every continent and every era. In 1939, through the generosity of the Norton family, a wing designed by the firm of Fetherstonhaught & Durford was added at the back of the building and the decorative art objects were reorganized. The galleries housing these collections were now called the "Museum".

Project drawing of the architects
Edward and W.S. Maxwell, front
elevation, 1910 (press clipping,
The Witness, undated)

WHAT MONTREAL'S NEW ART GALLERY WILL LOOK LIKE.

1939-1976 From Volunteer Association to Institution

The Museum's expansion and the diversification of its collections had an effect on the art school, which started offering courses in design. In 1940, the Art Association hired Arthur Lismer, a famous artist and an enlightened teacher under whose initiative the art school, in conjunction with the Art Centre, became a model for other institutions of its kind. The 1940s in Montreal also saw a new generation of "revolutionary" artists appear, rallying around John Lyman and Paul-Émile Borduas. The confrontations between academics and moderns escalated to the point where, in 1944, the Spring Exhibition had to resort to two separate juries. In 1949, the Museum made way for young artists by dedicating Gallery XII to new painting.

The appointment of a first director in 1947 reflected the changes the institution was undergoing. In 1948, the Art Association replaced the term Art Gallery – traditionally reserved for collections of painting and sculpture – with the Montreal Museum of Fine Arts, in order to better

Art Association of Montreal
The museum by Edward and W.S.
Maxwell (now the Michal and
Renata Hornstein Pavilion)
Entrance hall, 1913
Hall, second floor, about 1913-1914

Art Association of Montreal
Exhibition gallery, 1913

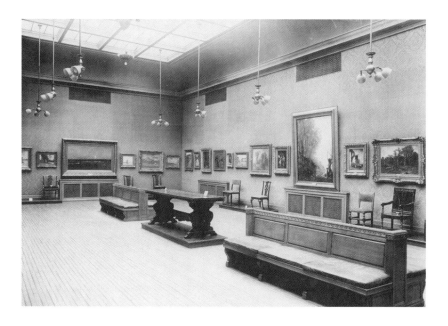

represent its collections, which were becoming increasingly enhanced with the decorative arts. The name became officially bilingual in the 1960s. To mark the institution's hundredth anniversary in 1960, a catalogue of paintings and a guide were published. At the same time, the Museum had a season of highly successful exhibitions aimed at the general public, including *Tutankhamun*, *Rodin* and *Picasso*, and annual attendance exceeded three hundred thousand visitors. However, the Museum suffered a blow when around fifty canvases were stolen in 1972. They have never been recovered.

Since its inception, the Museum had no other sources of funding but the contributions of its members. In the 1950s, it started receiving grants from the City of Montreal and the Canada Council. As a result of special legislation, the Government of Quebec granted the Museum a significant annual operating subsidy in 1972. Other public money, provincial and federal, permitted a new expansion to be built, a project further funded by private donations, notably from the Maxwell Cummings family. From 1973 to 1976, during the construction of a new pavilion on Avenue du Musée, designed by architect Fred Lebensold, the Museum remained closed to the public, but it began circulating travelling exhibitions across the country, bringing its collections to public attention.

1976-2003 Expansion and International Renown

When the Museum reopened in 1976, there were two exhibitions that showed equal respect for works from the past and the present: *Master Paintings of the Hermitage* and *Forum 76*, the latter representing contemporary artists. The following year, the art school closed down, five years shy of its centenary, and "visual arts" education was henceforth provided by various public teaching establishments.

The 1980s were a turning point in the institution's history. In 1981, the exhibition *Tintin's Imaginary Museum* drew a new audience, and in 1984, the *William Bouguereau* exhibition was organized in co-operation with the Petit Palais in Paris, a first step towards gaining an international reputation. A number of others followed: *Pablo Picasso: Meeting in Montreal* (1985), *Leonardo da Vinci: Engineer and Architect* (1987), *The 1920s: Age of the Metropolis* (1991) and *Lost Paradise: Symbolist Europe* (1995). The Museum also mounted major retrospectives of Canadian artists, including *Morrice* (1986), *Borduas* (1988), *Riopelle* (1991 and 2002), *Ozias Leduc* (1995) and *Françoise Sullivan* (2003).

The Riopelle retrospective of 1991 inaugurated a new building, the Jean-Noël Desmarais pavilion, on the south side of Sherbrooke. This large-scale expansion was made possible through the support of the governments, the business community and many private benefactors, among

Fred Lebensold's 1973-1976 extension, Avenue du Musée (now the Liliane and David M. Stewart Pavilion) View of second-floor galleries

The sculpture garden, Avenue du Musée, 1981, with a work by Antoine Poncet, Blancsœur (about 1968)

The 1976 extension, Avenue du Musée

them the family of Paul G. Desmarais. The architect was the world-renowned Moshe Safdie and the design reflects the Museum's concern for accessibility: the entrance is at street level and is transparent and filled with light. An underground gallery housing part of the permanent collection links the north and south buildings. The Museum reinstalled its collections and dispersed its activities on either side of Sherbrooke Street. It thus doubled its exhibition space and attracted over five hundred thousand visitors annually.

Today, the Museum organizes innovative and ambitious exhibitions that also circulate abroad: *Cosmos: From Romanticism to Avant-garde* (1999) travelled to Barcelona and Venice; *The Triumph of the Baroque* (2000) to Venice, Washington and Marseilles; *Hitchcock and Art* (2001) to Paris; *Picasso Érotique* (2001) to Paris and Barcelona; *Richelieu: Art and Power* (2002) to Cologne; *Vuillard: Post-Impressionist Master* (2003) to Washington, Paris and London.

With the creation of the Museum Foundation in 1994, and the International Friends of the Montreal Museum of Fine Arts in 1998, the Museum diversified its sources of private funding. At the beginning of 2002, following a highly fruitful fundraising campaign, the Museum announced a considerable increase in its acquisition fund and the creation of an exhibition fund (financed through the MMFA and the Paul G. Desmarais Fund). These increased resources will enable the institution to pursue its mission and expand its reputation. H.L.

The Jean-Noël Desmarais pavilion, by Moshe Safdie Entrance at night, 1991

A round window giving on to the 1912 building

Jean-Noël Desmarais Pavilion Main entrance hall, 1991

Interior with a work by Barry Flanagan, *Nijinski Hare* (1889-1890, priv. coll.)

A TRIBUTE TO DONORS

The three main pavilions of the Montreal Museum of Fine Arts were named in honour of three eminent patrons: the family of Paul G. Desmarais, Michal and Renata Hornstein, and Liliane and David M. Stewart. The entrance hall to the 1912 building is named after Benaiah Gibb, the Museum's first patron. This form of official recognition serves as a reminder that our Museum, the oldest and one of the largest in Canada, would not exist were it not for the indefatigable generosity of collectors and benefactors.

In 1892, John W. Tempest bequeathed sixty oil paintings and watercolours, along with a trust fund for art acquisitions. Until 1953, this fund remained the Museum's main source of income for the purchase of European paintings.[1] In 1909, gifts and the bequest from William John and Agnes Learmont added one hundred thirty-four paintings, a drawing by Rembrandt, and European and Asian ceramics to the collection. Rich in paintings of the Hague and Barbizon Schools, the Learmont collection represents "modern" taste in Montreal at the time. In 1927, a collection of more than three hundred items, including one hundred fifty paintings, was donated to the Museum by the heirs of Lord Strathcona.[2]

James Wilson Morrice
The Pond, West Indies (detail)
About 1921
Oil on canvas
Gift of the Louise and Bernard Lamarre family

1. p. 71, 92, 94, 95, 103, 121, 125, 131, 139, 153, 164, 165, 167, 177, 207

2. p. 128, 154, 155, 157

Florent Crabeels
Environs of Antwerp, Sunday Afternoon
About 1860
Oil on canvas
Benaiah Gibb Bequest

Jean-Paul Riopelle
Vertigo
1962
Oil on canvas
Gift of Power Corporation of Canada

Entrance to the Museum of
Decorative Arts, 1997

Although the parcelling out of estates often resulted in
the breaking up and dispersal of major collections, some
heirs turned to the Museum as a means of preserving
segments of those that Montreal was famous for at the
close of the nineteenth century. This is true of the Sir
George Drummond family,[3] R. B. Angus' daughters –
Mrs. W. W. Chipman, Mrs. Charles Meredith, Mrs. Charles
D. Martin and Mrs. R. Paterson[4] – Adaline Van Horne,[5]
daughter of Sir William Van Horne, and Olive Hosmer,[6]
daughter of Charles Hosmer. Related to the Hosmer family
were the Vaughan[7] and Pillow families.

Following the precedent set by John W. Tempest, many
benefactors designated funds for acquisitions of artworks.
Two of the largest were from William Gilman Cheney[8] in
1935, and Horsley and Annie Townsend[9] in 1955, enabling
the Museum to fill gaps in the collection and to set out in
new directions. Other notable donations of this type came
from David Y. Hodgson[10] and the Ivory[11] and Cummings[12]
families.

The Canadian collection grew slowly at first, through
individual gifts. The Museum began developing it in 1925
following a major donation of paintings by James Wilson
Morrice from the family of the artist. In 1929, Dr. Francis
John Shepherd,[13] former chairman of the board of the Art
Association, set up a fund for buying Canadian art. There
followed an acquisition fund established by Robert
Lindsay[14] in 1932, and gifts from A. Sidney Dawes[15] and
various members of the Morrice family. The extremely
generous support of the latter, initiated by David Morrice,
continued down the generations through his grandchildren
F. Eleanore (1901-1981) and David R. (1903-1978), who
bequeathed a rich collection of decorative art, sculpture

3. p. 152, 160, 166

4. p. 119, 208, 201, 286

5. p. 105, 117, 135, 136, 137, 147, 161

6. p. 100, 111, 278

7. p. 173, 226, 231

8. p. 29, 97, 115, 199, 207, 221, 266, 269

9. p. 27, 29, 33, 44, 46, 55, 56, 57, 59,
60, 66, 67, 69, 76, 87, 97, 98, 107,
110, 112, 113, 114, 115, 126, 133,
141, 150, 151, 173, 172, 179, 182,
183, 185, 191, 192, 194, 206, 208,
218, 220, 229, 230, 232, 233, 240,
246, 247, 248, 250, 253, 256, 258,
260, 261, 262, 263, 264, 270, 274,
289, 311

10. p. 26, 86, 133

11. p. 170, 292, 293

12. p. 173, 180

13. p. 198, 208, 216

14. p. 215, 225

15. p. 212, 216, 217

and Canadian painting.[16]

More recent funds – often oriented towards contemporary art – include donations from Mr. and Mrs. Maurice Corbeil[17] and the Succession J.A. DeSève,[18] as well as those from Saidye and Samuel Bronfman and Louise L. Lamarre, dedicated to the acquisition of artworks by young Canadian artists. Furthermore, the exceptional contribution of Max Stern to the Museum's collection[19] and to the dissemination of contemporary Canadian art throughout the country is manifested in the sculpture garden around the 1912 building, thanks to the Max Stern bequest.

In 1917, the Museum inaugurated a decorative arts department. With the impetus of F. Cleveland Morgan,[20] a connoisseur interested in all forms of art who became volunteer curator of the decorative arts from 1917 until his death in 1962, the Museum's collection became encyclopedic in scope. Apart from the hundreds of items offered by Morgan himself, there were donations from a new generation of collectors with more eclectic tastes: among them were Harry A. Norton[21] (Roman glass and Coptic textiles), Miss Mabel Molson[22] (traditional Quebecois art), David W. Parker[23] (textiles), Lucile Vaughan Pillow (eighteenth-century English porcelain)[24] and Harriet J. MacDonnell (who made a bequest for the purchase of First Nations art). Other gifts – like the three thousand Japanese incense boxes from Joseph-Arthur Simard,[25] and "primitive" art from Ernest Gagnon,[26] a Jesuit father – opened the Museum's horizons to Asia and Africa. More recently, the Honourable Serge Joyal[27] has considerably enriched the collection with silver and goldware, as well as an Egyptian sarcophagus dating from the seventh or eighth century B.C.

All of these gifts, which have constantly enlarged the

16. p. 197, 255, 290, 302

17. p. 219, 241

18. p. 175, 194, 297

19. p. 99, 129, 149, 176

20. p. 28, 31, 39, 48, 49, 50, 51, 53, 61, 63, 64, 65, 66, 77

21. p. 32, 36, 37, 40, 41, 44

22. p. 31, 294

23. p. 42, 43

24. p. 296

25. p. 72

26. p. 83

27. p. 30, 291, 319, 318

Gallery in the Museum of Decorative Arts designed by Frank Gehry, 1997

Ferdinand Hodler
Study for the first figure from the right of "View into Infinity"
1913
Graphite on paper
Gift of Michal and Renata Hornstein

breadth of the Museum's collections, culminated in 2000 with the addition of the modern design collection amassed by Liliane and David M. Stewart, which has long been identified with the Montreal Museum of Decorative Arts and was exhibited in the Jean-Noël Desmarais Pavilion from 1997 to 2000. In giving some five thousand objects[28] to the Museum, Mrs. Liliane Stewart carried through the work begun by F. Cleveland Morgan eighty years earlier. Together, these two collections tell the story of decorative art and design, from ancient times to the present.

The prints and drawings department, also founded in 1917, developed considerably in the 1960s with the support of David Y. Hodgson, Neil Ivory and Mrs. Gerald Bronfman. Its growth was furthered by, among others, Michal and Renata Hornstein, who gave the Museum one of the world's largest collections of drawings by the Swiss artist Ferdinand Hodler (1853-1918). However, this accounts for only a small part of what the Hornsteins[29] have donated in the way of exceptional artworks, especially old masters, and of generous financial support.

Paul G. Desmarais[30] is another important benefactor upholding his family's philanthropic tradition. In 1991, he made an exceptional contribution to the construction of the new pavilion, named after his father, Jean-Noël Desmarais, founder of Laurentian University in Sudbury, Ontario.

For the past twenty years, the Museum has benefited from the wholehearted support and expertise of Bernard Lamarre, Chairman of the Board from 1982 to 1991 and again from 1997. Knowledgeable collectors, Mr. Lamarre and his wife Louise shared their passion for art by donating one of Montreal painter James Wilson Morrice's finest canvases, *The Pond, West Indies* (ill. p. 18).

This generosity is a true testament to the strong commitment and unfailing support the Montreal Museum of Fine Arts has always enjoyed. There is unfortunately not enough space here to cite all the Museum's benefactors. Even so, we would like to take this opportunity to express our deepest appreciation for their support, and that of our anonymous donors, Friends of the Museum and devoted volunteers.

Thank you everyone.

28. p. 300, 303, 310, 312, 314, 316, 320, 326, 322, 323, 324, 328, 329, 330, 331, 332, 333, 335, 339

29. p. 113, 116, 118, 120, 123, 127, 132, 122, 148, 163

30. p. 239

PATRONS

Their exemplary generosity has fostered the development of
The Montreal Museum of Fine Arts.

1860-1912

R. B. Angus

Sir George A. Drummond,
K.C.M.G., C.V.O., and Lady
Drummond

Benaiah Gibb

William John and Agnes Learmont

James Ross

Dr. Francis J. Shepherd

Donald Alexander Smith, 1st Baron
Strathcona and Mount Royal

John W. Tempest

Sir William Van Horne, K.C.M.G.

1912-1939

A. Sidney Dawes

Sir H. Vincent Meredith, Bart.,
and Lady Meredith

Mabel Molson

F. Cleveland Morgan, M.A.,
D.C.L., LL.D.

Harry A. Norton

Mrs. R. MacD. Paterson

1939-1976

Murray G. Ballantyne

William Gilman Cheney

Sir Mortimer B. Davis and
Lady Davis

Huntly R. Drummond

Elwood B. and Olive Hosmer

Dr. Charles F. Martin and
Margaret Martin

The J.W. McConnell Family
Foundation

The Hon. Hartland de M. Molson,
O.C., O.B.E.

David R. and F. Eleanore Morrice

David W. Parker

Neil and Ivan E. Phillips

Lucile Pillow

Joseph-Arthur Simard

Horsley and Annie Townsend

Adaline Van Horne

1976-1991

Volunteer Association of the
Montreal Museum of Fine Arts

BCE Inc.

Samuel and Saidye Bronfman
Family Foundation

Maurice and Andrée Corbeil

Cummings Family

Nathan Cummings Foundation

Succession J.A. DeSève

Paul G. Desmarais, P.C., C.C.,
and Jacqueline Desmarais, C.M.

Michal Hornstein, O.C., O.Q.,
and Renata Hornstein

Paul Ivanier, C.M., Ph.D., and
Lily Ivanier

Dr. Paul Mailhot and Marielle
L. Mailhot

Dr. Ronnie McCall and
Dr. Frances McCall

Jacqueline Picasso

Max Stern, Ph.D., and Iris Stern

Ira Young

1991-

CIBC

Fondation J. Armand Bombardier

Nahum Gelber and Dr. Sheila Gelber

National Bank of Canada

Imperial Tobacco Group PLC

Mr. and Mrs. Neil B. Ivory

The Hon. Serge Joyal, P.C.,
O.C., LL.M.

The Macdonald Stewart Foundation

The Molson Foundation

Royal Bank of Canada

Sara Lee Corporation

Shire Biochem Inc.

Liliane M. Stewart, CStJ, O.Q.,
C.D., U.F.F., and David M. Stewart,
O.C., CStJ

ANCIENT CULTURES

Amlach
(Ancient Iran)

Female Steatopygous Figure

About 1000 B.C.

Terra cotta

53 × 20.3 × 20.2 cm

Purchase, gift of David Y. Hodgson
1963.Ea.1

■ This is one of a great many similar statuettes manufactured during the late second and early first millennia B.C. in the high plains and rugged mountains of northwestern Iran, just south of the Caspian Sea. It represents a nude woman, standing with feet apart and her short, fleshy arms extended in an age-old gesture of adoration and worship. The body is cylindrical, the neck long, the torso narrow. The legs, thick and wide, are positioned low on the body in a way that emphasizes the pubic area and the curvature of the hips. It is this feature that gives rise to the term steatopygous, from the Greek roots *steat-*, fat, and *pyge*, buttocks. The head is small in relation to the body, and the features show little detail other than a narrow nose and protruding eyes. The hair is tied back under a two-tiered tiara trimmed with a string of beads.

Such highly stylized terra-cotta statuettes of nude women were common in the ancient Near East. Most of them have been found in burial sites, particularly in graves of men. It is likely that the exaggerated sexual characteristics were taken as a powerful metaphor for life and rebirth, and that the presence of the statuettes was intended to magically facilitate the resurrection of the tomb's occupant. K.B.

Assyria, Nimrud

Genie before the Sacred Tree

877 B.C.
Bas relief, alabaster
128.3 × 129.9 cm
Purchase, Horsley and Annie Townsend Bequest
1964.Ea.3

■ This large wall panel was carved in the ancient kingdom of Assyria (northern Iraq) for the palace of King Ashurnasirpal II (883-859 B.C.) at Kalhu (modern Nimrud). An imposing muscle-bound genie with an eagle's wings and head stands at the right, dressed in richly embroidered, fringed garments that signal his semi-divine status. He stands before a stylized Sacred Tree. The right arm is raised in a gesture of ritual magic, blessing or anointing that is connected with the cone-like amulet in his right hand, probably the flower from a male date-palm tree. The metal bucket in the left hand is traditionally associated with magic rituals.

Images of genies are frequent on the wall panels at Nimrud. Strategically positioned alongside important doorways, they guarded the palace and its inhabitants against the intrusion of malevolent demons, disease and misfortune. The inclusion of the Sacred Tree in these scenes was reserved for the palace's innermost rooms, including the throne room, where it provided a visual metaphor for the king as the divinely appointed caretaker of the land and its people. The inscription in wedge-shaped cuneiform at the top of the relief records the king's many titles and achievements. K.B.

Egypt
12th Dynasty (1991-1786 B.C.),
Middle Kingdom (2040-1786 B.C.)

Statue of a Man

Wood, traces of polychrome
91 × 46 × 30 cm (with base)

Gift of F. Cleveland Morgan
1951.B.1

■ The pose of this young man standing tall, facing forward, the left foot advanced, is in keeping with ancient Egyptian convention. The broadness of the shoulders and the long length of the arms in proportion to the waist give him a lanky, almost spindly appearance. The only indication of musculature is on the torso. The round face is dominated by the wide-open eyes and full-lipped mouth. The man is wearing a high-waisted kilt and the short, rounded wig of Egyptian officials. Whatever the hands may have held is no longer extant; perhaps the right held a spear or carrying pole. Traces of polychrome suggest the statue would have been painted in antiquity.

Sizeable, good quality wood was difficult to find in the Egyptian desert, making this untypically large piece a rarity. It is also among the earliest of its type; the large eyes and slight build associate it with a group of statues introduced during the Late Old Kingdom, Egypt's great age of pyramid building. It was never intended to be seen; instead, it would have been placed in the tomb of an official. The idealized, youthful – even childlike – character is typical of such funerary sculpture, referring perhaps to the deceased's hope for rebirth and eternal youth. K.B.

Egypt, Akhmim region
26th Dynasty Saite (664-525 B.C.)
Coffin of Isis-Weret
Carved and painted plaster-coated wood
40 × 53 × 180 cm
Gift of the Honourable Serge Joyal, P.C., O.C.
1999.36

■ In ancient Egypt, preserving the body for survival in the afterlife involved elaborate methods of mummification and enshrouding. This richly decorated coffin, or sarcophagus, is that of Isis-Weret, a musician devoted to the cult of the fertility god Min. The cover portrays the goddess Nut with her wings unfurled, surrounded by various divinities and guardians of the underworld. Mother of the sun and personification of the celestial vault, Nut was often represented on sarcophagus lids, for the regeneration of the dead depended on her.

This sarcophagus is from the region of Akhmim in Upper Egypt, which had a temple sacred to Min. The inscription reveals not only the name of the deceased, but also her parents' names: her father was Neb-mose, a priest of the temple, and her mother was Mut-hotep. Mother and daughter both played the sistrum, a type of rattle that had the power to ward off evil spirits.

The history of Egypt was long that of the Nile Valley and its inhabitants. But over the centuries, contact with neighbouring empires increased until Egypt was absorbed by the most powerful among them: the Persians under Cambyses, the Greeks under Alexander and, finally, the Romans under Caesar. Isis-Weret would have lived during the relatively prosperous 26th Dynasty, the so-called Saite period, which was ancient Egypt's last era of total independence. H.L.

Egypt

Persian period (525-332 B.C.), 30th Dynasty (378-341 B.C.)

Nektanebo II and Osiris

359-341 B.C.
Bas relief, granite
104.1 × 137.2 × 61 cm

Purchase, Horsley and Annie Townsend Bequest and William Gilman Cheney Bequest
1964.B.1

■ This bas-relief fragment is from a wall that would have decorated the interior of the temple devoted to the Egyptian cat goddess Bastet at her holy city Bubastis, in the eastern delta of the Nile. The relief portrays King Nektanebo II (reigned 360 to 343 B.C.), the last native Egyptian to rule his land before being driven out by the Persians. Like all the kings of Egypt, Nektanebo fulfilled the varied roles of chief military official, head of the government and high priest. As high priest, he acted as intercessor between gods and men, presiding over cult offerings and sacrifices to the gods in order to ensure their favour upon those he ruled.

The scene on the relief typically depicts such an interaction between king and deity. Wearing traditional regal garb – the short kilt known as a *shendyet* and the *afnet* head-dress of the pharaoh – Nektanebo stands at the centre, between two gods, his hands raised in a gesture of offering. No suitable offering can be seen, however, which suggests that the relief may be unfinished. The fine carving technique shows the sleek refinement of over three thousand years' experience of stone craftsmanship. K.B.

■ The earliest figure-decoration on Greek vases was created essentially by silhouette and dark outline painting over the natural red clay background. About 700 B.C. came the addition of internal details to the silhouettes by means of incised lines and a small range of overlaid colours. This "black-figure" style remained in vogue until about 500 B.C., when two fresh developments occurred. One involved painting the black figures onto a white ground rather than the natural clay-coloured ground. An example is this lekythos, whose painter may in fact have had much to do with the growth of the white-ground style. The other development was the reversal of colours, setting red figures against a black ground and using black for the internal details, as seen in this kylix.

Lekythoi were used to hold perfumed oil. Since athletes would anoint themselves with such oil, they were an appropriate subject to be painted on this vase shape, though during the fifth century B.C., it was increasingly reserved for burial with the dead, and funerary scenes became the standard decoration. Kylikes were drinking cups, and so scenes involving Dionysos, the god of wine, were appropriate decoration for them.

Because the real names of vase painters are only occasionally known, it is conventional to devise names for them. These may refer to a site where their work has been found, hence Ancona Painter, or a museum where an important work of theirs is located, hence Edinburgh Painter. J.M.F.

Greece, Attica
Edinburgh Painter, active about 500 B.C.
Lekythos with black figures on white ground

Athletes
Pottery, painted and incised decoration
27.5 cm (h.); 10 cm (diam.)
Purchase, gift of Miss Mabel Molson
1925.Cb.5

Greece, Attica
Ancona Painter, active about 465 B.C.
Kylix, red-figure decoration

Dionysos, Mainads and Satyrs;
Courting Couple (interior decoration)
Pottery, painted decoration
13.6 cm (h.); 31.8 cm (diam.)
Purchase, gift of F. Cleveland Morgan
1959.Cb.1

Mediterranean Region (Greece)	Roman Empire, Germany (Cologne?)	Probably Jerusalem
Aryballos	**Pitcher with Trefoil Mouth**	**Flask**
Late 6th-5th c. B.C. Core-formed glass, combed decoration 6.4 cm (h.); 5 cm (diam.)	About 200 A.D. Blown glass, applied snake-thread decoration 13.7 cm (h.); 7.7 cm (diam.)	6th-7th A.D. Mould-blown glass 15.5 × 10.5 × 7.5 cm
Gift of Harry A. Norton 1953.Dg.6	Gift of Harry A. Norton 1953.Dg.86	Gift of Harry A. Norton 1953.Dg.61

■ Glass – a mixture of sand, soda and lime – was invented in ancient Mesopotamia in the third millennium B.C., but the industry only began to flourish in 18th-dynasty Egypt (1570-1293 B.C.). Glass remained a luxury item until the first century B.C., when the discovery of the technique of glass-blowing allowed faster and cheaper production of entire sets of tableware. Throughout the Roman empire, glass vessels were commonplace, new decorative techniques were invented, and occasionally pieces were even signed by the artists.

Each of these three glass vessels illustrates a different technique of glass-making. The earliest – a small, plump cosmetic container called an aryballos – is core-formed, meaning decorative threads of molten glass of contrasting colours were trailed onto a sand core built up over a metal rod. During most of the last three-quarters of the first millennium B.C., jars of this particular shape, also made in clay, were used almost exclusively to store unguents or perfumed oils. The translucent Roman pitcher was formed by inflating a molten glass bubble with a blowpipe. Abstract decoration was then applied to the surface in the form of "snake threads" of coloured glass. The latest vessel, a Christian pilgrim flask, was made by blowing molten glass into a mould. The flask's decorated panels bear lozenges and the Cross of Golgotha set atop three steps. Sold to pilgrims to Jerusalem, these flasks probably contained oil and served as souvenirs of the Holy City. J.N./J.M.F

Italy, Rome

Portrait of Cnaius Domitius Corbulo or of Caius Cassius Longinus

Late 1st c. A.D.
Marble
27.5 × 18 × 23 cm (without base)
Purchase, Special Replacement Fund
1974.55

Portrait of Emperor Alexander Severus (222-235 A.D.)

2nd quarter of 3rd c. A.D.
Marble
28 × 12 × 12 cm (without base)
Purchase, Horsley and Annie Townsend Bequest
1968.1600

■ Portraiture represents one of the principal achievements of Roman art. The penchant for realistic representation of people found expression on coins, in funerary portraits painted on wooden panels and, above all, in sculpture in the round. So interested were the Romans in the sculpted portrait that, while the bodies of life-size statues might be mass-produced, provision would be made for inserting an individually carved portrait head onto the shoulders. From the first century B.C. through the third century A.D., subjects of portraits made in stone (generally marble) were prominent political and military figures, with members of the imperial family dominating from the late first century B.C. The realism of the portraits died out somewhat in the fourth and fifth centuries A.D. with the introduction of frontality and the resulting flatness of faces.

The Museum's collection includes two fine Roman portrait busts: a first-century A.D. head, possibly of Corbulo (d. 66 A.D.), who held several high offices under the emperors Claudius and Nero, or a copy of an earlier portrait of Cassius (d. 42 B.C.), one of the assassins of Julius Caesar; and a third-century portrait of the emperor Alexander Severus (reigned 222-235 A.D.) as an adolescent.

These portraits are from two periods when short-cropped hair and clean-shaven faces were the fashion for men. In the intervening second century, longer hair and beards, introduced by the emperor Hadrian, were the norm. J.M.F.

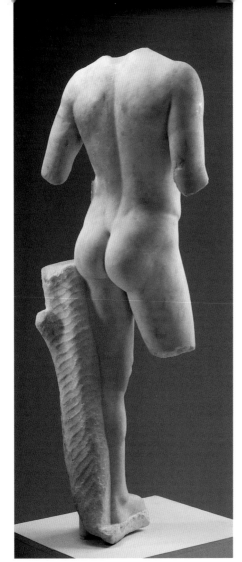

Italy, Rome

Statue of Chigi Apollo

2nd quarter of 2nd century A.D.
Marble of Paros
136 × 56 × 35.5 cm

Purchase, The Museum Campaign 1988-1993 Fund,
The Montreal Museum of Fine Arts' Volunteer
Association Fund and anonymous gift

2003.44.1-5

■ This hitherto unpublished piece now brings to five the number of works of this type formerly known as the "Centecello Adonis" but recently identified rather as an Apollo and named after the Chigi Palace collection to which one of the others formerly belonged. Of the other four, the Museum's statue is closest to that at the Ashmolean in Oxford, where the identification with Apollo is made clear by the arrow held in the right hand. On the Montreal Museum of Fine Arts' piece, a small portion of the lower curve of a bow is preserved against the tree trunk support, again indicating that it represents Apollo. Of the remaining three examples, the two in Rome (Vatican and National Museum) do not hold attributes at all, and the one in the Hermitage is depicted rather as an athlete (discus thrower).

This statue has two noticeable features. One is the high quality of the marble, from the Aegean island of Paros, and one of the most sought after and most expensive marbles in antiquity. Its use for this piece suggests a very important commission. The second feature is the striking quality of the carving itself and the thoroughly natural modelling of the body. Produced a little before the middle of the second century A.D., this is a Roman work derived from a Greek original of the early fourth century B.C. The Greek piece was probably carved by a follower of Polykleitos, a leading sculptor of the later Classical period; it may originally have been inspired by a late Archaic statue in the Severe style. J.M.F.

Persia
Seljuq period (1038-1194)

Bowl

Early 13th c.
Pottery, overglaze painted enamel colour decoration (Minai ware)
8.5 cm (h.); 21 cm (diam.)

Gift of Harry A. Norton
1934.Ea.4

■ Of all the techniques introduced by the prolific potters of the Seljuq period, in what was the heyday of Islamic ceramics, the most spectacular is the highly prized Minai, which means "enamelled" in Arabic; in Iran, the technique is called *haft rang*, or "seven coloured". To obtain the desired polychrome effects and detail needed for figural representation, the twelfth-century potters had to fire these fine wares at least twice: first at a high temperature for the underglaze colours, and one or more times again at a lower temperature to fix the less stable pigments added over the glaze for decoration. No effort or expense was spared in this delicate and risky process, and these exquisitely executed Minai wares, still considered to represent the height of sophistication, continue to inspire skilled imitators.

Much influenced by the prestigious art of miniature painting, the iconographic themes of Minai wares are taken from court scenes – enthroned rulers, hunters, riders, musicians, conversing couples – and epic tales illustrated in books. This bowl is decorated with imagery related to a princely cycle: an enthroned figure flanked by two attendants on one side and a rider on the other, with symmetrically placed harpies above and griffins below the group of figures. The quality, technique and decorative vocabulary of this bowl make it a fine example of the prolific production of the Seljuq kilns. H.S.L.

Persia
Ilkhanid period (1256-1353)

Lajvardina Ewer with Rooster's Head

About 1300
Earthenware, painted enamel colour and gilt decoration over blue glaze *(lajvardina)*
30.2 cm (h.); 16.2 cm (diam.)
Gift of Harry A. Norton
1934.Ea.6

Lajvardina Bowl

About 1300
Earthenware, painted enamel colour and gilt decoration over blue glaze *(lajvardina)*
10 cm (h.); 21.8 cm (diam.)
Gift of Harry A. Norton
1934.Ea.7

■ The Mongol invasion of 1220 A.D. devastated the Near East and destroyed many of the renowned centres of ceramic production. Artists, whose lives were often spared, were resettled in Central Asia to serve the Mongol overlords. Patrons for luxury goods in Persia became fewer and were mostly interested in miniature paintings, an art form that flourished with the arrival of the invaders. However, under the Ilkhanid branch of the Mongols (1256-1353), a revival of the arts and fine ceramics came about.

This ewer and bowl represent the most innovative and luxurious category of Mongol production, known as *lajvardina*. The name derives from the Persian word *lajvard*, meaning lapis lazuli, and refers to the deep blue of the glaze. Over this glaze, decoration was applied in a range of colours limited to red and white enamel and gold leaf, which was used for the main motifs, like the plants and birds seen on these two vessels.

Distinctive colours, shapes, motifs and execution make these fine blue wares of late thirteenth- to early fourteenth-century western Iran easy to date because of a well-known treatise on ceramics written in 1301 by the potter Abu al-Qasim, who said that in his day, *lajvardina* had replaced Minai wares as luxury items. H.S.L.

Syria
Ayyubid period (1176-1250)

Bowl

Mid-13th c.
Engraved brass, originally
inlaid with silver
23.5 cm (h.); 52 cm (diam.)

Gift of F. Cleveland Morgan
1917.Ea.1

■ This large, hemispherical yellow-brass bowl was the first object to enter the Museum's Islamic collection in 1917 and remains today its single most important piece. According to the decorative inscription it bears, it was made for al-Nasir Salah al-Din Yusuf, Sultan of Aleppo (1236-1250) and Damascus (1250-1260), and the great-grandson of Saladin, the founder of the Ayyubid dynasty. The golden age of Islamic metalwork was during the Ayyubid period.

Originally inlaid with silver and other precious metals, this bowl is decorated on the inside by a meandering vegetal scroll and on the outside with inscriptions and an extensive iconography organized in three registers. In the top register, a calligraphic band identifies the patron, and representations of dancers and musicians reflect the cultural life at court. The middle register depicts courtly scenes – an enthronement, a princely feast and entertainment – and other activities, including the filtering of wine around a vessel akin to this bowl. The bottom register contains a script decoration with wishes to the recipient, in addition to representations of the planets and their attributes, testifying to the period's interest in astronomy and astrology. H.S.L.

Syria, Aleppo or Damascus
Mamluk period (1250-1517)

Mosque Lamp

Mid-14th c.
Blue glass, polychrome enamel and gilt
decoration
26.7 cm (h.); 17.8 cm (diam.)
Gift of Harry A. Norton
1934.Dg.5

Mosque Lamp

Mid-14th c.
Clear, yellowish glass, enamel and gilt
decoration
35.5 cm (h.); 24 cm (diam.)
Gift of Mrs. W. Durie McLennan
1960.Dg.1

■ Mosques, religious schools and charitable foundations in the Middle East were lit with great numbers of glass lamps. In the thirteenth and fourteenth centuries, mosque lamps with coloured enamel and gilt decoration, like those illustrated here, were especially popular. The ruling Mamluk aristocracy, with its seat in Cairo, ordered large numbers of them from Syrian workshops in Aleppo and Damascus to supply an ever-expanding building programme of sacred places.

Both these examples show the traditional profile of a bulbous body with tall, flaring neck. Handles have been applied for attaching chains so the lamps could be suspended. At least three handles are necessary for stability, but sometimes there are more. The yellowish lamp, decorated with abstract and plant motifs, is of clear glass, which is quite common for these lamps. The dark blue glass of the other lamp is much rarer. Its decoration consists solely of inscriptions in thuluth script. The Islamic religion, intimately bound to its sacred writings, spawned a highly literate culture, and inscriptions that serve as decoration as well as sources of spiritual enlightenment are ever present on Islamic artefacts. Here, the band on the neck displays the beginning of the customary Koranic verse about light: "God is the Light of the Heavens and of the Earth . . ." (24:35), which often figures on mosque lamps. H.S.L.

Turkey, Iznik
Ottoman period (1281-1923)

Plate

About 1575
Earthenware, polychrome underglaze decoration
6.8 cm (h.); 33 cm (diam.)

Gift of Harry A. Norton
1939.Dp.19

■ This plate exemplifies the polychrome wares that made the kilns of Iznik world famous. The techniques and styles developed during the age of Suleyman the Magnificent (1521-1566) were to have a long-lasting impact on Islamic and Western ceramics.

The high silica content of the Iznik clay ensured an intense vitrification of the enamel and a brilliance of colour admired by the Ottoman court and sought after in Europe. Tableware for the court and tiles for mosques and imperial buildings was in such high demand that an enormous body of work exists today for the study of the stylistic evolution of techniques, which falls into three main periods: from about 1450 to the 1520s, a blue-and-white period heavily influenced by Chinese porcelain; from the 1520s to 1557, the time of the "Damascus style", where the colour scheme was enriched with the addition of turquoise and, in the 1540s, sage green and purple; and from 1557 to 1700, when the "Rhodes style" predominated, characterized by a raised tomato-red colour.

The colour scheme of this plate and its floral decoration of tulips, rose blossoms and buds, bluebells and leaves arranged in a balanced composition within a border of stylized Chinese-inspired waves are typical of the third Iznik type.

In the eighteenth century, when imperial patronage fell off and mass production was instituted, Iznik pottery went into decline. H.S.L.

Persia
Safavid period (1502-1722)

Garment Fragment

About 1600
Double cloth, silk with silver thread
15.8 × 14.5 cm
Purchase, D. W. Parker Fund
1950.51.Dt.2a

■ Textiles form a valuable part of the Museum's Islamic art collection. They were highly valued in the Islamic world, where the decorative arts had great symbolic and social significance. This garment fragment is one of some sixty in the Museum, which testify to the weavers' range of complex and ingenious techniques.

Persian weavers of the Safavid period attained a virtuosity rarely equalled. Figural representations, which enjoyed wide popularity in sixteenth-century Persia, appear on fabric used for garments and palace furnishings, as well as in religious and funeral ceremonies. In this "Boats at Sea" fragment of reversible double cloth, two textiles have been produced simultaneously, one over the other, in an offset repeat pattern of remarkable intricacy and detail: sailboats with four sailors alternate with simpler rowboats carrying three figures on a sea filled with fish and ducks. The overall composition achieves vertical stability through the repeating sails, and a rocking movement through the diagonal placement of the rowboats. H.S.L.

Turkey, Bursa

Ottoman period (1281-1923)

Cushion Cover

17th c.
Silk voided velvet, gold and
silver filé
105 × 61.5 cm
Purchase, D. W. Parker Fund
1950.51.Dt.15

■ The early Ottoman capital of Bursa was renowned from the fifteenth to the eighteenth century for luxurious brocades and velvets, which were used in clothing, banners and home furnishings. This cushion cover belongs to a group of textiles characterized by bold red, blue and green patterns, representing stylized tulips, hyacinths, carnations and pomegranates; figural representations became less common in 17th-century Islamic textiles. It is easy to recognize such items because imperial workshops in Ottoman Turkey, known as *nakkashanes*, employed artists and designers who produced a unified style for all decorative art with a distinctive repertoire of floral motifs. Ottoman textiles were admired in Europe, where they were often presented by sultans as royal gifts and were also sold in large quantities to royal and clerical figures. H.S.L.

Spain, Manises
Hispano-Moresque

Albarello

2nd half of 15th c.
Tin glazed earthenware, painted lustre decoration
38 cm (h.); 19.6 cm (diam.)
Purchase, gift of Harry A. Norton
1944.Ea.21

Plate

Mid-15th c.
Earthenware, painted blue and lustre decoration
7.6 cm (h.); 43.1 cm (diam.)
Purchase, Annie White Townsend Fund
1951.Dp.70

■ Art produced in Spain that shows Islamic influence is referred to as Hispano-Moresque. The term is most closely associated with ceramics decorated with lustre painting to create effects of gold and copper. This technique originated in ninth-century Iraq and Egypt, and moved westward with the Islamic conquest to Spain. Skill in the lustre technique established Málaga, in the fourteenth century, and Manises (near Valencia), in the fifteenth century, as ceramic centres unparalleled in Europe and the Arab countries. Countless families of the European ruling classes commissioned these immensely popular wares and had them decorated with their coats of arms.

At the time this large lustre-painted plate without base or rim was made, the Christian reconquest of Spain was nearly complete, and much of the work executed at Manises by Muslim craftsmen was for Christian patrons. The plate is decorated with stylized vegetal and floral motifs and tendrils, and with the coat of arms of the Aragons combined with that of a private family at the centre.

The origin of the albarello, or apothecary jar, has been traced to the Middle East, particularly Syria, where, from the twelfth to the fourteenth century, they were used as storage and for transporting spices and herbs to the West. Albarellos were admired by Europeans, and were generally used in pharmacies. Those from Manises were especially popular in Valencia; by the fifteenth century their production seems to have ceased. The form and decoration of this albarello are typical, but the glazed label with a symbol indicating its contents, rather than the customary handwritten cloth or parchment label pasted on the jar, makes this piece a rarity. H.S.L.

Iran, Shiraz
Safavid period (1502-1722)

Sprinkler

About 1700
Blown glass, spiral fluted design
34.9 cm (h.); 8.3 cm (diam.)

Purchase, Mabel Coghlin Bequest
1963.Dg.1

■ During the reign of Shah 'Abbas the Great (1587-1628), a period known for its artistic refinement, the industry of glass-making in Iran was revived thanks to Venetian craftsmen. Characteristic types of this late Persian glass are bottles, vases, ewers and sprinklers. They are almost always mould-blown, quite thin, of a single colour and decorated in the Venetian manner with fluted, trailed threads.

This rosewater sprinkler illustrates the finest technique of late Persian times. It has a fluted design and is made of clear blue glass, the colour most favoured. The bulbous body sits on an applied concave base made of glass, and the stretched slender neck ends in a teardrop pouring spout with pinched lip. Islamic culture laid great emphasis on scents, and vessels of this type were used for sprinkling guests upon their arrival at a ceremony or other special occasions.

According to Sir John Chardin, who published an account of his travels to Persia during the 1660s and 1670s, luxury glass was being produced in both Shiraz and Isfahan, but that made in Shiraz was far superior. Because of its fine craftsmanship, this sprinkler can be attributed to Shiraz. The shape and technique remained popular in Iran and the West through the nineteenth century and came to influence American Art Nouveau glassmakers. H.S.L.

Mexico
Preclassic (1600 B.C.-300 A.D.)
Olmec

Seated Figure
1200-900 B.C.
Buff clay with white slip and traces of pigment
28 × 23.3 × 14.8 cm
Purchase, Horsley and Annie Townsend Bequest
1973.Ac.3

■ The earliest civilization in Mexico, known as Olmec, flourished in the lush subtropical lowlands of the east-coast states of Veracruz and Tabasco. The Olmec were perhaps the first highly successful farmers, fishermen and traders, and their goods and influence, including their art style, spread widely. They built carefully laid-out ceremonial complexes with monumental stone sculptures in the form of both colossal heads that were portraits of rulers, and large relief carvings that anticipated Maya stelae.

Like most Olmec ceramic figures, this piece has narrow eyes, a downturned mouth, a sexless infantile body and an elongated head; the elite class practised cranial deformation to indicate special status. Like most of the larger seated figures, this one is hollow. A relief pattern indicates the hair, and there is a design on the ears. Both areas have some pigment, and a darker painted area defines a kind of loincloth.

Children, often with supernatural traits, were important in Olmec art and religious thought, and babies with this or similar poses have been found in many parts of Mexico, where the Olmec had contact. Such figures are generally thought to be related to the rain god as a weeping child. E.P.B.

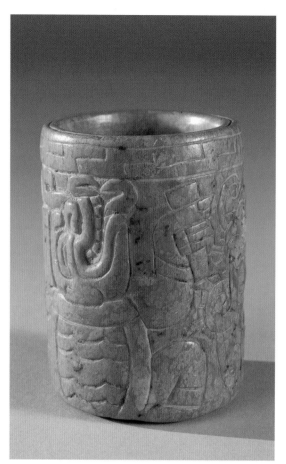

Peru, North Coast

Early Horizon (900-200 B.C.)
Cupisnique

Cylinder Vase

900-600 B.C.
Steatite
6.3 cm (h).; 4.7 cm (diam.)

Gift of F. Cleveland Morgan
1960.Ad.2

■ This vase dates to one of Peru's first great civilizations, a north-coast culture called Cupisnique. Its people constructed irrigation canals for farming in the desert, built impressive ceremonial centres of adobe or stone, and made objects of hammered copper, gold and silver, which depicted gods and supernatural beings. Another closely related early culture, whose great stone ceremonial centre lies on the other side of the Andes, was the Chavín. Both Cupisnique and Chavín architecture was adorned with incised and low-relief sculpture of the same general style as this vase.

A frequently encountered subject has been identified as a supernatural spider decapitator. This cylinder vase displays two different spider creatures. The schematic face on the back of one of them represents a severed human head. Ritual human sacrifice was a part of Andean religions, but human sacrificers are rarely depicted; the sacrificer is usually a supernatural being like this one. The spider's association with sacrifice may be due in part to the poisonous nature of many spiders. E.P.B.

Peru, South Coast

Early Intermediate
(1-700 A.D.)
Paracas Necropolis

Mantle

1-200 A.D.
Embroidered wool
254 × 147 cm
Gift of F. Cleveland Morgan
1947.Ad.19

■ The huge embroidered mantles of the Paracas culture are a major Andean art form. Their design usually consists of repetitions of a single embroidered motif, with bright colours that vary from figure to figure, often in diagonal patterns. There are also patterns of upside-down and right-side-up figures. On the whole, the figures are basically human with animal attributes, and most depictions are decorated with trophy heads decapitated in sacrificial offerings. This mantle's figure, which is repeated in seven colours in seven rows (four of eleven figures alternating with three of ten, for a total of seventy-four figures), has human legs and a falcon tail.

The size of these mantles indicates that they were made as the outer wrapping for the large *fardos*, or funerary bundles, found in a cemetery in the desolate desert sands of Peru's south coast. *Fardos* could be as tall as 1.5 metres, with the same measurement for the base. Although their contents varied, the bundles generally held a body in fetal position, food and objects of shell, metal, cloth or feathers, all wrapped in plain and more elaborate cloth and placed in a basket. The amount of labour that went into the intricate embroidery of this mantle shows the importance of objects taken to the other world. E.P.B.

Peru, South Coast

Early Intermediate (1-700 A.D.)
Paracas-Nazca

Mantle

100-200 A.D.
Wool with embroidery
141 × 64 cm
F. Cleveland Morgan Bequest
1962.Ad.6

■ In the Andes, cloth had a value and a symbolism that are hard for us to imagine. Cloth served for garments that expressed high status, royal gifts and important grave goods. Cotton and wool were used, the latter from tame llamas and alpacas, and from wild, hunted guanacos and vicuñas. Cloth was woven on a backstrap loom, which was in widespread use by 1000 B.C.; it is still used today. One end of the loom is tied to the weaver's waist, the other to a pole or a tree. The loom produces narrow panels, which are sometimes sewn together to make a wider cloth. Garments in the ancient Andes were not cut or tailored; cloth was woven in the shape of a mantle, tunic, loincloth, headband, turban, and so forth.

The repeated motif on this beautiful and unusual mantle is an animal figure with attached scrolls that may indicate vegetation; up-and-down orientations of the figure alternate by row. The mantle shows a transition from the Paracas Necropolis style to the Nazca style. The figures and their placement relate to Paracas designs, as does the embroidery, yet the colours and shapes are more simplified and subtle, and the plain weave of the basic cloth is more open. E.P.B.

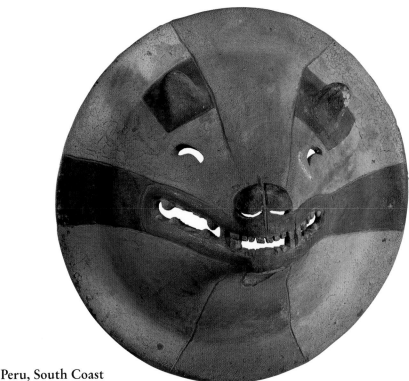

Peru, South Coast
Early Horizon (700-1 B.C.)
Paracas Necropolis

Fox Mask

100-50 B.C.
Clay with resin-based paint
11.9 × 19.8 × 12.5 cm
Purchase, gift of F. Cleveland Morgan
1948.Ad.32

■ The Andean fox is a sharp-snouted hunter and scavenger that lives in regions from the coastal desert to the highlands above the treeline. A frequent subject in ancient Andean art, especially on the coast, the fox was associated with the mountains, from which water comes for irrigation in the coastal desert. Foxes are still thought of as the helpers, or dogs, of the mountain gods. Myths about the origins of agriculture often include a fox that falls from a great height and scatters plants. Fox-skin headdresses have been found in Paracas burials, and at least one mummy bundle had a fox skin over the "head" and down the back of the *fardo*, or funerary bundle. Later in the same south coast region, Nazca textiles and effigy vessels depict a human figure with a fox skin on the head. Sometimes these figures hold plants. In Inca times, fox skins were worn by human guardians of crops, and this still occurs in some highland places.

Masks come from many cultures, but round ones, like this fox-face mask, are unusual. It is cone-shaped, with ears and snout projecting; the tongue is an incised triangle below the mouth. There are openings at the eyes, nostrils and mouth. This mask could have been worn, but the wide rim makes that unlikely. Holes on an underlying circular ledge allow for attachment, perhaps to a mummy *fardo*. The paint colours, derived from plant sources, are typical of Paracas ceramics. E.P.B.

Peru, South Coast

Early Intermediate (1-700 A.D.)
Nazca

Double-spout-and-bridge Bottle

350-450 A.D.
Clay with polychrome mineral paint
15.5 cm (h.); 17 cm (diam.)
Purchase
1981(?).Ad.1

■ The most brilliantly colourful ceramic tradition in the ancient Americas was the poly-chrome pottery of the Nazca culture. More than a dozen colours of mineral slip paint were used in these ceramics, which were fired in shallow pits. The double-spout-and-bridge bottle is the most important typical shape for fine Nazca pottery.

Nazca art could be quite realistic, but its mythical creatures were elaborately fantastic, especially the frequently encountered personage depicted around the dome-shaped body of this bottle. Under its supernaturally large head with elaborate ear ornaments, this Myth-ical Anthropomorphic Being, as it is sometimes known, holds a small, severed human head. The sacrificial offering of heads was widespread in the Andes, but it played a par-ticularly important role in the rites, cosmology and art of the Nazca region. Severed and ritually treated heads, found in greater quantity there than anywhere else in the Andean area, were preserved in caches in the desert sands. Trophy heads were also a common motif in Nazca textile designs. This being's basically reptilian form, decorated with trophy heads, is supported by a human lower torso and legs. Often, it sprouts vegetation or is draped with plants, demonstrating a belief in the cause-and-effect relationship between offered blood and successful agriculture. E.P.B.

Peru
Postconquest (1532-1650)

Beaker

Wood, traces of paint
19.3 cm (h.); 15 cm (diam.)
Purchase, gift of F. Cleveland Morgan
1948.Ad.36

■ Wooden goblets or beakers, known as *keros*, had a long history of ritual use in the Andes, and many still exist because much of Peru is desert, which makes conditions good for their preservation. This beaker was made not long after the Spanish conquest of the vast Inca empire, which stretched down western South America from Ecuador more than four thousand kilometres to Chile and Argentina. The beaker's form combines that of Inca metal vessels in the shape of a human head – it has ears, nose and chin carved in high relief – with that of a flared wooden *kero*. Earlier wooden *keros* were decorated with incised designs; later ones, like this, were painted.

While the shape is basically Inca, the painting on it reflects Spanish influence. Inca and colonial motifs are combined in a two-level scene. Below (under the chin of the carved face), two figures face each other, one holding a spear and shield, the other a bow and arrow. Behind each are two figures carrying similar weapons. On the back at the top space between the ears is a striding figure blowing a conch-shell trumpet and holding a staff with feathers on the end. The feathers hang over the head of a seated figure holding a staff, who faces another figure seated under a fan held by a standing figure. These scenes probably refer to a specific meeting during Colonial times between two leaders or groups, one Spanish and the other indigenous. E.P.B.

Probably Honduras or El Salvador

Late Classic (600-900 A.D.)
Maya

Tripod Plate

700-900 A.D.
Clay, polychrome painted decoration
8.1 cm (h.); 38.3 cm (diam.)

Gift of Mr. and Mrs. Gerald Benjamin
1972.Ac.1

■ Large, shallow polychrome plates with tripod supports were a typical Late Classic form in the Maya lowlands. However, the four-part composition painted on this one is unusual. It fits the Mesoamerican cosmological diagram of the four world directions, or quadrants, and a fifth direction, the centre, but the seated figure repeated in all five spaces is hard to identify. The black lower part – perhaps a garment – and the bare head with what looks like a long braid are not typical. Black circles on the flesh usually indicate a dead person in Maya paintings. The design in front of the nose may represent a nose ornament or may be a sign for breath or life, which is sometimes put before the face of a depicted dead or dying person to indicate that there is life in the other world. The object in this person's hand looks like a mirror. In palace scenes on fine Maya ceramics, the main seated figure sometimes has a mirror placed in front of him as a sign of kingship. The repeated motif around the sloping inner wall of the plate is also unusual. The Maya were the only people in the Americas who had a true form of writing in ancient times, and many Maya objects have texts inscribed on them. However, the design based on a face in the frame surrounding the four figures probably does not have a particular meaning. E.P.B.

Guatemala, Highlands

Late Classic (600-900 A.D.)
Maya

Urn

Buff clay with pigment
26.8 cm (h.); 39 cm (diam.)
Purchase, Horsley and Annie Townsend Bequest
1974.Ac.1

■ The Maya area covered a large and varied territory, from southernmost Mexico through Guatemala, Belize and into Honduras. Ceramics from the highlands of Guatemala differ from lowland ceramics in style and technique (notably, the kind of colour and the relief modelling), but the subject matter is much the same. Themes of agricultural fertility and successful hunting are always of primary importance.

Four full-length, frontal figures of gods, with heads in high relief, are spaced around the outside of this urn. Of the four, one apparently has the face of the Maya sun god. Another holds a cacao tree (chocolate, which comes from the cacao tree, is native to the Maya area). Another holds a plant that might be corn, an important Maya crop; he may also have a tuber such as manioc or a squash tucked in his loincloth. A fourth figure wears a helmet with a deer head on it. Between the figures are two projecting feline heads – symbols of power – and two quetzals with heads in high relief. The quetzal is the long-tailed bird whose feathers were used to decorate royal headdresses and precious objects. Its bright green feathers associate it with fertility. In pre-Columbian times, this species of quetzal was plentiful in cloud forests near where this object was made. E.P.B.

Mexico, Yucatán

Late Classic (600-900 A.D.)
Maya

Vase

700-900 A.D.
Fine Orange ware with incision and slip
15.8 cm (h.); 11.7 cm (diam.)

Purchase, Horsley and Annie Townsend Bequest
1973.Ac.12

■ Tobacco comes from the Americas. In the past, it was a sign of power and had various ritual uses. It was smoked, snuffed or chewed in curing ceremonies, as well as in other divination rites, some of which are still practised today in some parts. This is still true today in some places. In Classic Maya art, underworld gods are often shown smoking cigars. These gods were not only death gods and the lords of the world where the dead are buried, but also the gods of the earth from which plants grow to feed the people. The important Classic Maya deity known as God K is depicted with a cigar projecting from his brow.

On this vase, the incised design shows the head and upper torso of a figure, probably a ruler, who is smoking. He wears what must be jade jewellery and his simply combed hair is decorated with feathers. Vases of this style come from Yucatán, the northern Maya area, which is famous for such sites as Chichén Itzá and Uxmal. This vase is made from a fine-grained, untempered ware that became widely prominent towards the end of the Classic period and in the Early Postclassic, about when the great Classic Maya civilization was dying out in the central area to the south, where it had built great cities of stone. The civilization continued in the Yucatec region, but with many changes. E.P.B.

Central Mexico
Classic (300-900 A.D.)
Teotihuacán

Tripod Cylinder Vase

500-650 A.D.
Clay with post-firing paint on stucco
14.1 cm (h.); 14.5 cm (diam.)
Purchase, Horsley and Annie Townsend Bequest
1959.Ac.2

■ In 600 A.D., Teotihuacán was the world's sixth largest city. This metropolis of Classic-period Mesoamerica lay in the highlands just north of modern Mexico City. Its construction, extending for twenty square kilometres, includes the massive Pyramids of the Sun and the Moon, and the broad Avenue of the Dead, five kilometres long. The temples and houses there are richer with murals than at any other ancient Mesoamerican site.

The tripod cylinder vase with designs incised and painted, after firing, on a paper-thin layer of stucco originated at Teotihuacán. Vessels of similar shape also appeared in the Maya area and elsewhere, which testifies to Teotihuacán's influence. The Teotihuacán people had a symbolic notational system that approached true writing. The wall of this vase provides an example: a device known as the Rain God-Jaguar motif appears inside a feather-edged cartouche; to either side are four-petalled flower motifs. The openwork designs of the feet are a common feature. Although this vessel has no lid, some Teotihuacán tripods do. Perhaps all had lids originally, and their disappearance would be due to their great fragility. E.P.B.

Mexico, Veracruz
Late Classic (600-900 B.C.)
Ballgame Yoke
Stone
12 × 38 × 42 cm
Purchase
1949.50.Ac.1

■ The modern Mexican state of Veracruz, on the Caribbean coast, has been a major producer of rubber from very early times. Rubber balls were made in pre-Columbian times for use in a ritual ballgame. Ball courts are placed in the heart of ceremonial centres all over the region archaeologists call Mesoamerica – southern Mexico, Guatemala, Belize and parts of Honduras and El Salvador. The ballgame was particularly prevalent in Veracruz: the site of El Tajín, the major city there, has at least twelve ball courts. The ballgame was taken seriously, and led to human sacrifice.

In Veracruz, ballplayers wore a U-shaped yoke made of light, perishable material. Stone yokes like this one were a common form of sculpture in Late Classic Veracruz, and though too heavy to wear – they fit sideways at the waist and rest on the hips – they were probably made to be put in graves, where they have been found. This yoke, like many others, represents a personification of the earth in the form of a toad-like monster. Eyes, mouth and brows are carved at the front; the legs are shown at the sides. It may refer metaphorically to the passage from life on earth to the underworld. E.P.B.

Mexico, Veracruz

Late Classic (600-900 A.D.)

Seated Man

Buff clay with traces of pigment

33.8 × 29 × 29 cm

Purchase, Horsley and Annie Townsend Bequest

1975.Ac.5

■ Old men or gods appear often in Mesoamerican art. It is frequently the fire god who is depicted, an old god (the Aztecs called him Huehueteotl, "very old god"), and he came from the heart of the earth – Mesoamerica is volcanic territory. This seated old man represents someone of high status, perhaps an ancestor or a priest of the fire god, but he does not appear to be the god because he lacks the brazier that fire-god depictions usually have on their heads for burning incense. However, the figure is hollow and bottomless, and has openings at the nostrils and mouth, so it could have been used as a censer.

In a typical Mesoamerican cross-legged pose, with his hands on his knees and bent forward with age, this old man is realistically depicted. His back is finely modelled, and his dress shows elegant details. He wears an elaborate pectoral, and large, flaring ear ornaments mark his high status. When pre-Columbian people – usually men – had their ears pierced, holes were made in the lobe for large-diameter ornaments or ornament-holding tubes. Ear-piercing was often a ritual occasion. E.P.B.

India, Gandhara
Kushan period (50-320 A.D.)

Standing Bodhisattva or *Bodhisattva Maitreya*

3rd c.
Grey schist
186.5 × 42 × 30.2 cm

Purchase, Horsley and Annie
Townsend Bequest
1976.Eb.1

■ According to the doctrine of reincarnation, the Bodhisattvas are human beings who, having achieved the final stage of earthly perfection, refuse the supreme annihilation of Nirvana and choose to remain on earth in the service of others. As the Bodhisattvas also represent the historical figure of Buddha – the Indian prince Gautama, who lived in the sixth century B.C. – they are usually portrayed richly dressed and bedecked with jewels. The Museum's Bodhisattva wears three necklaces and amulets around his neck; the top-knot of hair and the halo with two praying figures are signs of his sacred status. Other details, like the beaded net covering the hair and the mark of enlightenment in the middle of the forehead, indicate that the figure represents Maitreya, a Bodhisattva who will renew the world's faith.

In spite of being sacred figures of Buddhism, some Bodhisattvas recall aspects of classical Greek statuary, especially in the profile and the rendering of the draped garment. These pieces come from the ancient kingdoms that sprang up along the Silk Road following the conquests of Alexander the Great. The Museum's example comes from Gandhara, one of the "interchanges" between Europe and the East, a cosmopolitan centre where, for centuries, products, styles and ideas were exchanged. H.L.

China, Shaanxi province
Early Western Zhou dynasty (about 1050-1000 B.C.)

Gui (ritual food container)
Cast bronze
15.5 × 28.5 × 20.5 cm
Purchase, gift of F. Cleveland Morgan
1947.Ed.2

■ Ritual bronze food and wine containers are the distinguishing art form of Bronze Age China (about 1600-300 B.C.). The political elite commissioned a great many pieces, often in sets, for use in state, religious and clan ceremonies. Because of the vast human resources required to mine and smelt the raw materials, operate the foundries, and produce the decorated clay moulds, such wares belonged exclusively to the most powerful and prosperous members of society. Their importance as status symbols meant these ritual containers were often buried with their owners to serve them in the afterlife. The excavation of large numbers of these vessels has provided a major source of information on the religious, social and political life of Bronze Age China.

This two-handled meat or grain container was probably cast for a member of a noble clan who lived in the western part of China, along the middle reaches of the Yellow River. Around 1050 B.C., they became powerful enough to challenge and ultimately defeat the Shang kings, whose capital lay further to the east. A new dynasty was established: the Zhou. While continuing the tradition of using ritual bronze vessels for worship, innovative shapes and decorative motifs were introduced under the Zhou kings and nobles. The imaginary creatures with curled muzzle and large spiral body seen in confrontation here are found only on bronze vessels from the early decades of the Zhou dynasty. J.F.S.

China, Shaanxi province
Tang dynasty (618-906)
Funerary Figures

Horse
7th-8th c.
Buff earthenware, three-colour glaze
(Sancai) and pigment
49.5 × 15 × 46 cm
Purchase, subscription
1918.Ed.4

Entertainer or Dancer in Court Costume
7th c.
Buff earthenware, pigment
43 × 12.8 × 12 cm
Purchase, General Capital Morgan Fund
1952.Dp.2

■ The custom of burying clay and wooden figures, instead of human beings, to attend the dead began in late Bronze Age China (about 4th c. B.C.). By the time of the Tang dynasty, some eleven centuries later, clay funerary figures were being mass-produced throughout northern China. They were often cast in moulds, and individually sculpted embellishments were added later.

This standing female figure, probably one of a group of attendant figures buried to serve the occupant of a tomb in the afterlife, is representative of the most elaborately costumed and coiffed funerary figures made during the Tang dynasty. The thickly painted face and the vestiges of pigment – suggesting embroidered or brocade patterns down the centre of her garment – hint at the opulence of the figure's original appearance.

Magnificent steeds were prized by the Tang nobility, who used them for hunting, playing polo and ceremonial parades. Favourite horses – their manes beautifully clipped and tails braided – received special treatment at court, and the foreign trainers and grooms who accompanied them to China from their Central Asian breeding grounds were often accorded special status. This earthenware horse is among the more elaborately caparisoned examples known. The moulded and applied decoration is highlighted with green and amber glazes against the pale cream-coloured glaze that covers the rest of the body. This combination constitutes the famous three-colour glaze, known as Sancai, seen on many Tang-dynasty funerary wares.

Figures like these provide a vivid image of the luxurious lifestyle during the Tang dynasty, considered a golden age of Chinese history. J.F.S.

China, Hebei province
Northern Song dynasty (960-1127)

Ding Bowl
12th c.
Porcelain, ivory-coloured glaze, copper-reinforced rim
5.1 cm (h.); 21 cm (diam.)
Gift of F. Cleveland Morgan
1949.50.Dp.12

China, Zhejiang province
Five Dynasties period (907-960)

Yue Vase
10th c.
Grey porcellaneous stoneware, celadon glaze
29.8 cm (h.); 15.2 cm (diam.)
Purchase, General Capital Morgan Fund
1951.Dp.55

■ This elegantly shaped vase – with a broad, dish-shaped mouth, small loop handles and a subtly lobed ovoid body – is typical of the wares from a wide variety of kilns in South China, and represents the height of a long tradition of green-glazed ceramics that had been produced in Zhejiang and Fujian provinces from the late first millennium B.C. By the tenth century A.D., when this vase was made, Yue wares were being produced as utilitarian articles for the court and literati. The finest glazed wares from the south continued to be sent north as tribute to the courts during the late Tang (618-906) and Northern Song (960-1127) periods. Production declined towards the end of the eleventh century.

In northern China, wares with ivory-coloured glazes, which had been produced as early as the sixth century, were revived during the Northern Song dynasty. The best northern kilns, near Dingzhou, in modern Hebei province, became the main suppliers of the court. The everyday and special wares they made for imperial use, probably the earliest imperial ware of the Northern Song dynasty, epitomize the elegant taste of its rulers. The shape, design and glaze of this modest bowl are typical of Ding wares from the Northern Song period. The interior is decorated with a boldly incised peony encircled by sprays of leaves. Unconfined by the interior shape, the design seems to spread effortlessly from the bottom of the bowl to the slanted walls. This suggests that such designs may have originated in two-dimensional art forms of the time – bird-and-flower paintings, for example. The rim is unglazed because the bowl was fired mouth down; a copper binding was added to protect the rim. J.F.S.

China, Fujian province
Southern Song dynasty (1127-1279)

Jian Tea Bowl

12th-13th c.
Dark brown stoneware, mustard brown "hare's fur" glaze,
copper-reinforced rim
7.1 cm (h.); 12.4 cm (diam.)
F. Cleveland Morgan Bequest
1962.Ed.23

■ During the Tang dynasty (618-906), tea drinking became an important activity of the court and the literati. Association with Buddhist and Daoist beliefs eventually elevated the experience to near-mystical levels. The bowls that the fragrant infusion was drunk from assumed a fundamental importance, and much was made of the exact colour and shape of the perfect bowl. The most coveted tea bowls have traditionally come from southern kilns. During the Southern Song period, the most highly prized bowls were produced in what is today Fujian province.

This deeply conical bowl on a straight foot is typical of these wares. The thick, lustrous brown glaze that forms a finely streaked pattern as it runs from the rim and gathers into a large teardrop just before the unglazed foot is a classic example of what came to be called "hare's fur" glaze.

This type of tea bowl was highly favoured by devotees of the tea ceremony in Japan, where it was known popularly as *temmoku* ware. The main users were Zen monks and disciples, who saw in their rustic simplicity and unstudied glaze effects a mirror of their faith. Some of the many tea bowls that were exported to Japan during the twelfth and thirteenth centuries acquired an almost sacred status because of their connection to famous Zen tea masters over the centuries. J.F.S.

China, Hebei province

Jin dynasty (1115-1234)

Cizhou Pillow

13th c.
Pale grey stoneware, black painted decoration over white slip
9.8 × 29 × 19 cm
Purchase, gift of F. Cleveland Morgan
1957.Ed.2

■ The earliest pillows in China were probably made of wood. Ceramic pillows like this one began to appear in large numbers only in the sixth and seventh centuries. This pillow is octagonal and slopes from back to front. The top is decorated with a bird on a branch; around the sides are free-flowing floral scrolls executed in dynamic black brushstrokes against a cream-white ground. The piece is covered with a glaze to protect the painting. Headrests of this type were made for general consumption, not for the demands of imperial taste. Although these wares may be less refined than the closely contemporaneous Ding wares, their lively calligraphic decoration sets them apart from other northern Chinese wares of the time.

It is unusual to be able to associate a Chinese ceramic object with a specific family of potters, but the unglazed underside of this piece bears a rectangular pillow-shaped stamp that reads *Zhang jia zhen* (Pillow of the Zhang family). The Zhang family were noted ceramic pillow-makers who worked and sold their goods near Cizhou in southern Hebei province. Founded in the late eleventh century, the family shop made pillows for nearly three centuries. J.F.S.

China, Jiangxi province, Jingdezhen

Ming dynasty (1368-1644), Hongzhi period (1488-1505) and mark

Dragon Saucer-dish

Hard-paste porcelain, incised reserve decoration enamelled green
on the biscuit *(anhua)*
4.5 × 20.1 cm

Purchase, Horsley and Annie Townsend Bequest, in replacement of a gift of F. Cleveland Morgan
1998.54.1-2 (1949.50.Dp.10)

■ This saucer-dish is decorated with the five-claw dragon, symbol of the Chinese emperor, emblem of the East and dispenser of fertility (it is associated with water and the arrival of rain). The decoration is of a type known as *anhua*, or secret. The dragon motifs were first incised on the surfaces of the piece and then covered with wax. The dish was then given a coat of clear glaze and fired at about 1,350 degrees Celsius, a temperature high enough to vitrify the glaze and fuse it with the porcelain body. At the same time, the wax is melted, exposing the unglazed dragon motifs to the heat of the kiln. These incised motifs were then painted in green enamel, and the bowl was fired again at a somewhat lower temperature, to vitrify the enamel without damaging it. The result is a brilliant white ground against which the dragon's shape appears in a rich green that partially hides and reveals the incised decoration underneath, depending on the light.

Coloured enamel decoration fired at lower temperatures was an innovation of mid-fifteenth-century China. This development, which made possible more naturalistic and permanent polychrome decoration on porcelain, was to change the course of ceramic production both in China and elsewhere. R.L.

China, Jiangxi province

Qing dynasty (1644-1911), Yongzheng period (1723-1735) and mark

Imperial Vase

Porcelain, overglaze *famille rose (fencai)* colours
51 cm (h.); 37 cm (diam.)

Purchase, gift of Neil F. and Ivan E. Phillips, and Horsley and Annie Townsend Bequest
1962.Ed.45

■ The Manchu emperors of the Qing dynasty were great patrons of the imperial workshops at Jingdezhen, Jiangxi province, in southern China. Particularly favoured wares were those decorated with the colourful pigments introduced into China by Jesuit missionaries at court, of which this large vase provides a most striking example. Experiments with these new colours, and the products using them, are a distinguishing achievement of early Qing-dynasty porcelain manufacture.

The shape, size and decorative scheme of this vase were popular throughout the eighteenth century. The pastel colours on a white ground decorating the bulbous body and straight neck depict peach tree branches with leaves, blossoms and eight ripe peaches, as well as five bats in flight. Every element has been realistically painted with utmost care, the subtle shadings of colour painstakingly applied. Although the vase bears the mark of Yongzheng, the third Qing-dynasty emperor, it was not necessarily part of his personal possessions. The imperial mark on the bottom of this vase, coupled with its auspicious symbolism – the peach is a traditional Chinese symbol of longevity, and the Chinese pronunciation of bat – *fu* – is a homonym for good fortune – would have made it an appropriate birthday gift to a deserving official, who could display it in his banquet or ancestral hall on special occasions. J.F.S.

China

Probably Shen Zhou (1427-1509)

Travelling in Wu

15th c.

Handscroll, ink on paper

31.8 × 165 cm

Purchase, special replacement fund and Horsley and
Annie Townsend Bequest

Dr.1986(1975.Ed.2).122.1-5

■ Shen Zhou ranks among the greatest painters of the Ming dynasty (1368-1644). He is considered the founder of the Wu school, a small group of literati painters who portrayed everyday scenes in an unaffected style for their own pleasure and for a select circle of friends. Their work contrasts with that of the Zhe school's professional painters, who were attached to the Ming court and produced sumptuous decorative works, in keeping with imperial taste and the grandeur of palatial settings.

This handscroll is typical of Shen Zhou's style. Painted in shades of grey and black, it depicts a lone scholar, cane in hand, walking along a narrow footpath that winds its way up the hilly terrain. Behind him, a low curved footbridge suggests that the blank space is a river. Groves of trees dot the spare landscape.

Above the footbridge, an inscription in a slanted script commonly associated with Shen Zhou expresses a modesty typical of the Wu school. It records how baffled the artist is at the praise of a fellow painter, who compares his work to that of great masters of the tenth century.

The matter-of-fact placement of the colophon illustrates an ambivalence towards realistic description that is a distinguishing feature of literati paintings produced after the thirteenth century. While the arrangement of the landscape creates the illusion of space, the colophon serves as a rude reminder of the two-dimensional nature of the medium. J.F.S.

Japan
Edo period, 1615-1867

Kobako (incense ceremony box)

About 1800-1850
Maki-e lacquer and gold, pewter on a wood core
4.4 × 15.3 × 12.1 cm
Gift of F. Gerald Robinson
1962.Ee.2

■ This lavishly decorated box in the shape of three overlapping books was part of the equipage of the incense ceremony, a traditional Japanese game in which its aristocratic participants had to guess the type of incense being burnt by the scent emitted, as well as the literary allusions the essence suggested. A discriminating olfactory sense and an extensive knowledge of Japanese literature were presumed of the participants. This box, used for storing the precious incense, would have been admired during the ceremony for its visual and tactile qualities, as well as for the aptness of the literary references it suggests. The top book, the *Kokin waka shu*, is an early tenth-century anthology of ancient and modern poetry, a pillar of Japanese literature. The depiction on its cover of a bush warbler perched on a flowering plum tree and a frog jumping across a nearby brook alludes to a poem from the book, as do the calligraphic characters in gold. R.L.

Katsushika Hokusai

Edo (now Tokyo) 1760 - Edo 1849

The Yoshitsune Horse-washing Waterfall

About 1831-1832
Woodcut
37.6 × 25.9 cm
Purchase, John W. Tempest Fund
Gr.1986(1932.Dv.2).15

■ Montreal collectors and the Museum's benefactors were by no means indifferent to the fashion for Japanese art that took hold in the West towards the end of the nineteenth century, as the wealth of the Museum's collection demonstrates. Like this woodcut, most of the Museum's Japanese textiles, ceramics, lacquers and sword guards date from what is called the Edo period (1600-1867), after Tokyo's old name. The period was characterized by the social rise of rich merchants who were connoisseurs of beautiful things and inspired by the heroic stories performed at the theatre and popularized in the form of prints. Nature was another favourite subject, and Katsushika Hokusai was one of the most skilled printmakers to depict it, successfully blending grandiose landscapes, genre scenes and legendary tales.

Here, for example, where the modern viewer might see only two men washing a horse under a waterfall, Hokusai's patrons would have recognized the association with Minamoto Yoshitsune (1159-1189), a rebel military chief with a tragic destiny. Despite the historic references, this print is not part of a cycle devoted to Yoshitsune but is rather from a series inspired by the most famous waterfalls in all the provinces of Japan. The depiction of the falls, bold in both composition and colour, is a very free interpretation of the water's movement, not a realistic transcription. Modern artists of the nineteenth century, the Impressionists and Postimpressionists, were fascinated by the graphic virtuosity of Japanese prints. H.L.

Gifu
1800
Buff earthenware, green and
transparent glazes, brown
painted decoration
3.3 cm (h.)
1960.Ee.980

Edo period (1615-1867)
Fuzo
About 1800
Blue and white porcelain
2.8 cm (h.)
1960.Ee.1261

Kyoto
1800
Porcelain, blue, brown and grey
glaze
4.4 cm (h.)
1960.Ee.190

Edo period (1615-1867)
Minato-yaki
About 1850
White earthenware with straw-
coloured glaze and green,
brown and white painted
decoration
4 cm (h.)
1960.Ee.921

Japan
Kogos
(Incense boxes)

Gift of Joseph-Arthur
Simard

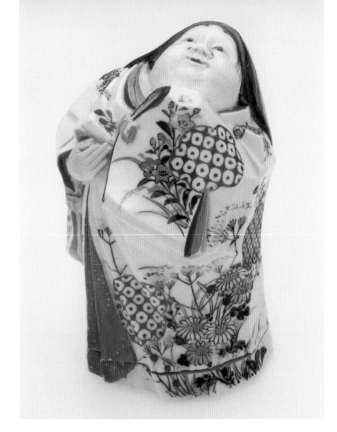

Edo period (1615-1867)
Minpei-yaki or Awaji-yaki
About 1830
Porcelain, polychrome enamel decoration
6.5 cm (h.)
1960.Ee.500

■ The Museum has an exceptional collection of nearly three thousand kogos – small incense boxes used in the Japanese tea ceremony. The collection was originally amassed by the French politician Georges Clemenceau (1841-1929). Under the influence of the late nineteenth-century fashion for Japanese prints and decorative arts in France, Clemenceau's interest in these tiny ceramic works became a near obsession. Montreal shipping magnate Joseph-Arthur Simard purchased the collection from the Clemenceau family in 1939, ten years after the French statesman's death, and gave it to the Museum in 1960.

Kogos were created by potters from all over Japan. Most of the kogos in the Museum collection date from the first half of the nineteenth century, but a few are older. The earliest, from about 1600, may be traced to the venerated tea master Furuta Oribe; they are of stoneware, with a green glaze and painted dark brown decoration. Kogos are usually made of glazed earthenware or white porcelain with blue or polychrome painted decoration.

The animals, plants and human figures fashioned in the form of miniature boxes, measuring an average of six centimetres reveal the artists' imagination, humour and keen eye for observing nature. The kogos pictured here offer a sampling of the wide variety of their shapes, and illustrate the attention paid to detail in each piece. R.P.

Benin Kingdom (Nigeria)
Edo

Plaque
16th-17th c.
Brass
46.5 × 18.5 × 5.6 cm

Gift of F. Cleveland Morgan
1962.F.1

■ The origins of the Benin Kingdom begin with a pre-fourteenth century legend in which the son of a god and a woman becomes the kingdom's first *oba*, or king.

Between the mid-sixteenth and mid-eighteenth centuries, in part due to the availability of brass and in part inspired by illustrated books, both acquired through trade, the Edo produced more than nine hundred cast-brass plaques. The plaques were mounted on pillars that supported the roofs over open gallery-altars across the end of a compound and, like most Benin art, they depict individuals, symbols and scenes of court life, and served to reinforce the power of the *oba*. Features typical of Benin art include a relatively large head, wide eyes, a segmented nose and frontal presentation.

Not only the facial scarification, but also the clothing and adornments seen in this plaque indicate a high-ranking individual: the costume was worn by nobility, and the many coral necklaces and anklets were a kingly prerogative. The three crocodile heads refer to the power and strength of these "police of the waters" and, by extension, to that of the *oba*. The incised foliate patterns refer to a river plant with healing properties. The hat is modelled on a type imported from Portugal during the sixteenth century. The object in the figure's right hand has broken off and cannot be identified. W.T.

Benin Kingdom (Nigeria)

Edo

Tusk

Late 19th c.
Ivory
92.5 × 10 × 24 cm
Purchase, Decorative Arts Fund
1956.F.1

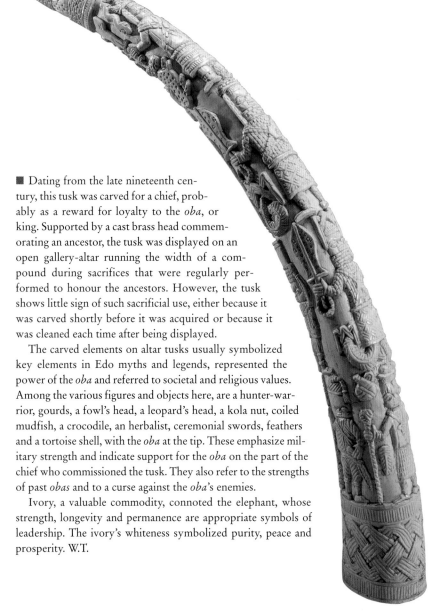

■ Dating from the late nineteenth century, this tusk was carved for a chief, probably as a reward for loyalty to the *oba*, or king. Supported by a cast brass head commemorating an ancestor, the tusk was displayed on an open gallery-altar running the width of a compound during sacrifices that were regularly performed to honour the ancestors. However, the tusk shows little sign of such sacrificial use, either because it was carved shortly before it was acquired or because it was cleaned each time after being displayed.

The carved elements on altar tusks usually symbolized key elements in Edo myths and legends, represented the power of the *oba* and referred to societal and religious values. Among the various figures and objects here, are a hunter-warrior, gourds, a fowl's head, a leopard's head, a kola nut, coiled mudfish, a crocodile, an herbalist, ceremonial swords, feathers and a tortoise shell, with the *oba* at the tip. These emphasize military strength and indicate support for the *oba* on the part of the chief who commissioned the tusk. They also refer to the strengths of past *obas* and to a curse against the *oba*'s enemies.

Ivory, a valuable commodity, connoted the elephant, whose strength, longevity and permanence are appropriate symbols of leadership. The ivory's whiteness symbolized purity, peace and prosperity. W.T.

Mali
Dogon

Seated Figure
19th c.
Wood, metal
94 cm (h.); 40.6 cm (diam.)
Purchase, Horsley and
Annie Townsend Bequest
1960.F.1

■ Tracing their beginnings to the ancient Mali Empire, the Dogon of Mali have inhabited the Bandiagara Cliffs since the fifteenth century and, more recently, the Séno Plain to the south. In their society governed by elders, with numerous priestly cults dedicated to the gods of the sky, earth and water, sculptures were commissioned from the blacksmith-carver and placed on altars, where their constant presence served as intermediary between people and gods.

This figure's ogival eyes and mouth, arrow-shaped nose, low-set ears and attenuated limbs are characteristic of Dogon art. The pendant, numerous bracelets and armbands, hairstyle and beard suggest that the figure represents either a *hogon* – the oldest male villager and priest of the earth god – or an individual with aspirations to high rank.

The stool reflects the Dogon understanding of the universe: the roof of the universe connected to the earth by the central post. The zigzags on the upper disk refer to the path the sacred ark followed when it brought the first people to earth. The figures on the legs refer to twins, the first Dogon created by the spirit Nommo. The crocodiles are protective figures. The strong horizontal and vertical lines refer to the complementarity of male and female and suggest increase. The use of columns creates negative space and a sense of monumentality. W.T.

Democratic Republic of the Congo (formerly Zaïre)

Pende

Costume and Mask

20th c.
Raffia, reed, paper, string, pigment
Jacket: 68 × 61 cm
Mask: 23.1 × 41 × 48 cm
Pants: 92 × 42 cm
Gift of Alan Brandt in memory of F. Cleveland Morgan
1963.F.1

■ The Pende people have inhabited the Kwilu River area in present-day Congo since the seventeenth century. Elders and chiefs traditionally governed the villages, and there was no central authority.

Young male dancers, their identity kept a secret, were sewn into masks and costumes for various occasions. The type of mask and costume illustrated here, for example, might have appeared in the village at ceremonies concerning the chief, at the rectification of a broken ancestral law or at a *mukanda*, a highly secret initiation camp. Every ten to twelve years, adolescent boys left the village to spend several months at a *mukanda*. During their stay, they were circumcised and learned ancestral laws and adult responsibilities. Masked dancers played different social characters to demonstrate appropriate behaviour or acted as "police" of the *mukanda*. When their training was over, the boys underwent a ritual death and rebirth as adults, and then returned to the village to be celebrated.

This particular costume is made almost entirely of the dried bast of the leaf of the raffia palm tree. Without the accompanying accessories, music, dance and words, we cannot know its full meaning, although it likely represents a *munganji*, or ancestral spirit. W.T.

Côte d'Ivoire
Senufo

Bird

19th-20th c.
Wood
147.6 × 50.8 × 38 cm
Purchase, gift of Mrs. Wilson G. McConnell
1970.F.2

■ The Senufo arrived in their present home in Côte d'Ivoire, Mali and Burkina Faso in the eighteenth to nineteenth centuries. Subsistence farmers in a harsh environment where the threat of famine has been constant, the Senufo not surprisingly have linked their art with initiation, divination and funeral rituals. Initiation into adulthood prepared adolescents for social, religious, political and economic responsibilities, on which the society's survival depended. Through divination, the community determined the cause of and sought help for a problem, thus enhancing social control. Funerals effected the transition from the living world to the world of the ancestors and spirits, and were a means of honouring the ancestors.

The large standing bird, based on the *porpianong* (hornbill), was an element of the initiation societies. Carried by young men during activities emphasizing values of social responsibility, the statue embodies Senufo values. The bird maintains a human stance, its long beak suggests a phallus, and the rounded belly evokes pregnancy. According to Senufo myths, the hornbill was the first creature killed for food. The combination of human male and female elements with a link to nourishment symbolizes the continuity of society and life, which is an unending struggle in a severe climate.

Although this *porpianong*, carved from one piece of hardwood, is very heavy, its proportions are slender compared with other examples. W.T.

Gabon
Obamba, Kota

Guardian Figure
(mbulu-ngulu)

Late 19th c.
Wood, brass, copper
67.7 × 28 × 19.3 cm
Purchase, gift of Dr. J. Douglas Morgan
1950.51.F.1

■ The Kota people are known to have inhabited the tropical forest of central and north-west Gabon since the sixteenth or seventeenth century. The culture placed great importance on family, lineage and respect for ancestors. Ancestral and other spirits played a role in the daily lives of the Kotas; they were propitiated and turned to for explanations of many events.

When a person of high status died, their bones were carefully cleaned and stored in a basket. A carved wooden figure, covered on the front with hammered brass and copper, was placed on the top of the basket to guard the relics. Guardian figures were probably first created in the mid-nineteenth century, when brass became available through trade. The practice was largely discontinued in the mid-twentieth century, in part due to the influence of Christian missionaries and migration to cities.

Various features of this figure indicate that it is from the Obamba subgroup: the oval face; the crescent-shaped hairstyle; the lateral projections, which are believed to be cheeks; and, below the head, the crosshatched patterning on the lozenge, which is said to represent shoulders. The lower half of the lozenge is bare where it would have been concealed from view. W.T.

New Zealand, North Island
Maori

Pare (Door Lintel)
About 1840
Wood, shell
106.6 × 26.5 × 2.5 cm

Purchase, gift of F. Cleveland Morgan
1956.Pc.4

■ Polynesian voyagers first settled New Zealand by the beginning of the eleventh century. The styles today referred to as Classic Maori developed between the fifteenth and eighteenth centuries. The Maori place primary importance on knowledge and commemoration of the ancestors and lineage. Within the lineage structure, art was produced by and identified with the *hapu*, or sub-tribe.

In a climate cooler than that of the tropical islands of Polynesia and Melanesia, the Maori built dwellings and meeting houses of wood, as opposed to less durable materials like reed. This above-the-door lintel is from the east coast of the North Island, from a house called Rongomaiwahine, near Gisborne. Depicting an ancestress, it contains references to the lineage history of the Ngati Kahungunu tribe and to their myths and beliefs. The central figure, with its protruding tongue, is characteristic of such lintels and may represent Tumatauenga, the god of war and man. The openwork spirals symbolize the entry of light and knowledge into the world when the god Tane separated his parents, Papa (Earth Mother) and Rangi (Sky Father). The two elongated fish-like forms flanking the central figure are very unusual in Maori door lintels, as the only earthly elements commonly seen are the human figures Papa and Rangi. The side figures are also unusual, as these are normally presented in profile rather than frontally. W.T.

Indonesia, Irian Jaya
Lake Sentani

Dish

19th-20th c.
Wood, pigment
131.2 × 27.3 × 4.5 cm
Purchase, gift of F. Cleveland Morgan
1949.Pc.8

■ According to linguistic evidence, Lake Sentani, near coastal northwestern Irian Jaya, may have been first settled approximately eight thousand years ago through migrations from southeast Asia across the then-existing land bridges. Archaeological evidence indicates more recent arrivals, about twenty-five hundred years ago. The society of Lake Sentani was structured in hereditary chiefdoms, with the men belonging to secret societies that built impressive meeting houses on posts over the lake. The people engaged in trade with the coast that, over the centuries, saw the exchange of cultural practices as well as objects and designs. By acquiring a strong design from a neighbouring culture, one could increase the power of one's own objects.

This food dish, carved in the shape of a shield, is covered with patterns similar to those found on tapa, barkcloth, support posts for the meeting houses, drums and daggers. The curvilinear patterns typical of the art of Lake Sentani – interlocking S-shapes, spirals and concentric circles – are stylized representations of fish, birds and other animals. The incised areas have been painted white with lime. This dish would have held sago, a staple of the local diet. It was probably carved with an iron adze, indicating a manufacture date after initial contact with the West, which occurred in the 1880s. W.T.

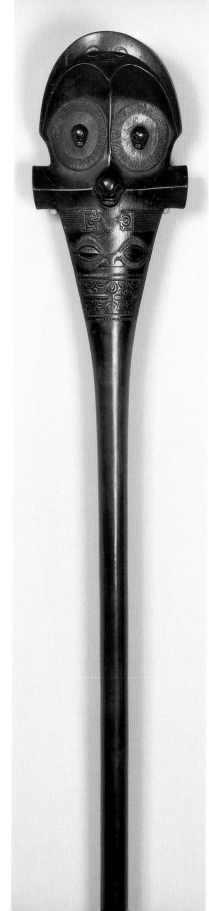

French Polynesia protectorate, Marquesas Islands

U'u Staff/Fighting Club

19th-20th c.
Wood
150 × 18.1 × 11.5 cm
Gift of F. Cleveland Morgan
1948.Pc.7

■ Linguistic and archaeological evidence points to the earliest Polynesian settlements around 1500 B.C. – probably in Fiji and Tonga, whence migrations continued eastward. The Marquesas Islands were first settled by 200 B.C.

Fierce warriors, the men of the Marquesas Islands used this type of club as both a weapon and staff (the top is rounded to fit one's armpit). This example displays typical elements of Marquesan art, such as low-relief carving, large eyes and wide mouths. The curvilinear patterns recall the tattoos for which the Marquesas Islanders were well known. The similar facial representations on the front and back of this club refer to the protective qualities of an all-seeing spirit. The notion is reinforced by facial features that are composed of human heads: the largest eyes are formed from small heads, as is the "nose" on the horizontal ridge. There are five pairs of eyes: one each on the top ridge and the face itself; and below the central horizontal ridge, three – one of which forms the rectangular mouth. Multiple representations of the head enhanced the warrior's *mana* – the spiritual force, or mind, that is believed to reside in the head. Skulls refer to the ancestors. W.T.

Papua New Guinea
Middle Sepik River

Mask

20th c.
Wood, pigment, cowrie shells, fibre
116.6 × 28.8 × 13 cm

Collection Ernest Gagnon, gift of La Compagnie de Jésus
1975.Pc.17

■ The island of New Guinea, settled by successive waves of migrants over the past several thousand years, has more than eight hundred languages. The Middle Sepik River, in northern Papua New Guinea, is an area rich in culture and art. Shields, suspension hooks, figure sculptures, masks and gable masks for the men's meeting houses, or "big houses", are among the better-known carvings.

In preparation for adulthood, young boys were taught the clan's history and rituals at an initiation camp. At its completion, masks of this type were danced in pairs that represented the mythical brother and sister of the clan. An elaborate fringed costume concealed the dancer, who played the sacred bamboo flute, the voice of the ancestor. Today, the masks appear on several important occasions.

Carved from a soft wood, this mask is painted in strong two-dimensional designs typical of Middle Sepik art. The scrolled curvilinear patterns were painted not only on masks, but also on the faces of initiates and the clay-covered skulls of ancestors and powerful enemies who had been killed in head-hunting raids for their power and soul. Opposing faces are also found in many Sepik masks and carvings. This mask lacks eyeholes; it was carried in front of the dancer, who could see out through his costume's fringe and feathers. W.T.

EUROPEAN ART

Italy

Crucifix

About 1100
Polychrome wood
121 × 104 × 20 cm
Purchase, gift of David Y. Hodgson
1965.Df.7

■ Wooden crucifixes as old as this one – dating to about 1100 – are exceedingly rare. Thought to be Tuscan, possibly from Siena, it would be among the earliest surviving examples of Italian origin. Because it is intended to be viewed frontally, it may originally have been suspended above an altar.

Carved in the stylistic tradition of the eleventh century, this devotional work blends two crucifix types: Christ suffering and Christ triumphant. Its moderate scale, severely posed head and arms, and open eyes relate it to early medieval and Carolingian traditions, while at the same time the heavy, drooping eyelids relate it to a later tradition of representing the crucified Christ in a way that suggests his mortality. The severe simplicity of the symmetry and the expressive presentation of the emaciated, elongated body of Christ with rows of ribs embody the non-realistic stylizations of early Romanesque art. They also effectively and impressively underline the spiritual message of Christ on the Cross, eternally alive and suffering for mankind's sins.

The two arms of Christ, of different woods from the rest of the body, are probably early replacements. H.T.G.

France, Burgundy

Head of Christ

About 1150
Limestone, traces of polychrome
23.2 × 14.8 × 16 cm

Purchase, Annie White
Townsend Fund

1950.51.Dv.10

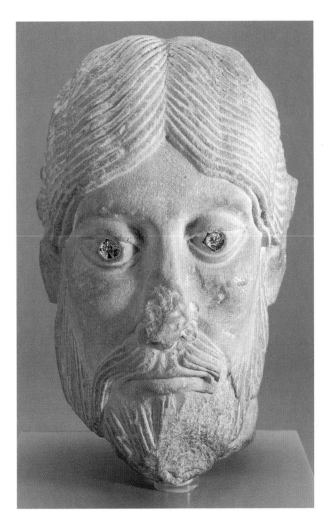

■ Dating to the late Romanesque period, when figures were becoming more naturalistically sculpted, this *Head of Christ* is notable for its sensitive modelling of the cheekbones, lips and lower face. While the hair is carved in the usual manner of parallel incisions, the plaiting is rendered elegantly. A comparison of this head with the earlier Romanesque crucifix illustrates the change of style.

The flat, unsculpted back of the head suggests that it was placed against a vertical architectural element such as a column. Nothing about the piece foreshadows the spatial independence and sense of individualized movement found in early Gothic sculpture at the end of the century.

This head has been related to figures in the tympanum of the Cathedral of Saint-Lazare in Autun (1130-1135). The carving of the hair and the facial expression recall the *Christ in Majesty* there, as well as the *Christ in Majesty* of about the same date from the tympanum of Sainte-Marie Madeleine, Vézelay. Typical features of such Burgundian Romanesque sculpture seen here are the downward mouth, very oblong face, almond-shaped eyes and large, stylized ears pressed against the head. The face would originally have been painted; traces of black pigment survive in the drilled eyes. H.T.G.

Meuse region

Virgin and Child

About 1230
Polychrome and gilt wood
66.6 × 22.2 × 24 cm

Purchase, the Montreal Museum of
Fine Arts' Volunteer Association and
Junior Associates funds
1973.Df.18

■ According to medieval theology, the Virgin in Majesty, seated on the Throne of Solomon with the adult Christ on her lap, is herself the Throne of the "New Solomon", the seat of divine wisdom (*Sedes Sapentiae*). These "Thrones of Wisdom" were devotional objects, and sometimes served as reliquaries as well.

This fine piece is Mosan, from the Meuse River valley intersecting modern France, Belgium and Germany. It exemplifies Late Romanesque sculpture. The deeply carved drapery folds are here still highly stylized with regular chevron patterns in the figures' laps, but they now fall more naturally around the bodies they cover. The faces, softened by gentle smiles, herald the more individualized representations of the relationship of Mother and Child. The Virgin's crown alludes to her role as Queen of Heaven and Bride of Christ. In his left hand, the Christ Child holds a pomegranate, symbol of the unity of the Church as well as of immortality and resurrection. H.T.G.

France, Lorraine
Virgin and Child
1st third of 14th c.
Limestone, traces of gilt and
polychrome
111 × 55 × 36 cm

Gift of Ishou Khanna and Juliette
Fallu in honour of Mr. Antoine and
Mrs. Anna Fallu

1999.203

■ This sculpture is characteristic of the Gothic style of Lorraine. Typical are the facial expressions, large foreheads, narrow almond-shaped eyes, wide noses and tightly drawn lips, as well as the Virgin's short, broad hands and laced cloak, and the drapery falling in wide pleats. Stylistically, a striking comparison can be made with the *Standing Virgin and Child* at Saint-Dié, also attributed to a Lorraine artist. The modelling of the faces and heads of both sculptures is nearly identical, as are the crowns and veils on the representations of the Virgin.

The fact that the figures are set on a plinth, the Child seated on the Virgin's proper right knee, rather than left, with the Virgin looking slightly downward and the Child to one side, suggests that they once formed the central group of an *Adoration of the Magi* or similar ensemble placed at a height above the viewer in a chapel or on an altar. There are several examples of this type in France. Such a protected setting would also account for both the survival of extensive traces of gilt and polychrome, and the lack of detailed carving on the back. H.T.G.

Russia, School of Moscow

Scenes of the Life of Saint Nicholas of Velikoretsk

Mid-16th c.

Tempera and gold on panel prepared with *lefkas*

56 × 47.5 × 4.2 cm

Gift of Graham and Elise Nesbitt

2002.113

■ This icon is a fine example of the refined taste of the Russian capital. The graceful elongated figures with the sensitively modelled small heads and extremities, the lush colour scheme with a wide range of blues and pinks, and the lavish use of gold for the background and the details, leave no doubt of the artistic milieu that produced it.

Stylistically, it recalls the art of Master Dionysij around 1500, but historical information points to a date half a century later, when Ivan the Terrible ordered the transfer of the miracle-working icon of *Saint Nicholas of Velikoretsk* from Khlynov (now Kirov) to Moscow. There, in the capital, a new iconography was developed, which the Museum's piece follows closely. One icon of this Muscovite production (Museum of History and Ancient Monuments, Kostroma), painted in the late 1550s and iconographically almost identical to this one, was offered in 1581 to the Ipatyevsky Monastery *in memoriam* of the elder son of Ivan the Terrible, whom the latter had killed in a fit of rage. The Museum's *Saint Nicholas* should then be attributed to this Muscovite production around the middle of the century. The luxury of materials, the nobility of the style and the incredible amount of detail, some of it barely visible to the naked eye, indicate that this *Saint Nicholas* must have been produced by a miniaturist in the sphere of the tsarist ateliers a generation or so before the famous Strogonov production. G.K.

Russia, School of Moscow with Northern influences

Dormition of the Most Holy Mother of God

2nd half of 16th c.
Tempera and gold on panel prepared with *lefkas*
70.1 × 60.5 × 6 cm

Gift of Graham and Elise Nesbitt
2002.114

■ Although traditional in its iconography, this icon demonstrates the infiltration of secular tenets into icon-painting in the later sixteenth century. Christ is no longer the imperturbable God of earlier representations, but is now emotionally engaged with his Mother, by turning towards her and blessing her body. The cherubs in the mandorla are rendered in expressive profiles, and the standing angels in three-quarter turns. The background buildings remain fantastic, but the two groups of mourners are shown as though filing out of arched openings. Figuring in the story of Jephonias, whose hands were severed when he tried to upset the funeral cortège, is the angel, whose armour is depicted with affection.

Yet despite these secondary instances, the work radiates a solemnity and deeply felt spirituality. In the grisaille zone of the mandorla, the flames of the torches have been depicted in fiery red, like the seraph in the apex, alluding to the eternal divine light and living force. The mourning Apostles maintain a profound psychological presence. The sacred history is here experienced in depth and not just illustrated. The sombre colours in saturated hues betray a Northern training of the artist, while the physiognomy and calm sorrowfulness of the faces derive from the Muscovite tradition. Such a blending occurred in Moscow in the second half of the sixteenth century, which no doubt corresponds to the date of this icon. G.K.

Niccolò di Pietro Gerini

Active in Florence,
1368-1415

The Coronation of the Virgin

About 1390
Tempera on panel
89.9 × 53.2 cm

Purchase, John W. Tempest Fund
1951.1059

■ Niccolò di Pietro Gerini executed important church commissions in Florence, Prato and Pisa from the 1380s through the early fifteenth century. A century earlier, the stylistic innovations of Giotto – whose student Taddeo Gaddi had taught Gerini – had brought an emergent realism to Florentine painting. Three-dimensional space was more convincingly depicted, subjects seemed to truly exist in light and space, while human sensibilities were conveyed through gestures and expressions.

The Coronation of the Virgin is conventionally presented in a stylized and hieratical manner. In this painting, however – despite the composition's symmetry, balance and serious presentation – the subject is invested with greater naturalism. Christ and Mary sit on a bench-like double throne beneath a baldachin of sumptuous fabric. Before them is a vase of flowers. The faces of the attendant angels and saints are individualized. The artist appeals to the viewer's delight in the physical world through the rich patterning of the draperies and the foreground field in which the saints stand and the charming angel musicians kneel.

The size of the panel suggests that it was created for a private chapel or as a small guild altarpiece. H.T.G.

Bernat Martorell

Active in Barcelona, 1427-1452

The Annunciation

1427
Oil and tempera on panel
76.2 × 52.7 cm

F. Cleveland Morgan Bequest

1962.1363

■ Among the Museum's Spanish medieval paintings, the *Annunciation* by Catalan artist Bernat Martorell is perhaps the finest. The panel depicts the moment when the Archangel Gabriel tells the Virgin Mary that God has chosen her to bear the Christ Child (Luke 1: 26-38). The subject had proliferated throughout Europe since the twelfth century, when devotion to the Virgin became particularly popular. The angel's greeting, inscribed here in Latin between the two figures, provided the opening of a prayer to the Virgin: "Hail, Mary, full of grace . . ."

Commissioned in 1427, this Annunciation is from a large altarpiece, or retablo, at the Franciscan Monastery of Santa Maria de Jesús in Barcelona and shows several sources of influence. Barcelona was a thriving city, and Catalonia, united with the kingdom of Aragon, was an international maritime power that conducted trade throughout Spain and Italy. Thus, Martorell was trained in the current International Gothic style, characterized by graceful courtly figures and sumptuously patterned textiles. He also delighted in naturalistic details and dramatic perspective. The geometric floor and ceiling decorations incorporate Mozarabic influences, reflecting the centuries of Arab rule in Spain. H.T.G.

Andrea Mantegna
Padua 1431 – Mantua 1506

Dido
About 1500-1505
Tempera and gold on linen
65.3 × 31.4 cm
Purchase, John W. Tempest Fund
1920.104

Judith with the Head of Holofernes
About 1500-1505
Tempera and gold on linen
65 × 31 cm
Purchase, John W. Tempest Fund
1920.103

■ Mantegna's *Dido* and *Judith* form part of a series representing famous heroines of the past; two others, *Tuccia* and *Sophonisba*, are at the National Gallery, London. The story of Dido, Queen of Carthage, is told in Book IV of Virgil's *Aeneid*. Dido fell in love with the Trojan hero Aeneas. After he abandoned her, she pretended to build a pyre to burn his belongings. Instead, she climbed onto the pyre and killed herself with his sword. The Old Testament heroine Judith saved her people from subjugation to Assyrian rule by seducing the enemy leader Holofernes and then decapitating him as he lay asleep.

Mantegna received his training in Padua, a university city and centre of humanist studies. Subsequently, he was appointed painter to the court of the Gonzagas in Mantua. His work was influenced by the sculpture of antiquity and by his classical studies. The head of *Dido* derives from a Roman statue or bust. Both figures shown here were painted to suggest highly polished gilt bronze against veined marble backgrounds. They also reflect the style of Mantegna's contemporary, the sculptor known as Antico: *Dido* recalls in particular that artist's bronze of Cleopatra at the Museum of Fine Arts, Boston. Antico had also executed statuettes for Isabella d'Este, the celebrated Renaissance noblewoman in Ferrara; it is furthermore recorded that she owned figures "painted in feigned bronze . . . by Master Andrea Mantegna". H.T.G.

Neri di Bicci
Florence 1419 – Florence about 1491

Virgin and Child with Saint Michael and Saint Blaise
About 1460
Oil and tempera on panel
255.2 × 254 × 37 cm

Purchase, special fund
1962.1374

■ Neri di Bicci ran a large and successful workshop in Florence and his style was conservative. It is an indication of Florentine popular taste that, at the same time his stiffly populated and strongly coloured paintings were being commissioned, artists like Botticelli, Perugino and Leonardo were coming to the fore. Yet Neri's style gradually adapted to the earlier innovations of the Florentine painters Filippo Lippi, Fra Angelico and Domenico Veneziano. Reflecting these sources here are the strongly modelled blond figures and the throne's architectural characterization and heightened three-dimensionality. In the 1460s, Neri began introducing the sort of illusionistically cast shadows found in this altarpiece.

The inscription at the base of the main panel, following medieval convention, identifies the figures. The Virgin and Child are accompanied by Saint Blaise and the Archangel Michael. Blaise holds an iron comb, the instrument of his martyrdom; Michael holds scales balancing two souls – one is blessed, the other damned and thrown to the devil held beneath Michael's foot. Kneeling at either side of the throne are the donors, depicted diminutively in profile. In the centre of the altarpiece's predella, or lower panel, is Christ rising from the sepulchre. At the left are Tobias with an angel, Saint Peter and the Virgin, and at the right are Saint John the Evangelist, Saint Lawrence and Saint Francis of Assisi; they may represent name saints of members of the donating family, whose crests are at either side of the predella. H.T.G.

Hans Memling
Seligenstadt 1433 – Bruges 1494

Portrait of a Man

About 1480 or later
Oil on panel
33.4 × 22.8 cm

Purchase, Horsley and Annie Townsend Bequest and William Gilman Cheney Bequest
1956.1129

■ Born in Germany, Hans Memling settled in Bruges in 1465 and became one of the leaders of that city's school of painting. The Netherlandish painters Rogier van der Weyden and Thierry Bouts influenced his work, which is characterized by a lyrical tranquillity. This painting, dating from the latter part of Memling's career, exemplifies the artist's talent for employing atmospheric perspective to create deep space and gentle modelling of his subjects, while providing the precise and realistic detail so typical of Netherlandish painting of this period. The market for Memling's paintings in Italy influenced painters there in their depictions of landscape backgrounds.

Holding a paper scroll in his hand, the subject is posed before an open landscape, in keeping with Netherlandish tradition. The style of the young man's haircut, fashionable in Southern Europe, and his distinctive black cap suggest he was a member of the Italian merchant community in Bruges. The turn of the figure towards the right could mean that the painting was originally one of two joined panels, the other portraying the man's wife or some religious subject. This panel has been cut down on all four sides. H.T.G.

■ Tilman Riemenschneider, one of the most successful German sculptors of his time, spent most of his career in Würzburg, where he was elected to several civic posts and became mayor of the city. Riemenschneider's essentially conservative, late Gothic style closely complements the achievements in painting of Netherlandish artists like Hans Memling. His figures are elongated, refined and delicate-limbed, with oval faces, narrow almond-shaped eyes and sunken cheeks that reveal the shape of the skull, all of which gives them an introspective quality. Hair tends to be expressively tousled.

The ethereal, spiritual character of Saint Sebastian is further accentuated in this statue by an emaciated body and protruding Adam's apple. According to tradition, Saint Sebastian was a third-century Roman soldier sentenced to be shot with arrows when his Christian faith was discovered.

This *Saint Sebastian* is among the rare examples of Riemenschneider's art outside Germany and is one of three surviving studio models Riemenschneider carved for workshop assistants to copy. It is extraordinary as an exploration of the male nude by the artist, and it served as the model for ten extant sculptures. The figure's missing left hand would originally have supported the raised drapery. It was customary to paint such sculptures, and this piece was probably not painted until it had ceased to be used as a studio model. H.T.G.

Tilman Riemenschneider

Heiligenstadt about 1460 –
Würzburg 1531

Saint Sebastian

About 1510
Wood, traces of polychrome
71 × 25 × 12 cm

Purchase, Horsley and Annie Townsend Bequest
and gift of L. V. Randall
1971.8

Master of the Legend of Saint Barbara

Active in Brussels, about 1470 – about 1500

Virgin Enthroned with Angels

About 1490
Oil on panel
61.6 × 43.8 cm
Gift of Dr. Max Stern
1986.14

■ The name by which this unidentified artist is known refers to the altarpiece that forms the nucleus of the group of thirteen works attributed to him. Influenced by Rogier van der Weyden, the renowned painter at Bruges in the mid-fifteenth century, the Master of the Legend of Saint Barbara distinguishes himself in his idealized females, with their high, plucked foreheads and doe-eyed expressions, and the dynamic narratives he creates out of religious events that are traditionally presented more staidly.

In this panel, the Virgin and Child are seated on an ornately Gothic throne symbolizing the Church, and two angels appeal for the Infant's attention. On the left, a window ornamented with the patrons' coats of arms reveals a landscape, while on the right, the space opens onto a chapel interior. The picture is replete with religious symbolism: the maiolica vase with a lily alludes to the Virgin's purity; the angel extending a fig to the Infant alludes to original sin; and the bright red of Mary's robe alludes to her role as Queen of the Church and to Christ's Passion. The panel is painted in brilliant colours of jewel-like intensity, and the minutely studied details are compelling reflections of the Netherlandish fascination with the surfaces of the phenomenal world. But the perspective is still inconsistent, and the interior is architecturally untenable.

The painting was originally the central panel of a triptych that would have been used in a private chapel or as a portable altarpiece. H.T.G.

Albrecht Dürer

Nuremberg 1471 – Nuremberg 1528

Adam and Eve (The Fall of Man)

1504
Engraving, state IV/V
24.9 × 19.2 cm
Purchase, Miss Olive Hosmer Fund
Gr.1961.81

■ In the early sixteenth century, German art developed two strains. One was closely tied to Northern European traditions of realism and accepted only certain Italian compositional devices. The other, oriented towards Italy and the classical balance of the Renaissance, was exemplified by the painter, printmaker and theoretician Albrecht Dürer.

Dürer was apprenticed at the workshop of the local woodcut printmaker Michael Wolgemut in Nuremberg; he was influenced as well by the art of Martin Schongauer. Dürer made extended trips to Italy in 1494-1495 and from 1505 to 1507. These travels, during which he studied the works of Mantegna, Giovanni Bellini and Raphael, were critical to his development by bringing a theoretical understanding of underlying structure to his firm grasp of the outer forms of the natural world. Yet an immediately recognizable Gothic preoccupation with surface detail remains characteristic of his work.

Nowhere are these diverse currents better exemplified than in *Adam and Eve*, executed just before his second trip to Italy. The frontally defined Adam, noble and sinless, reflects Italian idealization and standards of proportion, as does the softened generalization of Eve. In fact, the figures are inspired by the Belvedere Apollo and the Medici Venus, known to Dürer through prints. Yet the richly detailed and highly naturalistic landscape of this Paradise is typically Northern. H.T.G.

Jacopino del Conte
Florence 1510 – Rome 1598

Portrait of Bindo Altoviti

About 1545-1550
Oil on panel
128.5 × 103 cm

Purchase, Edward Cleghorn Memorial Fund
2000.14

■ Jacopino del Conte trained in Florence under Andrea del Sarto. About 1536, he moved to Rome, where he was influenced by Michelangelo and the Mannerism of Francesco Salviati and Daniele da Volterra. Jacopino had evolved his complex and elegant mature style by the early 1540s. In addition to his religious paintings, he was particularly renowned for his portraits of prominent Romans. Among these was Bindo Altoviti (b. 1491), under whom the family's bank had by 1528 become the most powerful in Rome, managing accounts for the Vatican, Henry II of France and Cosimo I de' Medici. Despite his anti-Medici political stance, Altoviti was appointed a Florentine consul and, in 1546, a senator of Florence.

Raphael had portrayed Altoviti as a handsome youth with long blond hair about 1515 (National Gallery, Washington). The Florentine court sculptor Benvenuto Cellini executed a bronze bust of him about 1550 (Gardner Museum, Boston), the same period as this picture. The statue Altoviti is pointing to in the painting is a figure of Fortitude, entwined around a pillar, a symbol of strength; the same device appears on the reverse of a portrait medal of Altoviti attributed to Cellini. In the background, a storm may allude to the vicissitudes of life.

This portrait remained with the Altoviti family in Florence until about 1940. H.T.G.

**Jacopo Robusti,
called Tintoretto**
Venice 1518 – Venice 1594

Portrait of a Member of the Foscari Family

About 1550
Oil on canvas
109.6 × 91.6 cm

Purchase, John W. Tempest Fund
1954.1097

■ Venice, the most opulent city in sixteenth-century Europe, produced an inimitable school of painting through a synthesis of an Italian idealization of form and an appreciation of the sensuous surfaces of the physical world, heightened by the faceting properties of Venice's watery atmosphere. The sixteenth century witnessed a golden age in Venetian painting, with the artistic giants Giorgione and Titian in the first generation, followed by the dominant figures of Veronese and Tintoretto, a pupil of Titian. Tintoretto's art was influenced by the highly mannered and psychologically remote refinement of mid-century Central Italian portraiture: the viewer is not invited to enter into the sitters' character and private concerns but is summoned instead to respond to their position in society.

In this portrait, Tintoretto's rough, animated brushstroke brings an evocation of rich tactility to the lushly patterned, fur-trimmed velvet senatorial robes, which, brilliantly highlighted, cascade down the breadth of the canvas, asserting the sitter's self-assured authority. Although the identity of the subject remains unknown, he has been associated with the Foscari family because the portrait was formerly in the collection at the Palazzo Foscari. H.T.G.

Pellegrino Tibaldi and studio

Puria di Valsolda 1527/28 – Milan 1596

Ten Scenes from the Story of Joseph:
The Discovery of the Cup in Benjamin's Sack of Grain

1560-1561

Fresco glued to canvas

75 × 69 cm

Gift of Roberto Ferretti di Castelferretto

1998.47.9

■ Pellegrino Tibaldi's fresco illustrations of the Story of Joseph (Genesis 37, 39-46) were created about 1560 as a decorative cycle for the palace of Angelo Ferretti in Ancona. The frescoes themselves were executed primarily by the artist's studio, however the designs are Tibaldi's – a preparatory drawing by him for *Joseph Released from Prison* survives (British Museum, London). They originally numbered twelve, but two were destroyed in the eighteenth century.

Tibaldi received initial training in Bologna. About 1545 he went to Rome, where he was influenced by the art of Michelangelo and the fluid Mannerist style of Perino del Vaga, whose studio he entered. In the 1550s Tibaldi returned to Bologna and became the most important artist there. He worked in Ancona between 1558 and 1561, before travelling to Milan and Spain, where he decorated the Escorial library and cloister for Philip II.

The style of Tibaldi's Ancona period shows a transition to greater simplicity and naturalism. The clarity and directness of the narrative reflect the current teachings of the Counter-Reformation. Although aspects of Tibaldi's earlier style survive in the narrative wit, certain foreshortened figures, elegant architectural details and references to Michelangelo and Raphael, the overall character of the Joseph cycle is of a touching simplicity that foreshadows his late unmannered work at the Escorial. H.T.G.

Domenikos Theotokopoulos, called El Greco
Candia, Crete, 1541 – Toledo 1614

Portrait of a Man of the House of Leiva
About 1580-1585
Oil on canvas
88 × 69 cm
Adaline Van Horne Bequest
1945.885

■ El Greco is renowned for the elongated forms, otherworldly brilliance of colours and spiritually evocative eccentricities of his style, derived to some extent from his early Byzantine-influenced training as an icon painter in the Venetian territory of Crete. Around 1558, El Greco went to Venice, where he studied with Titian and was influenced by Tintoretto and Bassano. By 1577, he had settled in Toledo, Spain.

Judging from similarities with other paintings of known date, this portrait was done not long after El Greco arrived in Spain. The subject, who retains an elegant pose, is portrayed in a limited palette of browns and blacks in the naturalist tradition of Venetian portraiture, and without the arch emotional intensity of the artist's later Spanish portraits. Yet the simplicity of the presentation of the subject, the flame-like contour of his head and the direct gaze anticipate El Greco's mature style and effectively communicate the subject's pride in his status. While his identity remains uncertain, the fragmentary inscription at the top of the painting, which was probably added later, refers to him as a "gentleman of the house of Leiva".

The painting has been cut down along the bottom, which explains why the fingers of the subject's left hand are missing. H.T.G.

Hendrick Goltzius
Mühlbrucht 1558 – Haarlem 1617

The Dragon Devouring the Companions of Cadmus

1588
Engraving, state I/IV
25.3 × 31.8 cm

Purchase, Wake Robin Fund in memory of Nelo St.B. Harrison

2001.9

■ Hendrick Goltzius, one of the most remarkable engravers in the history of print-making, was trained in Haarlem and established his studio there. His works demonstrate a sophisticated awareness of Italian and classical art (he visited Italy in 1590), and an encyclopedic knowledge of both the compositions and techniques of Italian as well as Northern prints. Though highly esteemed by his contemporaries, Goltzius suddenly stopped making prints around 1600 and devoted himself exclusively thereafter to paint-ing and drawing.

In the early 1580s, he was introduced to the Mannerist art of painters from Antwerp and Haarlem. Their influence is particularly evident in the Herculean muscularity of his male figures, and the exaggerated, twisting bodies.

The Dragon Devouring the Companions of Cadmus, one of Goltzius's most celebrated and horrific engravings, is based on a painting by Cornelisz. Van Haarlem (National Gallery, London); the composition is reversed from right to left. The print and the paint-ing are both dated 1588. The story of Cadmus is told in Ovid's *Metamorphoses* (3:1-137). Upon founding the city of Thebes, Cadmus sent his men for water to make a sacrifice to Zeus. They came upon a spring sacred to Ares, which was guarded by a fierce dragon that killed them all. The background of this print shows Cadmus, who will kill the beast, arriving on the scene. H.T.G.

Hendrick de Clerck
Brussels about 1570 – Brussels 1630

Moses Striking the Rock

About 1590
Oil on panel
86.4 × 86.4 cm

Purchase, Horsley and Annie Townsend Bequest
1969.1624

■ The subject of Moses striking the rock at Horeb with his rod to provide water for the Israelites (Exodus 17:5-6) was often paired with the Gathering of Manna. An octagonal *Gathering of Manna* by de Clerck, presumably the pendant of this painting, appeared on the market in 1999. These subjects seem to have been frequent in de Clerck's work, and in fact, the Museum owns another *Moses Striking the Rock* by him (1979.8), dating from about twenty years later.

Both themes are apt for a dining room. The decorative nature of this picture, in which the subject matter seems less important than the presentation of a complex and figure-filled composition, is further underlined by the abundance of serving vessels, the charming variety of the participants' poses, the forest setting and a brilliant colourism.

Early in his career, de Clerck visited Rome, but his style remains Flemish, profoundly influenced by Maarten de Vos, who is traditionally assumed to have been his master, although they may only have worked together. To de Vos he owes both his vibrant colours and the character of his Mannerist style. In Brussels, de Clerck became court painter to the governors of the Southern Netherlands. By 1594, he was serving Archduke Ernest in that capacity, and two years later, Archduke Albert and Archduchess Isabella. De Clerck maintained a very active studio and also collaborated with Jan Brueghel the Elder, executing figures for some of the latter's landscapes. H.T.G.

Jacques Callot

Nancy 1592 – Nancy 1635

The Stag Hunt

1619
Etching, state I/IV
19.8 × 46.7 cm

Purchase, Wake Robin Fund in memory of Nelo St.B. Harrison and gift of
Freda and Irwin Browns in honour of their 40th wedding anniversary
2001.72

■ Lorraine-born Jacques Callot was the most outstanding French printmaker of the seventeenth century. Working almost exclusively in etching, he revolutionized the technique. Instead of covering his copper plates with the brittle resin then being used, which was liable to flake off, he adopted violin maker's varnish, which not only overcame this defect but gave him far greater control over the character of the line. Callot also devised the echoppe, a steel cylinder cut off at an angle that permitted greater freedom in varying the width and character of the line.

Another of his innovations was to immerse the plate in the acid bath repeatedly, blocking out different areas each time so that some lines would print lightly and others deeply, thus creating atmospheric effects.

Callot employed his innovative techniques in *The Stag Hunt*, which was executed in Florence and is the largest and most beautiful of his printed landscapes. A sense of space is created through the shifting of light and dark planes and the convergence of lines towards the vanishing point, and scale is provided by the many figures moving within the landscape. H.T.G.

Pieter Brueghel the Younger
Brussels about 1564 – Antwerp about 1638

Return from the Inn

About 1620
Oil and tempera on panel
41.3 × 64.8 cm

Gift of the Maxwell family in memory of Mrs. Edward Maxwell

1955.1122

■ The death of the popular and highly esteemed Pieter Brueghel the Elder in 1569 did not mark the end of his family's association with painting, as his sons Pieter and Jan entered the profession with equal success. Pieter the Younger specialized in compositions based on his father's peasant-scenes, testifying to their popularity more than fifty years after their inception. But this painting is not simply a copy of a lost work by his father, unlike whose compositions it is organized along strictly drawn perspective orthogonals, leading back to the vanishing point of the village church. The painting also contrasts the peaceful church, birds pecking in the snow and peasant workers going about their business in the background with the drunken brawls before the inn, and the wife berating her husband as she escorts him home. The foreground abounds in sexual symbolism: the sloppy attire and grasped sword of the young husband being pulled away from the fight, the pipes carried by the accompanying boy and the slit tree trunk with a pole running through it would all have been readily interpreted by Brueghel's contemporaries. H.T.G.

Bernardo Strozzi
Genoa 1581 – Venice 1644

Eratosthenes Teaching in Alexandria

About 1635
Oil on canvas
78.9 × 99.4 cm

Purchase, Horsley and Annie Townsend Bequest
1959.1225

■ This painting depicts Eratosthenes of Cyrene (about 276-about 194 B.C.), a Greek astronomer, mathematician, geographer and philosopher who was the director of the library at Alexandria for many years. Although Eratosthenes is best remembered for the Sieve of Eratosthenes, a method he devised of finding prime numbers, he was also the first to accurately calculate the circumference of the Earth and the obliquity of the ecliptic, as well as to determine the size of the Sun and the Moon and their distance from Earth. The circumstances of the commissioning of this painting are unknown, but the choice of subject is intriguing, for even though it was painted in the intellectually liberal climate of Venice, it was done at the time when Galileo's teachings on astronomy were being condemned by the Church.

The conservative Mannerist style Strozzi had been trained in as a Capuchin monk in his native Genoa evolved through exposure to the work of Caravaggio, Anthony van Dyck (who resided in Genoa from 1623 to 1627) and especially Rubens, who painted a major altarpiece for the city in 1620. In 1630, Strozzi left Genoa and his religious duties to settle in Venice, and the further stylistic influence of Veronese and Domenico Fetti characterizes his later period. This is a fine example of Strozzi's mature work, reflecting the confluence of his sources. The rich colours and the evocation of surfaces and textures are Venetian and Northern Italian in character. The painterly treatment of flesh, particularly the hands, echoes that of Flemish masters. The dark background from which the figures emerge into strong light are Caravaggesque. H.T.G.

Salvator Rosa

Arenella (Naples) 1615 – Rome 1673

Jason Charming the Dragon

About 1665-1670
Oil on canvas
77.8 × 66.9 cm
Purchase, Miss Olive Hosmer Fund
1960.1251

■ The dark, often morbid character of Salvator Rosa's art reflects its Neapolitan origins and the influence of Jusepe de Ribera in particular. By the age of twenty, Rosa was studying in Rome, and he subsequently moved to Florence. The mingling of his study of antiquity and Baroque figure composition in Rome with the seventeenth-century Florentine taste for the bizarre resulted in an utterly unique style.

Rosa excelled in dramatic and mysterious compositions. This one was inspired by an illustration from a 1641 edition of Ovid's *Metamorphoses*, Book VII, which recounts the story of Jason and the Golden Fleece. With a typically Baroque proclivity for tales that incite wonder, Rosa depicts the mythical hero using the magic herbs the sorceress Medea gave him to charm the dragon guarding the object of his quest. Jason's pose heightens the aura of mystery and focuses the composition – in a powerful diagonal confrontation of the two figures – on the pouring out of the herbal brew.

Rosa was an accomplished printmaker and about 1663-1664, before painting this subject, he had made an etching of it. The etching's success no doubt led him to recast the subject, with minor differences, on canvas. This version of the painting, datable to the late 1660s, is unquestionably the finest of the several in existence that the artist produced. H.T.G.

Abraham Bloemaert

Gorinchem 1564 – Utrecht 1651

Harvest Scene

About 1625-1630
Oil on canvas
137.2 × 198.2 cm
Purchase, Horsley and Annie Townsend Bequest
1973.26

■ During his youth, Abraham Bloemaert spent three years in Paris, where he was greatly influenced by the late Mannerist art of the School of Fontainebleau. He was working in Amsterdam in the early 1590s, then settled in Utrecht, where the influence of Caravaggio's followers on him was mitigated by the elegant stylization of his earlier Mannerist idiom.

The largest of the artist's rural subjects, this *Harvest Scene* is datable to about 1625-1630. The large foreground figures resting and stretching on a small bluff at the left are dramatically contrasted with the smaller active figures in the middle ground. The sleeper provides a link between the two groups.

The painting is likely more than a simple depiction of harvesting. It uses motifs found in Bloemaert's own engravings of *July* and *August* from a series of the months of the year, which fits with the Flemish tradition of representations of the months and seasons. The subject may also be a personal combination of images derived from earlier prototypes inspired by the biblical Proverbs, reprimanding sloth while endorsing rest after diligent labour. Dutch art of the time commonly referred to both religious thought and popular proverbs as exemplified in daily life. H.T.G.

Matthias Stomer
Amersfoort (?) about 1600 – Sicily (?) after 1650
Christ and the Woman Taken in Adultery
About 1630-1633
Oil on canvas
101.6 × 137.2 cm
Purchase, Horsley and Annie Townsend Bequest and gift of Mr. and Mrs. Michal Hornstein
1993.16

■ The story of Christ and the Adulteress is told in the Gospel of John (8:1-11). The Pharisees conduct a woman caught in the act of adultery to Jesus, whom they test by asking how she should be punished. The punishment prescribed under Mosaic law is death by stoning, but Christ replies, "He that is without sin among you, let him first cast a stone at her." Stomer here depicts this dramatic moment.

Stomer received his early training in Utrecht, with such Caravaggisti artists as Honthorst and Baburen. *Christ and the Woman Taken in Adultery* uses a number of Caravaggesque effects, such as the contrasts of light and dark to isolate the figure of the adulteress and the Book of Moses. In a typical gesture of Caravaggio, Christ's hands articulate both his adjudication and mercy, while the passive contemplation of the adulteress anticipates her spiritual rebirth implied by Jesus' words to her, "Neither do I condemn thee; go, and sin no more."

Stomer spent from 1630 until about 1633 in Rome, where the Caravaggesque realism of his figures was further developed. That this painting belongs to the artist's Roman period is evident in its aggressive colourism, bold execution and certain physiognomic types – note the forceful realism that characterizes each of the Pharisees as they respond to Christ's words. H.T.G.

Nicolaes Maes

Dordrecht 1634 – Amsterdam 1693

The Adoration of the Shepherds

1658
Oil on panel
59.4 × 87 cm

Purchase, Horsley and Annie Townsend Bequest

1965.1520

■ Although it is not documented that Maes studied under Rembrandt, his early biographer, Arnold Houbraken of Dordrecht, attested that he did; at any rate, the influence of Rembrandt on his works is evident. Maes's fame rests on his genre scenes from the 1650s and his portraits. Only five religious paintings survive.

This evocative *Adoration* is a masterful synthesis of compositional elements derived from Rembrandt and other contemporary painters. In particular, it recalls Rembrandt's celebrated *Adoration* from 1646 and two of his etchings of the subject (about 1652 and about 1654), all three of which, like this painting by Maes, are set at night. Maes has built up layers of brown and black paint over a yellow ground to intensify the light and the colours of the figures caught in its glow. In addition to the lantern and the candle, there is an extraordinary effect of light emanating from the Infant that shows the influence of the Utrecht Caravaggisti. But Maes has also introduced inspired touches of his own, such as the cloud-covered moon seen through the open door and the focused gaze of the bespectacled shepherd on the Infant. H.T.G.

Gerrit van Honthorst
Utrecht 1590 – Utrecht 1656

The Duet

1623-1624
Oil on canvas
79.1 × 95.3 cm
Purchase, Horsley and Annie Townsend Bequest and William Gilman Cheney Bequest
1969.1639

■ After training in the Utrecht studio of Abraham Bloemaert, Gerrit van Honthorst began his career in Rome, where he was greatly influenced by the art of Caravaggio. In fact, the young Dutch artist lived in the household of Caravaggio's patron, Cardinal Vincenzo Giustiniani. While in Italy, Honthorst also encountered the artists Ribera and Valentin, and received commissions from Cardinal Scipione Borghese, a renowned collector and patron of the young Bernini.

This painting of a singing duo was executed after the artist returned to Utrecht in 1620, for a clientele attracted by both the subject matter and the modern style. Honthorst was particularly successful in creating candle- and torch-lit scenes. The key element of the composition, the centrally placed candle flame, contributes a subtle eroticism as it highlights the woman's breast. While the candle theatrically illuminates the merry singers, it is itself partly obscured by the dark band of the songbook, which enhances the contrast of light and darkness.

The painting is related to Caravaggio's early *Concert of Youths* (Metropolitan Museum of Art, New York) and certain pictures by Bartolomeo Manfredi. It also recalls other subjects in Dutch painting: the procuress and her client, and allegorical treatments of love and of the five senses (in this case, hearing). H.T.G.

Paulus Bor

Amersfoort about 1601 – Amersfoort 1669

Travel Pouch and Documents on a Table

1630
Oil on panel
56 × 76 cm
Gift of Mr. and Mrs. Michal Hornstein
2000.95

■ As a student in Rome in the early 1620s, Paulus Bor associated with Dutch painters of lively genre scenes, becoming a founding member of the raucous fraternity of painters known as the Bentvueghels. He returned to his native Amersfoort by 1626, after which time his work reflects his connections with the Utrecht Caravaggisti, as well as stylistic ties to Dutch classicism.

Born to a prosperous Catholic family of textile merchants and not dependent on painting for his livelihood, Bor was free to paint atypical subjects or well-known historical and mythological subjects in unusual contexts. The subject of this painting – one of his few surviving still lifes and the only one from this period of his career – is most unconventional. A worn ledger, pouch and other travel implements are arranged on a strangely angled table. The picture depicts the play of light and surface textures so well that one can almost smell the musty hides. The spider and flies – perhaps metaphorical? – add an enlivening detail.

Bor's relatively rare works are seldom signed or dated, but this one is both signed and dated 1630. The monochromatic palette recalls paintings done around that time by Heda, Claesz, Lievens and others, but the style is uniquely Bor's. H.T.G.

Jacob van Ruisdael

Haarlem 1628/29 – Haarlem 1682

The Bleaching Grounds at Haarlem

About 1670
Oil on canvas
55.5 × 68 cm
Adaline Van Horne Bequest
1945.920

■ This is one of Ruisdael's *Haarlempjes*, or little views of Haarlem, which are first documented in a 1669 inventory. It presents a panorama of the city from the vantage point of the linen bleaching fields that underpinned the city's prosperity. Indeed, from the late 1660s through about 1675, Ruisdael and his circle executed scenes of not only Haarlem but also the many surrounding towns whose dunes served the bleaching industry. The paintings appealed to the patriotic tastes of the Dutch burghers who bought them.

The Museum's signed canvas is closely related to another two of Ruisdael's pictures of the same subject (Mauritshuis, The Hague; Rijksmuseum, Amsterdam), both datable to about 1670. It is rich in identifiable landmarks of the seventeenth-century Haarlem skyline, including the ruins of the castle of Huis te' Kleef, Bakenesser Church, Saint John's Church, the Clock Tower, Saint Bavo's Cathedral, the Town Hall and Saint Ann's Church. The low horizon permitted Ruisdael to create a remarkable orchestration of lighting in the sky and on the dunes through the rich cloud clusters. It was Ruisdael's genius to convert city profiles into dynamic panoramas. H.T.G.

Barent Fabritius

Midden-Beemster 1624 – Amsterdam 1673

Saint Matthew and the Angel

1656
Oil on canvas
76.9 × 63.9 cm

Gift of Mr. and Mrs. Michal Hornstein in honour of Frederik J. Duparc
1990.13

■ Barent Fabritius painted portraits, genre scenes, and history and religious subjects. He was probably first trained by his brother, Carel, a student of Rembrandt. Rembrandt's direct influence can be traced to the 1640s, when Fabritius lived in Amsterdam.

This intimate depiction of Saint Matthew writing under the guidance of an angel focuses on the Evangelist deep in concentration as he pauses to ponder the interpretation of the divinely inspired words dictated to him by the angel before committing them to paper. The signed and dated painting may originally have been part of a cycle of half-length pictures of the four Evangelists. It also falls within the tradition of half-length character studies, so-called tronies, that were a specialty of other contemporary artists, including Rembrandt.

The vibrant colouristic highlights, notably red and black, are characteristic of Fabritius' mature paintings, in which he looked to the palette of Rembrandt's pupil Nicolas Maes. H.T.G.

Rembrandt Harmensz. van Rijn

Leiden 1606 – Amsterdam 1669

Portrait of a Young Woman

About 1665
Oil on canvas
56.3 × 48 cm
Mrs. R. MacD. Paterson Bequest
1949.1006

■ That Rembrandt was one of the greatest of all portraitists is universally acknowledged. His technical skill in the naturalistic depiction of his subjects – including himself often – was matched by his profound exploration of psychological types. By the end of his long and productive career, he could achieve these effects with remarkably limited and controlled means.

This portrait, executed in the last years of Rembrandt's life, provides an example of his masterful economy. The palette is restricted to a rich range of blacks, loosely applied flesh tones and rough strokes of white that convey the vivacity of the subject and the tactility of her dress. The light is carefully manipulated in the undefined space so that the face emerges out of a dark, enveloping atmosphere, which contributes to the introspective mood.

The tenderness and intimacy in this portrait have led some to propose that it depicts a member of the artist's immediate family. At the beginning of the twentieth century, W. Valentiner identified the subject as Magdalena van Loo, the second wife of Rembrandt's son, Titus. There is no solid evidence for this, however. H.T.G.

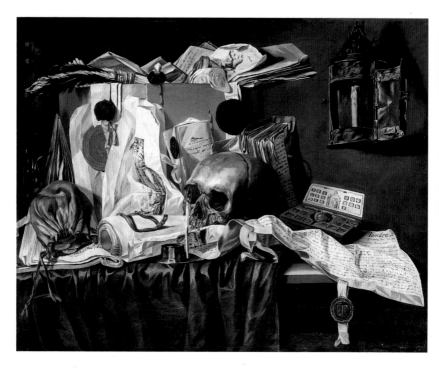

N. L. Peschier

Active in Holland 1659-1661

Vanitas Still Life

1660
Oil on canvas
70 × 89.5 cm
Gift of Mr. and Mrs. Michal Hornstein
2001.28

■ N. L. Peschier, a seventeenth-century painter active in Holland but possibly of French origin, signed and dated a handful of fine still lifes. This *Vanitas Still Life* is a particularly successful and intricate example of his work. A *vanitas* is intended to encourage the viewer to reflect on the vanity of worldly possessions and aspirations by depicting objects that symbolize the transience of earthly existence and pleasures.

The artist has included a rich diversity of objects to convey this theme. The skull is an obvious symbol of mortality, as are the hourglass and the lantern with a dying candle. The temporality of power and wealth is alluded to in the portable scale, the coins and purse, the quills, pen and inkpot, and the deeds and documents, one dated 1660, others bearing the seals of Philip II of Spain (d. 1598), who had ruled the Netherlands. Even the contemplative pleasures of art and music are implied: there are a music book open to a love song, a figure sketch and a book of landscapes after Van de Velde. The brilliantly rendered crumpled paper further emphasizes the impermanency of all things.

A rich palette orchestrates the disparate elements depicted in this work, and unity is achieved through the overall compositional pattern of the strongly lit papers. The canvas is signed along the lower right: *N. L. Peschier. F.* H.T.G.

Emanuel de Witte

Alkmaar about 1617 – Amsterdam 1692

Interior with a Woman Playing a Virginal

About 1660
Oil on canvas
97.5 × 109.7 cm
Purchase, John W. Tempest Fund
1894.41

■ Emanuel de Witte is one of the most renowned Dutch painters of architectural interiors. His paintings are characterized by their grand scale, elaborate perspective, strong sunlight and human activity. Although he specialized in church interiors, he also painted domestic interiors, imaginary harbour scenes, market scenes and even mythological subjects.

De Witte established himself in Delft before moving to Amsterdam around 1652. This painting was done in Amsterdam but strongly reflects his Delft training. The orthogonals of perspective meet in the distance through a succession of rooms and doorways. The alternation of sunlight and shadow, its effect enhanced by the floor pattern, guides the eye through the space while softening the severity of the geometric organization. The house depicted is probably imaginary, as such deep houses did not exist in Amsterdam, not even along the grand Herengracht canal.

In the left foreground a man, barely deciphered, lies in a bed, his clothes tossed on a chair, listening to the music being played. The canvas may depict an adage such as "Love teaches music" or "Music dispels care." The domesticity of the subject is underscored by the maid seen through the open doors diligently sweeping. H.T.G.

Godfried Schalcken
Made (Dordrecht) 1643 – The Hague 1706

Salomé with the Head of John the Baptist

About 1700
Oil on canvas
116.3 × 85.9 cm

Gift of Michal and Renata Hornstein in honour of Guy Cogeval, Director of the Montreal Museum of Fine Arts
2003.87

■ Godfried Schalcken trained between 1662 and 1665 in the Leiden studio of Gerrit Dou, a Rembrandt pupil who was a master of minute detailing and varnish-smooth finish. Dou tended to employ candlelight and indirect lighting to attain chiaroscuro effects. Schalcken further developed this aesthetic by enveloping his compositions in a unifying atmosphere, with half-length figures devoid of dramatic gesture. In the 1670s he became a renowned portraitist, influenced by Nicolaes Maes of Dordrecht and the Flemish artist van Dyck. From 1692 to 1699, Schalcken worked in England at the court of William and Mary, receiving distinguished international commissions. As Flemish art's influence on him intensified, his female figures became more monumental and idealized, while remaining highly sensuous – the light seems to caress their skin. These qualities are seen in *Salomé with the Head of John the Baptist*, a late work in which the artist achieves a new level of psychological insight, enhanced by the play of the artificial light on the figures.

According to Saint Matthew (14:3-11), King Herod took his brother's wife, Herodias, as his own. When John the Baptist criticized this illegal arrangement, the king had him arrested. For Herod's birthday, Herodias' daughter Salomé danced for him, whereupon he promised her anything she wished. At her mother's prompting, she asked for the head of John the Baptist on a salver. With the starry night visible through the prison window, the executioner stands behind Salomé, hand on his sword, as she, looking at her hand-maiden, bears the platter with his head. H.T.G.

Valentin de Boulogne, called Valentin
Coulommiers-en-Brie, France, 1591 – Rome 1632

King David with a Harp
About 1626-1627
Oil on canvas
70 × 60 cm

Gift of Mr. and Mrs. Michal Hornstein
1980.1

■ The dramatically innovative works of Caravaggio were an exciting source of inspiration to the impressionable young artists arriving in Rome from France and Holland in the early seventeenth century. Among the most talented of them was Valentin de Boulogne. He lived in the same neighbourhood as other French artists and the Dutch genre painters known as the Bentvueghels, with whom he associated. His emulation of Caravaggio was equalled only by Bartolomeo Manfredi, with whose works his have sometimes been confused. Valentin spent his entire brief career in Rome, his style enriched by exposure to such contemporaries as Saraceni, Honthorst and Ribera. His patrons included the eminent Cardinal Francesco Barberini.

This *David* is from about 1626-1627, when Valentin was at the peak of his artistic powers. It employs a rich Caravaggesque chiaroscuro so that the figure's sorrowful, introspective stare and hands holding the sceptre, harp and psalmatic sheet with Hebrew characters – all traditional imagery of David as king, musician, poet and psalmist – emerge dramatically into light. H.T.G.

Nicolas Poussin
Les Andelys 1594 – Rome 1665

Landscape with a Man Pursued by a Snake

About 1638-1640
Oil on canvas
65 × 76 cm
Purchase, special replacement fund
1975.15

■ Respected for his subtle erudition and his sober classical compositions, Nicolas Poussin is one of the most influential artists in the history of European art, particularly in regard to the development of French art during the second half of the seventeenth century.

Poussin created *Landscape with a Man Pursued by a Snake* in Rome in the late 1630s for his friend Cassiano dal Pozzo, who was a humanist, antiquarian and secretary to Cardinal Francesco Barberini. The painting adapts the landscape tradition of the Venetian Renaissance to evoke feelings and ideas. Against the passive panorama of an idyllic landscape inspired by the Roman *campagna*, a terrified man is pursued by a snake that is poised to strike him, unnoticed by a nearby woman and fisherman. The painting thus deals with two themes of great interest to Poussin: the arbitrariness of fortune, and the passions of the soul, ranging from terror to stoic calm. Nature is shown as a source of both life and destruction within the cycle of death and regeneration. Esoteric symbolism abounds. For example, snakes, which shed their skin, symbolize rebirth, and fish symbolize corruption. The subject may also derive from classical literary sources like Virgil's *Eclogues*. H.T.G.

Sébastien Bourdon
Montpellier 1616 – Paris 1671

Landscape with Classical Ruins

About 1635
Oil on canvas
50.2 × 64.5 cm
Purchase, John W. Tempest Fund
1953.1083

■ The mercurial career of Sébastien Bourdon, his facility in embracing a range of contemporary styles with equal mastery, and his adventurous life make him one of the most interesting figures in seventeenth-century French art. Born in Montpellier, he received his early training in Paris. At the age of fourteen, he left the capital for Toulouse, where he entered the military. In 1634 Bourdon arrived in Rome and worked in the styles of a surprisingly wide range of artists active there. Denounced as a Protestant by a fellow artist, he fled Rome in 1637. His subsequent career reflects the increasing influence of Poussin.

For all its geometric clarity, articulated through elements of classical architecture, this landscape retains a sense of spontaneity. The subject, to the extent that there is one, is an odd assemblage gathered at a country tavern, including gypsies and beggars by a tent, a gentleman, a soldier, lovers, a dog and a family setting off on horseback with their belongings. The poetic late afternoon light envelops the entire scene, conveying a sense of paused action. Executed in Rome about 1635, this work brings together the various influences Bourdon absorbed there: Castiglione's pastoral scenes, Pieter van Laer's low-life concerns, Claude Lorrain's atmospheric lighting of landscapes, and Poussin's classicism. H.T.G.

Laurent de La Hyre
Paris 1606 – Paris 1656

Landscape with Swineherd

1648
Oil on canvas
60.4 × 77.5 cm
Purchase, gift of Murray G. Ballantyne and Horsley and Annie Townsend Bequest
1972.4

■ The refinement and attenuated grace characteristic of the Second School of Fontainebleau marked the young Laurent de La Hyre. During the 1630s, and especially after Poussin's visit to Paris from 1640 to 1642, La Hyre's paintings took on an increasingly classical cast, with more severely structured compositions and idealized figures of more normative proportions. La Hyre's landscapes, which can be dated between the mid-1640s and mid-1650s, are the French equivalent of the views of the Roman *campagna* Claude Lorrain was creating at the time. Their magic lies in the balance of classicism and a more Northern naturalism. Thus, while the sculpture and the ruins of a temple (probably inspired by the Roman temple at Tivoli) in this *Landscape with Swineherd* allude to antiquity, the vast panorama in all its atmospheric splendour evokes the Seine Valley, with a chateau and town in the distance. La Hyre's interest in the science of perspective is reflected in both the panorama and the foreshortened horse.

The swine and young swineherd have led to the suggestion that this painting may portray the parable of the Prodigal Son; but La Hyre's mythological and religious subjects tend to be more explicit. While a moralistic subtext cannot be discounted, the work's appeal is fundamentally visual. H.T.G.

Jacques Linard
Paris about 1600 – Paris 1645

Still Life with Shells and Coral

1640
Oil on canvas
53.3 × 62.2 cm

Gift of Mr. and Mrs. Michal Hornstein
1999.149

■ Jacques Linard was one of the most important still-life painters in seventeenth-century France; his patrons included Louis XIII and Cardinal Richelieu. Linard's works balance fascinating detail with poetic compositions of a simplicity that distinguishes French still-life painting of the period from the lusher, more sophisticated works by Flemish and Dutch painters.

This fine dated canvas is one of only four among the artist's approximately forty surviving paintings to feature shells. The shells it depicts were exotic and very expensive. Part of their appeal would have been as *maraviglie* – rare objects pursued by amateurs for their collections of natural wonders, or *Wunderkammern*. Still lifes also delighted seventeenth-century owners for their implied moral and intellectual themes. Coral was believed to ward off the "evil eye" and, because its form recalls blood vessels, had long been associated with Christ's Blood of Redemption. The allusion to Christ's protection against the evils of the world gave coral a spiritual significance, while shells with pearly interiors suggested luxury and sensuality. Linard thus contrasted the physical and the spiritual in this painting. H.T.G.

Jean Lemaire

Dammartin-en-Goële 1601 – Gaillon 1659

Roman Senators and Legates

About 1645-1655
Oil on canvas
101.6 × 148.9 cm

Gift of Lord Strathcona and family
1927.313

■ Jean Lemaire established a successful career in Rome, specializing in imaginary antique scenes. In 1638 he returned to France, where he executed paintings, set designs and murals for a prestigious clientele that included Cardinal Richelieu, and assisted Nicolas Poussin in the decoration of the Grand Gallery of the Louvre.

In this painting, Lemaire creates an idealized city from an assemblage of scattered monuments. Lemaire's patrons would have delighted in recognizing these far-flung buildings, united in the inspiration of the artist. In addition to the Colosseum in the right background, the artist has brought together the Triumphal Arch at Orange, the portico of the Pantheon in Rome, one of Verona's town gates (the Porta dei Leoni), and the Septizonium (a late Imperial Roman seven-storey structure ornamented with colonnades). The monument at the right, blocking part of the Colosseum, is a free creation by the artist. The sculpture of the river god in the left foreground derives from the colossal figure of the Nile on the Capitoline Hill in Rome, and the reliefs decorating its base derive from the Forum of Trajan.

Lemaire's sources were the ruins themselves, as well as engravings and published reconstructions of ancient edifices. H.T.G.

Philippe de Champaigne
Brussels 1602 – Paris 1674

The Tribute Money

About 1655
Oil on canvas
138.5 × 188 cm

Purchase, Dr. and Mrs. Max Stern Bequest
1999.1

▪ After initial training in Brussels, Philippe de Champaigne worked in Paris, receiving commissions from Louis XIII, Cardinal Richelieu, Anne of Austria and various religious orders. Renowned for his sober religious works, he was also one of the most sought-after portraitists of his time.

The episode depicted in *The Tribute Money* is recounted in the Gospels of Matthew, Mark and Luke. Seeking to entrap Jesus while he taught at the temple in Jerusalem, a group of Pharisees asked him whether one should pay taxes – tribute money – to Rome. A negative answer would offend the Roman authorities, while a positive answer would upset the Jews, who opposed the occupation. Drawing attention to the image of Caesar on a coin shown to him by the Pharisee wearing a prayer shawl with a Hebrew inscription, Jesus responded, "Render unto Caesar the things that are Caesar's and unto God the things that are God's."

In this mature work, Champaigne has borrowed compositional elements from artists such as Raphael, Guercino and Valentin, while the composition's classicism and formality reflect the art of Poussin. The life-size figures in this monumental canvas seem to embrace the viewer within their circle. At the left, the Pharisee wearing a Hebrew-inscribed headband respectfully contemplates the scene. The figure at the far right is clearly a portrait, likely a self-portrait. H.T.G.

■ Michel Anguier played an important role in the development of the classical tendency in mid-seventeenth-century French sculpture. He received his initial training in Paris in the 1630s and was deeply grounded in the aesthetics of the Second School of Fontainebleau. He spent from 1643 to 1651 in Italy, studying the works of antiquity and working in the studio of Alessandro Algardi, whose refined classicism stood in marked contrast to the Baroque exuberance of his contemporary Bernini. During these pivotal years, Anguier evolved his own distinctive idiom – an elegant synthesis of the Mannerist stylization of Fontainebleau and the classicism he encountered in Rome – that was perfectly suited to the tastes of Paris upon his return.

This statuette of Amphitrite, wife of the sea god Poseidon, is based on a model executed in 1652 for a series of gods and goddesses to be cast in bronze, an ideal medium for conveying the elegant proportions, smooth surfaces and fluid, rhythmic outlines of figures. The evocation of tactility is enhanced by the dolphin on which Amphitrite stands and the lobster clinging to her hand. H.T.G.

Michel Anguier
Eu, Normandy, 1612 – Paris 1686

Amphitrite
About 1652
Bronze
65 × 21.5 × 19.5 cm (with base)
Purchase, gift of Mrs. Algernon Lucas
1965.1517

Charles Le Brun
Paris 1619 – Paris 1690

The Deification of Aeneas

1642-1644
Oil on canvas
81.3 × 97.7 cm
Purchase, John W. Tempest Fund
1953.1082

■ The story of the deification of Aeneas is told in Ovid's *Metamorphoses* (XIV:595-608). In this painting by Charles Le Brun, the goddess Venus is seen anointing her kneeling son Aeneas, before he fights Turnus for the possession of Rome. She holds the ambrosia and nectar she will apply to Aeneas' lips so that he may join the pantheon of gods. At the left, the river god who has cleansed away Aeneas' mortality looks on, and two nymphs peer out from the forest glade in the background. In the lower corners, putti play with the arms Vulcan forged for Aeneas at Venus' behest (Virgil, *Aeneid*, VIII:608-625).

This painting can be dated to Le Brun's Roman period. Profoundly influenced by Poussin, who was in Paris between 1640 and 1642, Le Brun followed him back to Rome, where they worked in close association until 1646, when Le Brun returned to France. The influence of Poussin is felt in the painting's measured classicism. As late as the eighteenth century, in fact, it was attributed to Poussin, whose *Venus Showing the Arms to Aeneas* (Musée des Beaux-Arts, Rouen) from 1639 depicts a related subject. The treatment of the landscape reflects the influence and possible intervention of Poussin's brother-in-law, the Roman landscape painter Gaspard Dughet.

In France, Le Brun became one of the most powerful and influential artists of his time. He was First Painter to the King, in charge of decorating the Château de Versailles for Louis XIV, and chancellor and "prince" of the French Academy of Painting. H.T.G.

François de Troy
Toulouse 1645 – Paris 1730

Presumed Portrait of Madame de Franqueville and her Children

1712
Oil on canvas
138.5 × 163.4 cm
Gift of Mr. and Mrs. Michal Hornstein
1982.21

■ Born in Toulouse, François de Troy received his artistic education and established his career in Paris. As a portraitist, he was rivalled only by the slightly younger Hyacinthe Rigaud and Nicolas de Largilliere. Although de Troy received major royal commissions, he enjoyed great popularity with the bourgeoisie and clergy. The somewhat less formal and more naturalistic character of his works in comparison with those of his two rivals probably contributed to this broader appeal.

De Troy was influential in promoting the family portrait as brilliantly exemplified in this monumental painting, which furthermore shows the artist's preference for setting his subjects in domestic interiors, though of certain grandeur. The identity of the family group portrayed here remains unconfirmed. According to a later inscription on the frame, the figures at the centre are the Marquise de Franqueville and the young Marquis; the child seated on the cushion and looking up from plaiting a garland of flowers is the Comtesse du Lys; and the elder sister standing behind her is the future Madame de La Baume. There is no independent confirmation of these identifications, however. A variant family portrait dating from 1711 in Douai is also said to be the de Franquevilles, but it is likewise undocumented. The oval portrait visible through the drawn drapes in the adjacent room at the left of the Museum's painting is likely a portrait of the deceased father of the family. H.T.G.

Nicolas de Largilliere

Paris 1656 – Paris 1746

Portrait of a Woman as Astrea, Probably Mary Josephine Drummond, Condesa de Castelblanco

About 1710-1712
Oil on canvas
140 × 106 cm

Purchase, special replacement fund, Horsley and Annie Townsend Bequest, anonymous gift in honour of Dr. Sean B. Murphy, gift of David Y. Hodgson, Dr. William L. Glen and other friends of the Museum
1977.1

■ Portraiture was a popular genre in the eighteenth century, and Nicolas de Largilliere was among its most renowned practitioners in France. Besides serving as a visual memorial, a portrait could express a patron's social position, sentiments and, allegorically, aspirations.

This portrait reflects changes in Largilliere's style in the early decades of the eighteenth century. Less dependent on the precedents of Peter Lely and van Dyck, and relying more on Rubens, Titian and various Dutch sources, his work features a lighter palette with brilliant colouristic accents. Unity is achieved here through suavely orchestrated shades of pink, blue and golden green in the dress, face, hair, landscape and attentive dog. Although essentially an allegory, the work conveys the vitality and warmth of the subject – a sensual woman, full of charm and possessed of great, subtly idealized beauty, in a spectacular brocade gown.

An inscription on the back of the canvas indicates that the subject was twenty years old on January 14, 1710, which corresponds to the age of Mary Drummond, who married the Conde de Castelblanco that year. The portrait was probably commissioned by her father, the Duke of Melfort, and his wife. The sitter is portrayed as the shepherdess Astrea, the heroine of a seventeenth-century pastoral novel, *L'Astrée*, by Honoré d'Urfé, a character who embodies chaste love – an appropriate, if contrived, image for a young woman entering marriage. H.T.G.

François Boucher
Paris 1703 – Paris 1770

The Assumption of the Virgin

About 1758-1760
Oil on canvas
143.2 × 75.3 cm

Purchase, The Museum Campaign 1988-1993 Fund
2003.88

■ Painter to Louis XV and director of the Royal Academy, François Boucher was the quintessential exponent of the French Rococo, and remains among the most esteemed artists of eighteenth-century France. He was at his peak when he painted this *Assumption of the Virgin*, and its open sketch work illustrates his superb draftsmanship. Boucher painted it in brown camaieu (monochrome), restricting his palette to salmon pink, red and brown with white highlights.

The purpose of this oil sketch is unknown. It is the first of three similar works, though the other two (National Gallery of Scotland, Edinburgh; Musée des Beaux-Arts, Dijon) represent the Glorification of the Virgin. Boucher may have produced this sketch in connection with a cycle on the Life of the Virgin for the Church of Saint-Sulpice, Paris. Or it may have been done in the hope of gaining a commission from Madame de Pompadour, Louis XV's preferred mistress and a major patron of the arts. About 1750 Boucher began executing large-scale religious paintings in response to her increasingly pious interests.

Yet the work apparently bears some connection to a commission for an *Assumption* received by the artist's pupil and son-in-law Jean-Baptiste Deshays in 1758. Although Deshays's altarpiece is lost, a sketch for it (Institute of Arts, Minneapolis) incorporates some of Boucher's composition. Because Boucher's oil sketches were popular with collectors, he may have produced this painting initially to aid Deshays and then sell. In any case, the work appeared in the auction of Deshays's estate after his death in 1765. H.T.G.

Giovanni Battista Tiepolo
Venice 1696 – Madrid 1770

Apelles Painting the Portrait of Campaspe

About 1725-1726
Oil on canvas
57.4 × 73.7 cm
Adaline Van Horne Bequest
1945.929

■ According to the story in Pliny's *Natural History* (35:10-36), Apelles, the most famous painter of ancient Greece, fell in love with Campaspe, the favourite of Alexander the Great, while painting her portrait. In homage, Alexander gave Campaspe to the artist. During the Renaissance, this story became an occasion for painters to praise the nobility of their art – and their patrons.

Tiepolo depicts himself as Apelles and his wife, Cecilia (sister of the Venetian painters Gian Antonio and Francesco Guardi), as Campaspe. Their servant, Ali, watches from the far right. One of the two paintings in the background of the studio illustrates *Moses and the Brazen Serpent*. Tiepolo painted two other more formal presentations of Apelles and Campaspe, one dating from the late 1720s (J. Paul Getty Museum, Los Angeles), and the other dating from about 1736 (Louvre, Paris). The version in Montreal has an endearing, affectionate humour and a domestic intimacy not found in the other versions. The detail Apelles is shown applying to the canvas has been selected with poignant wit. Tiepolo likely created the lighthearted picture for himself or a close acquaintance.

Considered the greatest Venetian painter of the eighteenth century, Tiepolo was also the last of the decorative and mythological artists in a tradition going back to Titian and Veronese, artistic mentors who had an indelible impact on his art. H.T.G.

Francesco Guardi

Venice 1712 – Venice 1793

Storm at Sea

About 1770
Oil on canvas
53.3 × 66.1 cm
Adaline Van Horne Bequest
1945.957

■ While Francesco Guardi is best known today for his atmospheric views of Venice, he also worked in other genres and subjects. However, this depiction of a stormy sea is an unusual theme not only for him but also in the Venetian painting tradition. The open brushwork and sketchily defined forms enhance the dramatic immediacy of the scene, further intensified by the monumental scale of the waves and sharp keel of the ships against the open sky. The ships depicted are of seventeenth-century design; evidently, Guardi looked to Dutch sources of the previous century including prints and, as some have posited, the naval battle scenes of Willem van de Velde the Younger.

Francesco and his elder brother Gian Antonio did not enjoy the esteem in their own time that they came to possess posthumously. Among their activities during the 1730s and 1740s, they executed a large number of copies of paintings, some based on prints, for the collection of Marshal von der Schulenburg in Venice. Perhaps this earlier broad exposure accounts for the unique character of this unusual depiction of a stormy sea. H.T.G.

Giovanni Antonio Canal, called Canaletto

Venice 1697 – Venice 1768

Interior of San Marco, Venice

About 1760
Oil on canvas
44.1 × 31.5 cm
Adaline Van Horne Bequest
1945.871

■ No artist is more closely associated with vedute, or views of Venice than Canaletto, who attracted the patronage of wealthy tourists at a time when the "Grand Tour" was becoming fashionable. His splendid paintings served as souvenirs – albeit of a high artistic order – for aristocrats and distinguished visitors, and were also prized by those who would themselves have wished to travel to Italy.

Canaletto's views of Venice are often composite studies, and he would convincingly manipulate perspective to enhance dramatic effect. These characteristics are apparent in this unusual interior view of the altar of the eleventh-century Basilica of San Marco. Rich in ornamentation, the painting is full of incident: a priest officiating at the left, praying worshippers and wandering visitors. Hanging at the centre is a banner that reads *VERONA FIDELIS*. The Senate had ordered such a banner upon the death of Scipione Maffei in 1755, a time when Verona was under Venetian rule. Ducal coats of arms, like those adorning the arches here, were removed from San Marco in the 1720s but may have been put back for special occasions; they may also simply reflect the imagination of Canaletto.

Another version of the painting was acquired by George III and is in Britain's royal collection. While both may be dated between 1756 and 1762, the Museum's picture is generally placed about 1760. H.T.G.

George Romney
Dalton in Furness 1734 –
Kendal 1802

Portrait of Sir Robert Gunning

1779-1795
Oil on canvas
239.9 × 148 cm
Purchase, anonymous gift
1967.1557

■ In 1762, with little early training, George Romney left Lancashire for London, where he became a leading portrait painter. His travels in Italy in 1773-1775 drew out his talent to a point that, upon his return, he was able to rival even Joshua Reynolds. While Romney's portraits of women sometimes exhibit a certain facile elegance, his portraits of men, like this handsome painting, can be quite powerful.

The subject, Robert Gunning (1731-1816) of Horton, Northamptonshire, had a distinguished diplomatic career as ambassador to Copenhagen (1765-1770), minister to Berlin (1771) and ambassador to Saint Petersburg (1772-1775). In 1773, he was made a Knight of the Order of the Bath (he is portrayed here with the star and collar of the order) and in 1778 he received the title of baronet. It is documented that Gunning sat for Romney repeatedly between 1779 and 1795. This particular picture was exhibited, unfinished, at the artist's residence in 1787 and 1788, and payment for it was recorded in March 1795. Romney had also made portraits of Gunning's wife and two daughters.

This canvas is remarkable for its depiction of fabrics and textures, bold treatment of whites and overall orchestration of colours. H.T.G.

Thomas Gainsborough
Sudbury 1727 –
London 1788

Portrait of Mrs. George Drummond

1779-1782
Oil on canvas
230.1 × 152 cm

Purchase, John W. Tempest
Fund

1951.1062

■ This painting portrays the eldest of the Honourable Thomas Harley's five daughters, Martha (1756-1788). Harley, a wealthy banker and merchant, was Lord Mayor of London and the younger son of the Earl of Oxford. This portrait was probably made to commemorate the marriage of Martha to George Drummond in 1779. Commissioned by her father, it was undoubtedly intended for his new residence, Berrington Hall, built between 1778 and 1781 with the fortune he had amassed supplying the British army during the American Revolution. In this magisterial painting – the only full-length portrait by Gainsborough in Canada – the suave, fluid brushwork of the artist's late style enhances both the richness of the white satin gown and the pastoral charm of the park. To create unity between sitter and setting, Gainsborough enframed the young subject within the trees in the background and gently silhouetted her head against their greenery.

Harley also commissioned a companion portrait of his son-in-law (Ashmolean Museum, Oxford), and the two portraits remained together until they were auctioned in May 1951. The young George Drummond is portrayed leaning against a tree and turning slightly to the right, presumably towards his seated wife, according to paired portrait convention. H.T.G.

Jean-Joseph Taillasson
Bordeaux 1745 – Paris 1809

Saint Mary Magdalene in the Desert

1784
Oil on canvas
205.7 × 195.4 cm
Purchase, The Museum Campaign 1988-1993 Fund
2003.1

■ Taillasson, a neoclassical history painter, was trained in Joseph-Marie Vien's studio – then thought very avant-garde – and came in third place in the Grand Prix de Rome in 1769. After spending time in Rome he settled in Paris, where in 1782 he was accepted by the Royal Academy of Painting. Thereafter he exhibited regularly at the Salon. As a respected artist who was also a percipient critic, he exerted considerable influence on the coming generation of Romantic artists.

Taillasson was more concerned with capturing emotion than ideal beauty. His work is characterized by a sentimentalized presentation of tragedy, achieved with a limited palette and elaborate composition reminiscent of both Greuze and Poussin. The imploring face of the penitent sinner harks back to his early success as a student painter, when he was twice winner of the prize for facial expression.

The sobriety of the composition is tempered by the delicate handling of details. The imposing rock in the background throws the saint's figure into a typically neoclassical kind of relief. This shaded and barren refuge expresses the agonies of the penitent, suggesting the influence of Rousseau's attitude to nature. Although the overall colour scheme is restricted to cool, muted shades, some notes of warm colour subtly heighten the emotional tone in an eloquent diagonal: the dawn, the reddened eyes and pleading lips, and the red sash lead the viewer's eye to the overturned jewellery box.

Exhibited in the Salon of 1785, this canvas belonged to a distinguished collector, the Abbé de Pradine, chaplain to the Comtesse d'Artois. Two preparatory drawings with slight variations survive (Ashmolean, Oxford; priv. coll., New York). N.B.

François-Xavier Fabre
Montpellier 1766 – Montpellier 1837

Portrait of a Man in a Red Cape
About 1795-1800
Oil on canvas
91.7 × 71 cm

Purchase, Horsley and Annie Townsend Bequest and J. Aldéric Raymond Bequest
2001.35

■ A pupil of Jacques Louis David and recipient of the prestigious Grand Prix of the Académie de France in Rome, Fabre was a royalist and did not share the revolutionary opinions of his studio colleagues. On moving to Florence, he struck a friendship with the Countess of Albany and her companion, the poet Alfieri, which brought him a considerable clientele of aristocrats and gentry from abroad who came to Italy as part of the Grand Tour. Although his ambition was to be a history painter, circumstances decreed otherwise, and he became a portraitist with numerous successful neoclassical portraits to his credit, from the sculptor Canova to King Louis XVIII. This *Portrait of a Man in a Red Cape,* until recently unknown, may represent one such transient foreigner, judging by the wide-brimmed travelling hat. Some have inconclusively identified this figure as Henri de Léon, silversmith to Louis XVI, or as Alfieri himself. Whoever it represents, this portrait was surely admired; at least one copy from the period exists (private collection).

Fabre, who was of a reflective turn of mind and a realist by inclination and by training, recorded every detail, including blemishes. His aim was to paint a "flattering likeness", hence a subtle idealization of the sitter. Here the youth's rosy cheeks, bright eyes, silky curls and half-open lips give him a sweet, dreamy look. The elegant treatment of costume and accessories is just as complimentary, as evidenced in the striking contrast between the lemon-yellow waistcoat and the scarlet cape, and the dim reflections in the gilt buttons of the coat. Although here he employs a uniform background that recalls David, Fabre later preferred to place his sitters in a landscape. N.B.

Nicolas André Monsiau

Paris 1754/55 – Paris 1837

Ulysses, after Returning to His Palace and Slaying Penelope's Suitors, Orders the Women to Remove the Bodies

1791
Oil on canvas
98 × 195 cm

Purchase, Edward Cleghorn Memorial Fund

2001.7

■ Monsiau studied under Pierre Peyron, a French leader of the Neoclassical reform. From 1776 to 1780, Monsiau was at the French Academy in Rome, where he studied the art of antiquity and the Renaissance and became acquainted with Jacques Louis David and Pierre de Valenciennes. Monsiau's subjects were mostly drawn from ancient history: the two works he presented for admission into the Academy of Painting and Sculpture were *Alexander Breaking in Bucephalus* and *The Death of Agis*.

At the Revolutionary Salon of 1791, Monsiau exhibited a portrait, a genre scene and this painting based on a passage from Homer's *The Odyssey* (Book XXII). After an absence of nineteen years, Ulysses returns to his palace in Ithaca to find it overrun by a group of men who, expecting him never to reappear, are suing for the hand of his wife, Penelope. Aided by his son Telemachus and his faithful swineherd, Ulysses slays them all and then orders those of the palace women who have been disloyal to him to remove the bodies and clean the area. After performing this task, they too are put to death.

The paintings's Neoclassicism is expressed not only in its moralistic subject from an antique source, but also in the great care taken to accurately render the historically specific architectural setting, furnishings, clothing and colours, and the theatre-like poses. To give the painting a surface reminiscent of ancient murals, the artist mixed sand into the undercoat. H.T.G.

Charles Meynier
Paris 1768 – Paris 1832

Milo of Croton, Attempting to Test His Strength, Is Caught and Devoured by a Lion

1795
Oil on canvas
61 × 50 cm

Purchase, The Montreal Museum of Fine Arts' Volunteer Association Fund

2002.38

■ Charles Meynier was trained in the studio of the Neoclassical painter François-André Vincent. In 1789, he won the Grand Prix for painting, which took him to the French Academy in Rome. On returning to Paris, he exhibited regularly at the Salon between 1795 and 1824. This official but unassuming artist was involved in the great building projects of the Empire and later of the Restoration.

The story of the ancient Greek athlete Milo of Croton is an allegory of pride and vanity. The aging Milo wants to show his strength by pulling a split tree trunk apart. His hand gets caught and, unable to escape, he is devoured by wild beasts. Meynier's usual adherence to literary sources is apparent in the preparatory sketch for this *modello*, in which Milo is attacked by wolves (Musée Fabre, Montpellier). Here, however, following the celebrated *Milo of Croton* by the sculptor Pierre Puget (Louvre, Paris), Meynier decided to replace the wolves with a lion, thus creating a pendant to his *Androcles,* who was spared by a lion he had cared for. The two works offered an iconographic contrast between vanity and violence on the one hand, and meekness and calm on the other. The final pair of large paintings no longer survive: only this very polished preliminary canvas remains.

Although a model of Neoclassicism, this painting strays from the tranquil grandeur advocated by the theoretician Winckelmann and leans towards a new sense of the picturesque and pre-Romantic. Milo's white hair stands out starkly against the turbulent skies; his expression's *terribilità*, screaming mouth, tensed muscles and spread-eagled body recall other mythological figures, like the Laocoon. N.B.

Hubert Robert

Paris 1733 – Paris 1808

Young Girls Dancing around an Obelisk

1798
Oil on canvas
120 × 99 cm
Lady Davis Bequest
1964.1464

■ Hubert Robert spent from 1753 to 1765 in Italy. Residing in Rome at the same time as the popular Piranesi, the famous printmaker of grand architectural schemes, Robert gained expertise in presenting vistas of ruins peopled by picturesque figures. In *Young Girls Dancing around an Obelisk*, he blends neoclassical elements with ancient Egyptian monuments. An interest in Egyptian motifs was already evident in the art of Piranesi; Robert himself had created an "Egyptian" landscape in 1760. The Egyptian Expedition and Napoleon's victory over Mamluk forces at the Battle of the Pyramids on July 22, 1798, revived this interest in Egypt. It is hardly surprising that this painting, with its image of the pyramids at Giza, dates to that same year.

Robert knew the country only through the many published illustrations of the period. This scene conveys an Egypt of the imagination. Musicians and dancers in classical drapery cavort around the base of an enormous toppled obelisk, their small size emphasizing the grandeur of the monuments set against the open sky; monuments that simultaneously evoke the awe of the sublime and the eternal, as well as an ideal architecture of simple volumes and forms. H.T.G.

Jacques Sablet the Younger
Morges, Switzerland, 1749 – Paris 1803

Family Portrait in front of a Harbour

1800
Oil on canvas
64.8 × 81.4 cm
Purchase, special replacement fund
1975.16

■ Son and brother of Swiss-born painters, Jacques Sablet was accepted into the studio of the fashionable artist Joseph-Marie Vien, who advocated a return to the antique in art. Sablet followed his teacher when in 1775 the latter was appointed director of the French Academy in Rome, and made his name as a portraitist. In 1793, he was forced to leave Rome by anti-French riots. Back in Paris, he obtained a stipend from the government and an apartment in the Louvre. He was intimate with the Bonapartes and was supported by great art lovers like Cardinal Fesch and Pierre-René Cacault. Since his career was contemporary with that of his brother Jean-François, there has been some confusion in the accounts of their lives.

Sablet the Younger exhibited regularly in the Salons; *Family Portrait in front of a Harbour* appeared in the Salon of the year VIII (1800). It is a typical "conversation piece", one of those outdoor group portraits made fashionable by the English in the mid-eighteenth century. The children dance spontaneously to the music of the violin under the fond gaze of their parents, who are likely aristocratic émigrés. The men are wearing the wigs, knee breeches and silver-buckled shoes of the *ancien régime*, while the women are arrayed in the antique manner, with loose hair and high-waisted pleated gowns, and the boys sport haircuts *à la* Titus.

The composition in two planes is Neoclassical: on the stage formed by the terrace, the figures are arranged in a frieze, and the landscape serves as a backdrop. Could this be Naples or Palermo where, fleeing the anti-French uprisings, this family would have taken refuge – the Two Sicilies ruled by the House of Bourbon? Regardless of the location, the long shadows of late afternoon and the soft light in which the scene is bathed demonstrate why this artist was known as "the painter of sunlight". N.B.

Nicolas François Octave Tassaert
Paris 1800 – Paris 1874

The Temptation of Saint Hilarion
About 1857
Oil on canvas
111.4 × 144.3 cm
Purchase, gift of Mr. and Mrs. Michal Hornstein
1991.19

■ Octave Tassaert, son and grandson of artists, was also a painter by vocation. After serving his apprenticeship in the Neoclassical studio of Guillaume Guillon-Lethière, he found his own style, somewhere between Romanticism and Realism. After his *Death of Correggio* was purchased by the Duc d'Orléans at the Salon of 1834, a number of official commissions were forthcoming from Versailles. But neither the resounding success of *An Unhappy Family* at the Salon of 1851 nor the faithful patronage of two collectors – Alfred Bruyas and Alexandre Dumas *fils* – could prevent the artist from plunging ever deeper into misanthropy, alcoholism and poverty. This Bohemian "Correggio of the garret", as Théophile Gautier called him, ended up committing suicide. He loved women and lived in poverty: in this way his art and life were one, as his favourite subjects were borrowed from the "frolicsome genre", as he called it, or else were sentimental, mawkish genre scenes.

In the course of his lifetime Tassaert returned more than once to the very Flaubertian subject of the temptation of Saint Anthony and of his disciple Saint Hilarion, the anchorite from Gaza who founded Palestine's first monasteries. According to Bernard Prost, the artist's biographer, the large dimensions of our canvas correspond to two paintings of the *Temptation of Saint Hilarion*. The one he believes to be the original (Barré sale, February 4, 1858) could be this one, as the other is dated 1848. There also exists a smaller version dated 1857 (Davin sale, March 16, 1874; collection of Alexandre Dumas *fils*; location unknown). In any case, Tassaert brings together here iconographic elements he was drawn to, counterbalancing the starving saint with a cloud of delectable female flesh. N.B.

Paul Delaroche

Paris 1797 – Paris 1856

Portrait of Ludmila Komar, Princess of Beauvau-Craon

1849
Oil on canvas
71 × 58 cm

Purchase, Dr. and Mrs.
Max Stern Bequest

1990.24

■ During his lifetime Delaroche was as famous as his contemporary Eugène Delacroix. His style lies somewhere between historical realism and Romanticism, embodying that golden mean of aesthetics during the July monarchy. His history paintings, widely known through prints, and his large decor for the hemicycle of the École des Beaux-Arts in Paris where he taught, brought him international renown and many students from abroad. At thirty-five, he was elected to the Institut, becoming its youngest member and its first Romantic artist. Although he was doted on by the Beaux-Arts administration, his distrust of critics was such that after 1837 he refused to participate in the Salons. In 1849, the already misanthropic painter became an inconsolable widower. When not travelling, he stayed in Nice, where his circle of friends included the Princess of Beauvau-Craon.

This noblewoman of Polish birth, née Potocka, and her sister Delphine played a leading role in the intellectual and fashionable life of Paris. Both adored reading, music (they were close to Chopin) and painting (both were taught by Ernest Hébert, a friend of Delaroche). It was out of affection for the sisters that the artist painted oval portraits of them that same year (the other is in a private collection in the United Kingdom). In 1851 he drew portraits of them (Musée Hébert, La Tronche). The princess's poetic, rather languid melancholy contrasts with the haughty look of her sister Delphine, who was notorious for her love affairs. Exemplarily Romantic in its frame of twined roses and sentimental pose, this canvas belongs among the few but outstanding portraits painted by Delaroche. N.B.

■ "Goddess, come again today, deliver me from my cruel torments, fulfil my heart's desire, and deny me not your all-powerful succour." Such is the supplication that Sappho, rejected lover of Phaon, addressed to Aphrodite. Her hand placed on a votive column at which she has just offered a desperate libation to the goddess of love, she meditates on her impending suicidal leap from the cliffs of Leucas. The Romantic era was more inclined to view Sappho as a tragic lover than as a woman of letters or courtesan.

When the model of this sculpture was shown at the Salon of 1848, poet and critic Théophile Gautier was effusive: "Suitably oxidized and covered in verdigris by an extended sojourn beneath earth or sea, which would give it an antique patina, it could pass for a work from the finest age of Greek or Roman art."

Pradier won the prestigious Prix de Rome and a residency at the French Academy there, essential steps for any artist on the way to success. The sculptor excelled in a half-classical, half-romantic – but always voluptuous – style, creating many graceful, even erotic, statues, which he sold as models to the producers who abounded during this time when statues were exceptionally popular. This *Sappho* is known in three sizes, and in various materials; in silver, bronze, plaster, alabaster and even painted unglazed porcelain. At the Great Exhibition of 1851 in London, founder Victor Paillard presented it in a silvered bronze version, some examples with gilt highlighting. N.B.

James Pradier
Geneva 1790 – Bougival 1852

Standing Sappho

1848
Silvered bronze
44.7 × 22 × 20 cm

Purchase, Horsley and Annie Townsend Bequest
1985.1

Lawrence Alma-Tadema
Dronrijp, Netherlands, 1836 – Wiesbaden, Germany, 1912

A Sculpture Gallery in Rome at the Time of Augustus

1867
Oil on panel
61.5 × 46.9 cm

Purchase, Horsley and Annie Townsend Bequest
1980.2

■ Familiar with his enthusiasm for archaeological accuracy, Alma-Tadema's colleagues defied him in his studio to depict an art gallery in ancient Rome. Rising to the challenge and basing his work on historical sources like Pliny the Elder, the Dutch painter trained in Belgium created in the summer of 1867 the first of his works with a Greco-Roman subject: the *Collector of Paintings at the Time of Augustus* (H. E. Finsness Collection, London) and its pendant, this painting. Jean Léon Gérôme's highly popular neo-Greek paintings that Alma-Tadema would have seen in Paris in 1864, were another source of inspiration for him, as were the recent excavations at Pompeii and Herculaneum, which created a craze for antiquity.

In the Sculpture Gallery, rich Imperial Roman art lovers are examining a bronze Sophocles, while, in a double reading, the viewer (and potential buyer) who knows antiquity will recognize celebrated ancient sculptures grouped together in the same place by sheer force of the painter's will: from left to right, the *Endymion Sarcophagus*, the *Laocoon*, *Penelope*, an ex-*Agrippina* and *Posidippus*.

Alma-Tadema took a keen interest in Greco-Roman art on his honeymoon to Italy in 1863. Every detail of furnishing and architectural setting derives from specific historical sources in this re-creation of the past, so in keeping with the spirit of the nineteenth century. This emphatic homage to patrons and collectors recalls seventeenth-century Flemish and eighteenth-century Italian cabinet paintings. The artist also portrays, not without a touch of humour, the group of friends who lost face, and himself, with the red beard. The painting's success at the Salon in Antwerp prompted the artist to reiterate the theme in ten variations over a decade. N.B.

Camille Corot

Paris 1796 – Ville-d'Avray 1875

L'île heureuse

About 1865-1868
Oil on canvas
188 × 142.5 cm

Gift of the family of Sir George A. Drummond in memory of Arthur
Lennox Drummond and Captain Guy Melfort Drummond
1919.30

■ *L'île heureuse* attests to the long friendship of two artist companions. Fellow combat-
ants in the battle against the Beaux-Arts academic system and administration, these two
landscape painters were precursors of Impressionism: Charles Daubigny and, as he called
his friend, "Le Père Corot." At Corot's suggestion, Daubigny moved to Auvers-sur-Oise,
near Paris, not far from Daumier's studio. Together, they undertook to decorate the new
lodgings with the help of Karl, Daubigny's son, and the architect Oudinot. Within this
confraternity of artists, brushstrokes and signatures mingled to create a collective work.
L'Île heureuse is the finest of the five panels Corot executed for the vestibule.

If Daubigny veered from Realism to colourful Impressionism in his landscape-portraits,
the elder Corot proceeded more from the classical spirit of seventeenth-century French landscape masters Claude Lorrain and Nicolas Poussin in the landscapes of his maturity, which
he called his *paysages-souvenirs*. This is one of the painter's infinite variations on the theme
of a placid lake in dawn mist under a flurry of foliage, the scene disturbed only by sketchily
rendered peasant figures. Is this the Italy of Lake Albano? Or the French countryside
around Ville-d'Avray? Regardless, the atmosphere is as always that of a reconstituted
dream, in which the painter-poet favours sensation over description, tone over colour.
N.B.

Henri Fantin-Latour
Grenoble 1836 – Buré 1904

Display of Enchantment

1863
Oil on canvas
98.5 × 131.4 cm
Purchase, John W. Tempest Fund
1936.658

■ *Display of Enchantment* is an ambitious canvas painted by a rising artist for the Paris Salon. According to his widow, it represents "a young fairytale princess" who "descends the steps of a fantasy palace and sees before her a young prince charming with his retinue, offering her precious gifts". What was viewed as the painting's unfinished appearance – created by its sketchy brushwork – kept it out of the official exhibition but it was included in the famous Salon des Refusés in 1863 alongside avant-garde works by the future Impressionists. Among those misunderstood artists were Manet, Cézanne, Pissarro and Whistler, who became Fantin-Latour's friend and the owner of this picture.

Fantin-Latour objected to being labelled an Impressionist. His work is at once belatedly Romantic and Symbolist before the fact. It also makes cultivated references to past masters, quoting from the Venetian Renaissance painting of Titian and Veronese, and the Rococo artist Watteau's *Embarkation for the Island of Cythera*, which Fantin-Latour had studied at the Louvre. Neither mythological nor realist, the subject falls in line with the "art for art's sake" decree of Théophile Gautier. The artist borrowed the flamboyant colouring of Delacroix, whom he honoured that same year with a painting. Creating a work comparable to no other, Fantin-Latour infused this canvas with a uniquely misty atmosphere, an effect contributed to by the lithographs he was making at the same time. His poetically musical lyricism drew inspiration from the music of Berlioz and especially the operas of Wagner, which he encountered in 1857, putting him well in advance of the *fin-de-siècle* craze for Wagnerian opera. N.B.

■ Carrier-Belleuse was a prolific artist and one of France's leading sculptor-decorators. He was especially popular during the Second Empire, seeming to embody the inclinations of the age. At the Salon of 1859 in Paris, he exhibited a bronze entitled *Jupiter and Hebe*. In classical mythology, Hebe, the personification of youth and cupbearer to the gods, was the daughter of Juno and Jupiter (here changed into an eagle). Seated between his wings, she is holding the *oinochoe* (wine pitcher) in one arm while with her free hand she gracefully offers him nectar.

The Mannerist spiral in the composition of this piece, half sculpture and half goldsmith's work, testifies to the contemporary taste for Renaissance art; it takes its inspiration from Benvenuto Cellini's goldwork. Carrier-Belleuse especially admired graceful longnecked beauties with skilfully braided hair, like the exaggerated elongation typical of the School of Fontainebleau. On the other hand, the draperies here are more neo-Baroque and the wine pitcher is obviously antique in style. The historical references are interwoven in a very Second Empire style.

The chasing work all over the piece is of outstanding quality. Its surfaces, sometimes like shot silk, sometimes rough, reinforce the contrast between the supple young limbs of the goddess and the massive, powerful body of the eagle. Copies identical to this version are extant but few in number. N.B.

Albert Ernest Carrier-Belleuse

Anizy-le-Château 1824 – Sèvres 1887

Hebe and the Eagle of Jupiter

1858
Chased and plated bronze, gilded plinth
69 × 32 × 27 cm

Purchase, The Montreal Museum of Fine Arts' Volunteer Association Fund

2002.10.1-2

Honoré Daumier
Marseilles 1808 – Valmondois 1879

Women Pursued by Satyrs

1850 (later additions made by the artist)
Oil on canvas
131.8 × 97.8 cm
Adaline Van Horne Bequest
1945.880

■ Although already famous for his political caricatures, Daumier hoped to be considered a painter when he exhibited this picture at the official Salon of 1850 in Paris. The vaguely mythological subject, unusual for a mainly realistic artist, was more of a pretext for depicting two bare-breasted women amid a whirlwind of draperies, attempting to escape from their pursuers. The canvas was coldly received by the critics: one found it to be "a pandemonium of colours". The artist himself was not satisfied with it and towards the end of his life retouched it, striping it with strident greens and orange tones. The result is certainly one of his most astonishing works.

Here, Daumier pays tribute to Flemish, Rococo and Romantic art. The opulent sensuality of these tipsy bacchantes echoes Rubens, in particular his *Kermesse*, which Daumier had copied at the Louvre. The strident colours and energetic brush work recall both Fragonard and Delacroix. Here, he goes beyond even Impressionism: in his way of using bold cross-hatching to establish the planes of colour, he seems to leap ahead to the Divisionist experiments of Seurat and Signac. N.B.

John Everett Millais
Southampton 1829 – London 1896

Saint Martin's Summer

1878
Oil on canvas
151 × 107 cm
Gift of Lord Strathcona and family
1927.325

■ Millais left the Pre-Raphaelite Brotherhood, of which he was a founding member, to join the English Aesthetic movement. Honoured by the highly prestigious Royal Academy, he was in demand as a portraitist. During hunting and fishing trips in Scotland, however, he painted a few, rare landscapes. Executed with astounding subtlety, this canvas gives a detailed view of a body of water around Rumbling Brig, near Dunkeld, Perthshire. Some off-put critics condemn it as "too prosaically literal" and lacking feeling.

In this period of artistic maturity, Millais shows a preference for the broad brushstroke of a Gainsborough over a close and careful execution in his landscape backgrounds. A highly personal work, *Saint Martin's Summer* harks back to his Pre-Raphaelite youth in his painting from nature and attention to detail, and the perspective foreshortened by the absence of a middle ground. This nature scene filled with water and rocks also reflects the precepts of his old friend, the critic John Ruskin, who was the movement's theorist.

However, beyond the apparently objective illustration of a late autumn mild spell and tranquil days foretelling peace, Millais fills this nature setting with a distant celestial light, evoking *fin-de-siècle* Symbolist visions. N.B.

James Tissot
Nantes 1836 – Buillon 1902

October

1877
Oil on canvas
216 × 108.7 cm
Gift of Lord Strathcona and family
1927.410

■ Businessman, painter and dandy, Jacques-Joseph Tissot was born in Nantes but exiled himself to London because of his involvement with the Paris Commune. Very much an anglophile, he thereafter went by the name James.

Mrs. Newton was twenty-two years old, the mother of two illegitimate children; when Tissot met her in 1876, she was also a beautiful divorcee. Theirs would have been a perfect happiness had tuberculosis not claimed the life of the painter's graceful and notorious muse six years later, leaving him inconsolable – shades of the Marguerite Gautier of Dumas fils's *Dame aux camélias* and Violetta of Verdi's *La Traviata*.

It is this comedy of manners, this tableau of social behaviour and fleeting fashion, that is captured in *October*, one of the finest and largest of the artist's works. Elegantly corsetted in the Princesse line she favoured, Mrs Newton turns towards the viewer, a touch flirtatiously, showing a well-turned ankle in the rustle of lace petticoats, her boot treading a carpet of autumn leaves. Dressed in black in this season of decline, she shines with the glow of her last fire.

Tissot began collecting Japanese art early on and also executed cloisonné enamels. Signs of Japanism here are the verticality inspired by kakemono scrolls, and the tumultuous background of chestnut trees, through whose leaves and branches can just be made out a small group of deer. N.B.

Jean-Paul Laurens
Fourquevaux 1838 – Paris 1921

"She Had the Happiness and Power of Brunhild Constantly before Her Eyes"

Illustration for *Récits des temps mérovingiens* [*Narratives of the Merovingian Era*] by Augustin Thierry. Fourth narrative: History of Praetextatus, Bishop of Rouen (577-586)

1877-1887
Pen and ink, black ink wash on paper
36 × 28.2 cm
Anonymous gift
2001.218.5

■ Jean-Paul Laurens, a leading figure of "pompier" art under the Third Republic, breathed new life into the great tradition of history painting, imbuing it with a republican, anti-monarchist and anti-clerical ideology. His depictions of medieval, but especially Byzantine, history demonstrate an insistence on accuracy and a dramatic approach to composition.

In 1877, when he was at the height of his fame, having received the Medal of Honour at the Salon, Laurens was commissioned to execute forty-two drawings to illustrate *Récits des temps mérovingiens* by the historian Augustin Thierry, which, though published in 1840, is still popular. The Museum possesses nine of these original drawings, the rest being in other public or private collections. The series was photo-engraved by Goupil and published at intervals by Librairie Hachette in large folio-volume instalments between 1881 and 1887; an inexpensive edition came out in 1887. It took the artist almost ten years to complete the commission, for which he made numerous preparatory sketches and paintings. The original series of drawings, including those now at the Museum, was then exhibited in 1889 at the Durand-Ruel gallery and later at the Chicago World's Fair of 1893.

Laurens remained faithful to these accounts of the sixth-century fratricidal wars of the Merovingians. The implacable Queen Fredegund, crowned to the throne through crime, punishes her son-in-law Merovech for having secretly married Brunhild; she will drive him to suicide. Laurens preferred thoughtful subjects rather than figures in action, and depicting the slow premeditation of the murder rather than the act itself. Silence is here given expression, somewhat in the manner of Sarah Bernhardt, the actress whose celebrated interpretation of Victorien Sardou's *Fédora* included eloquent miming and long silences. N.B.

Jean Joseph Benjamin Constant, called Benjamin-Constant
Paris 1845 – Paris 1902

Evening on the Terrace (Morocco)

1879
Oil on canvas
123 × 198.5 cm
Gift of Lord Strathcona and family
1927.243

■ Benjamin-Constant's studio in Paris was an Eastern bazaar, crammed with rugs, caftans, weapons and turbans brought back from his journeys to Spain and the Moroccan sultanate. The Orientalist painter recalled his journey to Tangiers in 1871: "On arriving, I only intended to stay a month and now I have spent two years here . . . since that day I have dreamed of one thing only: becoming a real Orientalist and following in the steps of Marilhat, Delacroix and Henri Regnault."

Working from the sketches he had made on the spot, Benjamin-Constant recreated that inaccessible world of Muslim women seeking cooler air on their terraces at the end of the day. Among his different, dreamed-of Orients was the Egypt of the Pharaohs, and the seated figure has the hieratic pose of the colossus of Memnon. His memories of Moorish Spain glow with colours inspired by the palette of Mariano Fortuny, a colleague whose work Benjamin-Constant admired.

At the Académie Julian in Paris, he taught many American and Canadian artists (including Suzor-Coté), and so exerted a certain influence on artistic taste in North America. His powerful compositions, reproduced in photographs and prints, became so popular that they were sought after by North American collectors during his lifetime, and that is how the Montreal Museum of Fine Arts acquired two of his finest paintings, the other being *The Day after a Victory at the Alhambra.* N.B.

Gabriel Max

Prague 1840 – Munich 1915

The Raising of Jairus' Daughter

1878
Oil on canvas
123.3 × 180.4 cm
Gift of Lord Atholstan
1920.117

■ When Jairus, a ruler of the synagogue, implored Jesus to save his daughter, Jesus answered, "Why do you make a tumult and weep? The child is not dead but sleeping." Then he said to the girl, "Talitha cumi", which means, "Little girl, I say to you, arise." (Mark 5:22-43). In the stifling alcove occupied by the bed, the miracle occurs: the dead girl's eyelids quiver, her cheeks flush, even as her cadaverous pallor and the macabre detail of the fly on her arm punctuate her recent brush with death.

If the palm and crown of roses are imagistic symbols of the Virgin's innocence and victory over death, the contrast between the mysterious shadow that surrounds Christ and the divine light that haloes the resurrected girl confers a dynamic and spiritual reading of this passage from one nature to another. In this regard, Max, an esteemed painter and teacher who trained at the academies of Prague and Vienna, recalls Rembrandt and Caravaggio. Subtly blending symbolism and realism, the work combines the artist's double penchant for the occult and spiritism on one hand, and science and natural history on the other.

Exhibited at the Paris Exposition universelle of 1878, *The Raising of Jairus' Daughter* was viewed as an attempt to revive grand-scale religious painting, then in decline. George Drummond, a prominent Montreal businessman and collector, bought the canvas and circulated it throughout Canada to great acclaim. Considering it one of the most important works in his collection, he had a special frame made for it, adorned with Passion flowers and the biblical inscriptions cited above, to hang over a fireplace in his opulent mansion. N.B.

William Bouguereau
La Rochelle 1825 –
La Rochelle 1905

Crown of Flowers

1884
Oil on canvas
162.9 × 89.9 cm

Gift of R. B. Angus
1889.17

■ "Paint as you see, and be accurate in your drawing", was the advice of Bouguereau, an official painter with a "photo-idealist" style. Indeed, the studio models in this painting – two children dressed as peasants – are depicted with virtuoso minuteness. To obtain an exact rendering of drapery, Bouguereau would arrange fabric on a mannequin and draw studies of it; to capture a figure's outline, so its form would stand out distinctly from its rustic background, he sometimes worked from sculptures. But the realism stops there. Although the life-size scale of the figures is a concession to the Naturalism of the period, this image is neither a pitiful plea for the peasantry nor a glorification of country life. For sheer love of the beautiful, Bouguereau idealizes the plump, perfectly foreshortened arms, the clean, fleshy feet, the porcelain complexions. These sweet little bucolic faces are imbued with a contemporary nostalgia for the happiness of the countryside and a stock-in-trade picturesqueness. Recollections of his academic training, the group composition and the girl's serious, meditative look recall Saint John the Baptist weaving a premonitory crown of thorns for the infant Jesus, and the stiff pose of an offering bearer from antiquity.

But what is the subject of this painting? Nothing if not the pleasure of anecdote and the accomplished workmanship that wealthy American buyers appreciated in the paintings of this "pompier" artist, honoured during his lifetime, forgotten and then discovered once again. N.B.

Auguste Renoir

Limoges 1841 – Cagnes-sur-Mer 1919

Young Girl with a Hat

About 1890
Oil on canvas
41.5 × 32.5 cm

Purchase, grant from the Government of Canada under the terms of the Cultural Property Export and Import Act and gifts of Mr. and Mrs. A. T. Henderson, the families of the late M. Dorothea Millar and the late J. Lesley Ross, the Bank of Montreal, Redpath Industries Ltd. and the Royal Trust Company, in memory of Huntly Redpath Drummond
1984.17

■ The year 1890 was a turning point for Renoir. Regular purchases of his work by his dealer Paul Durand-Ruel had brought him financial security, and he had married his mistress Aline, a seamstress with whom he already had a son, Pierre. The family moved into a roomier house in Montmartre, with a garden. During this happy though uncertain period, the artist abandoned the more rigid Ingres-influenced manner he had adopted some years earlier in reaction to the haziness of Impressionism. Taking up the latter style, he turned to French eighteenth-century painting. In the work of Watteau and Fragonard he admired the supple brushwork that draws and colours in a single stroke, moulding shape and space simultaneously. The severe rheumatism in his hands made it harder for him to paint but did not deter him. It was then that he created a new sort of iridescent impasto lit up by gleaming whites and layers of glaze.

The half-length paintings of young girls in hats, which he turned out for his dealer, appealed to a wide public. He sometimes ordered hats to be specially made for his models. About 1900, Durand-Ruel implored him in vain to give up such antiquated headwear. But whether the girls were modern or sham mattered little to Maurice Denis, who wrote as a discerning critic in 1892 that, "out of the delight of his eyes [Renoir] has created wonderful posies of women and flowers." N.B.

Paul Cézanne

Aix-en-Provence 1839 – Aix-en-Provence 1906

Roadway in Provence

About 1868
Oil on canvas
92.4 × 72.5 cm
Adaline Van Horne Bequest
1945.872

■ This is Cézanne's first large landscape. At the time it was done – a period he later referred to as "*couillarde*" to describe his foolish youth – he was an unknown artist aspiring to be a visionary, trying his hand at all formats, vacillating between religious and mythological subjects, portraits and still lifes. In Paris – where he had the support, albeit with a certain scepticism, of the future Impressionists, who had already committed themselves to landscape painting – he was looked upon as a lad from the south, rough mannered, reclusive, tempestuous and impassioned by nature.

Back in his native territory for the summer, the environs of Aix-en-Provence, he would paint out of doors like the Barbizon School. He had already done some small oil and watercolour landscapes, but nothing as radical as this. Although the perspective of a road is a commonplace point of view, no figure or animal, no picturesque detail enlivens this scene. Cézanne constructed his perspective with large areas of colour, openly and frontally juxtaposing the blues, whites, blacks and greens that were then the basis of his palette. He smoothed the broad impastos with his spatula, building up a solid, bold and disciplined way of painting that recalls Manet more than Courbet, two artists he admired. Because of its size, this canvas exceeds the boundaries of a sketch to become a full-fledged finished work. In this regard, Cézanne was following examples recently shown at the Salon by Pissarro, his loyal and supportive friend, with whom he would soon pursue landscape painting N.B.

Édouard Manet

Paris 1832 – Paris 1883

Head of a Young Woman (The Seamstress)

1881
Pastel on canvas
53 × 44.4 cm

Gift of the family of James Reid Wilson in his memory
1923.321

■ Towards the end of his life, Impressionist painter Édouard Manet's health progressively failed, and he abandoned oil painting for the faster, less taxing medium of pastel. He liked to be surrounded by pretty women, whether of the demimonde or fashionable society, whose conversation and coquetry raised his spirits.

Of eighty-eight pastels inventoried, more than seventy are quarter- or half-length portraits of women. With their hastily sketched features in a corolla of lace, ribbons and flowered hats, they seem to be portrayed as blossoms. The often neutral background, generally a pearl grey, brings out the brilliance of their pink complexion.

At the home of Méry Laurent – a glamorous beauty infatuated with society, a friend and love of artists from Mallarmé to Manet, and a muse of poetry and painting – Manet executed this portrait of a young woman who worked days as a seamstress. If at times he yielded to a facile prettiness that led to his being sought after by his delighted models, here there is no trace of Parisian chic, no artifice. There is only the sober black ribbon and plain tulle collaret, the bronze lustre of the chestnut hair and delicate red of the carnation, the wistful expression of a humble girl. N.B.

Edgar Degas
Paris 1834 – Paris 1917

At the Theatre: Woman Seated in the Balcony

About 1877-1880
Oil on canvas
24.5 × 32.7 cm
Gift of Mr. and Mrs. Michal Hornstein
1999.18

■ Degas found much of his inspiration in the world of ballet, theatre and café-concerts, focusing on the performers both on stage and in the wings. He often showed the audience – suggested by a lady's fan or opera glasses – in the foreground, to offset the action taking place on the stage.

This canvas is one of the few in which Degas makes the audience, whether in the stalls, the pit or the boxes, his subject. It is an intimate close-up of a seamstress, absorbed in the show, wearing a tip-tilted hat, the lace at her neckline and cuffs a band of light. The heaviness of the face, with its shadowed eyes and strong jaw, heightened by the small nose, recalls the gentle, rather sad and obstinate countenance of Ellen Andrée, one of the artist's favourite models at that time. Whoever the woman portrayed here is, Degas seems touched by her look of concentration. Unlike his predecessors, Daumier being an example, he does not make her a caricature.

The painting has a distinguished provenance. It first belonged to the Paris art dealer Jacques Seligmann, who owned seventy-one works by Degas. He bought this one at the first posthumous sale of works in the artist's studio in May 1918 (No. 23). In 1943, it passed into the remarkable collection of Impressionist canvases assembled by Erich Maria Remarque, author of *All Quiet on the Western Front*, and his wife, the actress Paulette Goddard. N.B.

Alfred Sisley
Paris 1839 – Moret-sur-Loing 1899

Road at By, Roches-Courtaut Woods – Saint Martin's Summer

1881
Oil on canvas
59.1 × 81 cm
Purchase, John W. Tempest Fund
1922.400

■ Sisley, whose English parents had moved to France, took part with Monet, Renoir and Pissarro in the first Impressionist exhibition in 1874. The Museum possesses another of his paintings that was also shown in that exhibition: *Autumn – Banks of the Seine near Bougival* (1945.924). In the early 1880s, the group split up, its members achieving varying degrees of success. Sisley, penniless and unknown, lived for a time in the village of By, south of Paris and close to the banks of the Seine, which never ceased to delight him.

Faithful to his Impressionist beginnings, he painted his canvases entirely from nature. With one exception, his landscapes are topographically accurate records. He had his favourite places, often characterized by trees and stretches of water, which he depicted in a poetic, personal manner directly influenced by the English Romantic landscapists and the Barbizon School. Here we see a path skirting a loop of the Seine. It is late afternoon during a mild spell in November, and the shadows are growing longer.

This painting is a typical work of Sisley's mature style. The bare branches are swiftly sketched in, almost calligraphic. To achieve the beautiful effect of depth he uses a thick, smudged brushstroke for the foreground to contrast with the smooth, light rendering of the background. His palette is dominated by pure shades of mauve, orange and blue. N.B.

Camille Pissarro
Saint-Thomas, Danish Antilles, 1830 – Paris 1903

View of the Cotton Mill at Oissel near Rouen

1898
Oil on canvas
65.3 × 81 cm
Purchase, John W. Tempest Fund
1942.145

■ In 1898, Camille Pissarro turned sixty-eight. The Impressionist revolution was over, but he continued to support the new generation of painters, including Gauguin, van Gogh, Seurat and Signac. He even considered new Neo-Impressionist theories but changed his mind. Comfortably settled in the country, he watched the prices of Impressionist canvases skyrocket. For the new generation, he belonged to the past: during this period he painted pictures of Rouen, leading the young Charles Angrand to call his work *Rouenneries.*

And yet, he renewed himself. The painter of meadows became the master of cityscapes bustling with human activity in Paris and the industrial port towns of Normandy: Rouen, Dieppe and Le Havre. Although as an Impressionist he was interested in modern life and as an anarchist he felt close to the working class, it was neither poverty nor bohemian nightlife that he depicted: what he wanted was to capture the atmosphere. Partly out of admiration for Monet's paintings of the Rouen Cathedral, he decided to go back there to work on a series of canvases. He painted the medieval town but was more attracted by the life of the port and the dense river traffic (five thousand ships a year). Turner's influence is also very apparent during this period.

Suffering from eye problems, he took to painting views from the open window of a hotel room. Pissarro stayed in Rouen in 1896, and between July and October 1898, which is when this view of the cotton mill at Oissel was executed. N.B.

Auguste Rodin

Paris 1840 – Meudon 1917

The Sirens

About 1887-1888
Marble
44.5 × 45.7 × 27 cm
Gift of the Huntly Redpath Drummond family
1958.1192

■ When Rodin conceived his monumental *Gates of Hell* (commissioned in 1880 for a future decorative art museum but never installed), he created an iconography of his own that he was to reuse endlessly, like a stock of words rearranged into new sentences. Although the gates are a tragic homage to Dante, this group, originally a high-relief for the left door, does not derive from the Italian poet.

Rodin first exhibited the plaster model of the free-standing version at the famous exhibition *Monet-Rodin*, organized in 1889 by the Georges Petit gallery in Paris, which brought these two great geniuses together during their lifetime. "Three intertwined sirens sing; each of a different stature and pose, they form an uneven group, staggered like Pan pipes," critic Gustave Geffroy wrote in the laudatory catalogue preface. Emerging voluptuously from the unfinished block, the bodies and hair of these women – sirens in name only (Rodin often conceived his titles after the fact) – are interlaced in a Sapphic weave that obsessed the sculptor in its eternal round.

The artist later transformed them into a poet's muses for the monument to Victor Hugo. The success of this model proved long-lived: eighteen copies are known, four in marble, this one ordered directly by the Montreal patron of the arts George Drummond. Under the close supervision of the master, the marble versions were carved by a workshop assistant, which explains the minor differences among them. N.B.

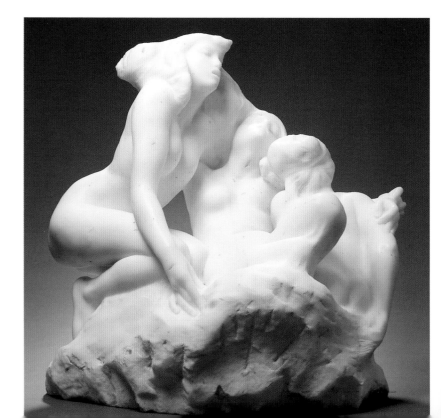

Claude Monet
Paris 1840 – Giverny 1926

The Cliffs at Pourville

1897
Oil on canvas
65.8 × 100.6 cm

Purchase, John W. Tempest Fund

1918.126

■ The Caillebotte Bequest of thirty-eight Impressionist paintings, which in 1897 entered the contemporary art Musée du Luxembourg, Paris, included eight Monets. At that time, the painter was fifty-seven years old and, from his residence in Giverny, held the role of Impressionism's patriarch, and was showered with praise despite the resistance of a few cantankerous voices at the Institut.

From January to March 1897, Monet stayed at a little inn in Pourville, not far from Dieppe, on the Normandy coast. During previous sojourns in the early 1880s, he had painted varied motifs; this time, he produced series. After grain stacks, poplars and cathedrals, he turned his attention to cliffs. He worked on several canvases at once, one for each time of day. He painted directly from nature, sheltered from the wind and exhilarated to again be witnessing the movement of the sea.

Critic Gustave Geffroy, Monet's biographer, wrote, "The clifftops are covered with low grasses, faded flowerets, woolly carpets hugging the curves of the ground. Softly upon the sand the waves spread their blue-green transparency, their fringe of foam. Vast skies rise from the water and breath in the ocean mass: it is an exchange, a commingling, that results in an admirable unity." He concludes his description of this new "air painting" of Monet: "No one had yet perceived this distant painting, as if 'within', that expresses the mists wandering on the cliffs of Dieppe, the cool and peaceful quiet of solitude." N.B.

Maurice Denis

Granville 1870 – Paris 1943

Yellow Evening over Fourqueux

About 1890
Oil on panel
16 × 26.8 cm

Anonymous gift
1998.57

■ Maurice Denis, a theoretician and a Catholic, started the group known as the "Nabis". These "prophets" of the avant-garde aimed at a new kind of art, "synthetist", idealistic and anti-academic. In pursuit of this goal, the young artist made two important discoveries. In 1888, Paul Sérusier, another Nabi, showed him *The Talisman* (Paris, Musée d'Orsay), a small landscape painted on a wood panel at Pont-Aven, Brittany, in accordance with the dictates of Paul Gauguin. The following year, Denis was deeply impressed by the exhibition of the Pont-Aven artists at the Café Volpini, Paris, and especially by the work of Gauguin and Émile Bernard; he later remembered, "the deformation of the drawing. The hint of caricature, the colours laid on so flat, it's all scandalous . . . initial amazement, and then, what a revelation!"

This painting came directly from the family holdings and belongs to this pivotal moment in the artist's career. Like many of his works, it is painted on a salvaged panel. With its flat layers of colour and whole, almost abstract shapes, it is an example of the earliest, highly experimental Nabi manner used by Denis at the age of twenty. It was at this time that he articulated his famous definition: "Remember that a picture – before being a war-horse or a nude woman or an anecdote – is essentially a flat surface covered with colours assembled in a certain order." N.B.

Édouard Vuillard

Cuiseaux 1868 –
La Baule 1940

Seated Woman in a Dark Room

About 1895
Oil on cardboard mounted on panel
36.7 × 26.3 cm
Purchase, The Museum Campaign 1988-1993 Fund
2001.111

■ To all appearances Vuillard led an uneventful life with his mother at his side. At the Lycée Condorcet in Paris, he met Maurice Denis, Lugné-Poe and Kerr-Xavier Roussel, his future brother-in-law. Later, at the Académie Julian, he was one of the first group of Nabis. From 1893 on, he executed many paintings of middle-class interiors in which the people dissolve into space. He also designed programmes and scenery for Lugné-Poe's Théâtre de l'Œuvre. After the art dealer Jos Hessel took the artist's finances in hand early in the century, Vuillard was able to lead a comfortable bourgeois life. In 1937, he was elected to the Institut de France.

The seated woman in this painting is Vuillard's sister Marie, left alone in the family apartment after being abandoned by Roussel. A veil of sadness seems to hang over this mysterious scene; the main figure emerges gradually from total darkness, barely broken by a few notes of colour – the light-coloured patterned dress, the red curtain, a stylized tree trunk. In this poignant composition, Marie is turned towards the window like Maurice Denis's princesses, looking out from a high tower for the improbable arrival of their knights errant. Here, Vuillard comes very close to the Symbolist mode. We know that his theatre sets were designed to accord with the imperceptible entry of the actors from the back of a stage plunged in complete darkness at the start. This small canvas also recalls Odilon Redon's painting, in which figures – women deep in thought, "profiles of light" – seem to explode into colour, silently and mysteriously, out of the depths of an ink black night. G.C.

Constantin Meunier

Etterbeek, Belgium, 1831 – Ixelles, Belgium, 1905

Toilers of the Sea

1898
Bronze
59 × 96 × 13.2 cm

Purchase, gifts of Mrs. Neil B. Ivory, Bruce McNiven, and anonymous donor
2000.7

■ This is the very cast of *Toilers of the Sea* that Belgian sculptor and painter Constantin Meunier chose over ten of his other works to present at the prestigious avant-garde exhibition of the Berlin Secession in 1900. At that time, he was one of the most highly regarded artists of the so-called Naturalist movement, which depicted peasant and working-class life.

Although the sculpture's title is also that of a novel by Victor Hugo, the subject is entirely original. At low tide, workers with sturdy horses are bringing sticks bound in bundles to repair the breakwaters that hold the beach sands in place. This common activity of the Belgian shoreline is treated as an episode from the saga of rural life and man's heroic struggle against the elements for survival. Belgian author Émile Verhaeren described it as "a very simple bas-relief, but of very great elegance… an everyday occurrence, a routine act, magnified by its epic conception." Meunier, his reputation at its peak, drew upon archetypes he had already created: the magnificent figure carrying the wood recalls *Labourer*; the peasant bending to his task like a beast of burden recalls *Glebe*. The artist's powerful social realism is tempered here by the sweeping lines of the sea, which are more typical of Art Nouveau's spirit.

Besides the casts at the Musée Constantin Meunier (his former studio on Rue de l'Abbaye, Brussels), two bronzes, produced by B. Verbeyst of Brussels, are inventoried at the Musées royaux des Beaux-Arts de Belgique, and the Musée de la Chartreuse, Douai. N.B.

Félix Vallotton

Lausanne 1865 – Paris 1925

Vuillard Drawing at Honfleur

1902
Oil on cardboard
81.7 × 59.9 cm
Purchase, The Museum Campaign 1988-1993 Fund
2003.75

■ Originally from Switzerland, Vallotton encountered artistic modernity while studying at the Académie Julian, Paris. In 1892 he became a member of the Nabi circle, joining its founding members, including Vuillard. His reserved character earned him the nickname *Nabi étranger*. The biting tone of his paintings of middle-class interiors and life, and his woodcut engravings for avant-garde publications in particular, earned him international notoriety. A firm friendship formed quickly between Vallotton and Vuillard, accompanied by a certain artistic affinity.

They were very close, and their manner of painting was similar – smooth and objective, with areas of flat colour in soft and luminous pastel tones. During visits to their summer vacation spot, they took pleasure in studying the landscape, and with portable Kodak and sketchbook, they explored the countryside before returning to the studio to compose their final pictures; a drawing exists for this work (private collection, Lausanne). In September 1902, Vallotton joined Vuillard on the Normandy coast, in Criquebeuf at the villa called "Les Étincelles", where the park went right to the edge of the sea cliff. This picture – part portrait and part landscape – was painted then.

The subject's face is shaded by the brim of the cap, but the angular features and the red beard reveal he is Vuillard. From his feet in the grass to the pencil between his fingers, artist and nature are shown as one. Like a great tree, he is a noble and powerful presence, defying the elements with cap and cape. Unlike Vallotton's other more abstract and distant portraits of the time, Vuillard is rendered with simplicity and in a spirit of comradery and friendship. This is an homage to vacationing artists – in other words, to themselves. N.B.

Vassily Kandinsky

Moscow 1866 – Neuilly-sur-Seine 1944

Study for "Betonte Ecken" or "Accentuated Corners"

1922
Watercolour on paper
46.9 × 41.8 cm

Purchase, Horsley and Annie Townsend Bequest and The Montreal Museum of Fine Arts' Volunteer Association Fund
1977.10

■ It was at the invitation of architect Walter Gropius, founder and director of the Bauhaus, that Kandinsky went to Weimar in March 1922. At the age of sixty-two, he had an established reputation. He was the inventor of Lyrical Abstraction and also a theoretician: his *Concerning the Spiritual in Art* was published in 1911. Before World War I he had founded and participated in several associations of avant-garde artists: Phalanx, then Der Blaue Reiter in Munich, Der Sturm in Berlin and the Jack of Diamonds in Moscow. During the Bolshevik Revolution, he took an active part in reorganizing the arts in Moscow.

Gropius offered him a teaching post with a class on the theory of shape and the directorship of a workshop for mural painting, a technique Kandinsky had never practised. However, because there was no room for easel painting in the Bauhaus programme, which combined architecture, the applied arts and theatre painting, he took up the position in June. There he renewed his friendship with Paul Klee, another teacher at this celebrated school, and met figures such as Lyonel Feininger, Georg Muche, Lothar Shreyer, Johannes Itten, Gerhard Marks and Oskar Schlemmer.

This watercolour, dated November 1922, demonstrates the artist's transition between Lyrical Abstraction and Bauhaus geometric austerity. The balanced, light-hearted composition is contained within a perfect square and held together by a central cross from whose centre a centrifugal force causes rectilinear and organic shapes to burst into pieces. In late 1922 or early 1923, Kandinsky painted an almost identical work (Nahmad Collection). A few weeks later, his *On White II* (Musée national d'art moderne, Paris), despite being similar in composition, already shows less spontaneity and greater severity. N.B.

Lyonel Feininger
New York 1871 – New York 1956

Yellow Street II

1918
Oil on canvas
95 × 86.1 cm

Purchase, The Maxwell Cummings Family Foundation, The Ladies' Committee of
the Museum, John G. McConnell, CBE, Mr. and Mrs. A. Murray Vaughan, Harold
Lawson Bequest, Horsley and Annie Townsend Bequest
1971.35

■ This typical Thuringian village, with its double-pitched roofs, is one of those in the
countryside around Weimar where Feininger so often found his subjects: architecture and
towns. It is, as he wrote in 1917, "a real Sunday morning full of luminosity, with a pale
golden light over the trees and roofs, not hard and glassy as in summer, a delicate haze medi-
ating between the sky and the world." A few well-dressed women and a flag (Belgian, oddly
enough) provide counterpoints of colour here and there to the chromatic division of the
canvas, and the shapes of the houses echo the wave-like curves of the sky. At the period
when he executed this canvas, the artist was alternating between unpeopled cityscapes verg-
ing on geometric abstraction and more picturesque scenes like this one. With its figures
sketched from life, it recalls his time in Paris and his past as an illustrator.

Feininger, born American of German parents, studied in Paris and was influenced by
Cézanne's crystalline constructions and Delaunay's solar Orphism. In 1911, he exhibited
with the Cubists at the Salon des Indépendants. However, he found the Cubism of Picasso
and Braque too mechanical and physical, preferring the atmospheric, poetic and lyrical
qualities of a way of painting he called "prism-ism": a violinist of some talent like Paul
Klee, Feininger compared his art to music and his paintings to fugues. Although he was
a member of the Der Blaue Reiter and Die Brücke groups, he has a unique place within
the German Expressionist movement. N.B.

Salvador Dalí

Figueras 1904 – Figueras 1989

Portrait of Maria Carbona

1925
Oil on cardboard
52 × 39.2 cm
Gift of The Montreal Museum of Fine Arts' Volunteer Association
1969.1640a

■ Dalí was only twenty-one when he painted this portrait of Maria Carbona. At the time, he was an obstreperous student in the Fine Arts, indifferent to the manifesto of Surrealism published that same year in Paris. A shy youth, the son of a notary, he nonetheless got himself expelled from Madrid's professional art school (now the Academia de San Fernando). In 1925, his first solo exhibition at the avant-garde Dalmau gallery in Barcelona was a success. In its classicism, his work echoes the post-war "return to order" movement and Catalan Noucentisme, and especially Italian Metaphysical Painting. Above all, Dalí revered the Neoclassicism of Ingres, as is apparent in the very finished preparatory drawing for this painting (Museu de Montserrat, Barcelona). It seems to have been done from life and cannot fail to remind us of Ingres's line drawings.

Maria Carbona was a member of the young intellectual circle in Figueras, the artist's birthplace in Catalonia. Her father, Juan Carbona, was a writer and mayor of the town. Her pose here suggests both shyness and poise, rendered by a combination of cool elegance and stark monumentality that recalls earlier portraits of Olga by Dalí's countryman Picasso and, to some extent, portraits by the German New Objectivity group.

The work is painted on the back of a fragment of a still life executed by the artist in 1924, which was later cut in four. This period of his career is called the Ana Maria period, after his sister, whom he often painted. In 1929, Dalí officially joined the Surrealists. N.B.

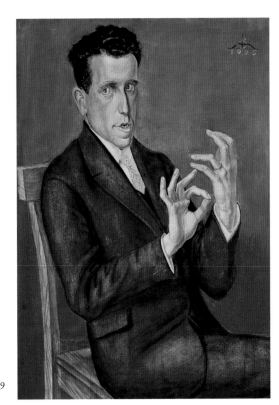

Otto Dix
Untermhaus 1891 – Singen 1969

Portrait of the Lawyer Hugo Simons

1925
Tempera and oil on panel
100.3 × 70.3 cm

Purchase, grant from the Government of Canada under the terms of the Cultural Property Export and Import Act, and the Succession J.A. DeSève, gifts from Charles and Andrea Bronfman, Mr. Nahum and Dr. Sheila Gelber, Phyllis Lambert, the Volunteer Association and Junior Associates of the Montreal Museum of Fine Arts, Louise L. Lamarre, Pierre Théberge, and the Museum's acquisition fund, through the Horsley and Annie Townsend Bequest

1993.12

■ When a client refused to pay for his daughter's portrait because he judged it a poor likeness, Otto Dix called upon attorney Hugo Simons, who won his case in the name of freedom of artistic expression. In gratitude, Dix made him this extraordinary portrait.

An exponent of the recently spawned Neue Sachlichkeit (New Objectivity) movement, Dix railed against the emblems of the military cult and bourgeois morality, and denounced the social malaise and decadent pessimism of Weimar Germany. If he retained the violence of Expressionism, he disciplined his painting by a thorough concern for objectivity and precision, following the example of Italian and Northern Renaissance masters, to such an extent that he was nicknamed Hans Baldung Dix, after Hans Baldung Grien! Just back from Italy, Dix experimented with a new mixed media technique for this panel: egg tempera covered with an oil glaze. In this warm portrait, devoid of caricature, the painter's memory retraces the essence of his model after studying him with his eye, for in Dix's opinion, it is better to paint without a model; otherwise one sees too much. Here, the mannered hand gesture, the feverishness of the face, the maroon of the suit and the coppery red of the background transcribe the lawyer's oratorical intensity. Everyone has a colour, according to Dix.

Condemned by the Nazis as a degenerate artist, Dix was forced to quit teaching, but he stayed in Germany and embarked on an "interior emigration". Simons and his family, at odds with the regime and stripped of citizenship, sought refuge in Montreal. N.B.

Kees van Dongen
Delfshaven 1877 – Monte Carlo 1968

Woman on a Sofa
About 1930
Oil on canvas
89.2 × 116.8 cm
Gift of Dr. Max Stern
1978.21

■ Van Dongen, Dutch-born but a naturalized Frenchman, became known as one of the outrageous Fauve painters, but in his work the Fauve riot of colour had little to do with the countryside: instead he focused on the world of acrobats and bohemian city life. As a portraitist of the elegant and the shady sides of urban life, he soon became famous. During the post-war period, aristocrats and muses of all sorts flocked to his studio to be painted by the tireless artist, who now displayed a less strident palette and at times a certain cynicism: "The basic rule is to make the women longer and above all thinner. After that, one has only to make the jewellery bigger. And they love it."

Who is this woman lounging in the corner of a sofa, wearing a fur stole that reveals the flawless cut of her dress? A respectable woman would pose in a more dignified manner; this is one of the many models who kept low company in what Van Dongen called "the cocktail era". The androgynous hair cut and the flowing line of the fabric are characteristic of the free-spirited style of the Roaring Twenties. Even so, this archetypal modern odalisque cannot be precisely dated. Vlaminck admiringly concluded, "Portraits of women? Portrait of the *woman of the inflation.* Wonderful, sinister portraits of a made-up woman, with hints of an unwholesome exaggeration exacerbated by the red of her lips, the yellow of her makeup base and the line of her eyebrows elongated and reshaped by a pencil."

Dr. Max Stern bought his painting directly from Van Dongen's studio and gave it, along with three other of the artist's canvases, to the Museum. N.B.

Henri Matisse

Le Cateau-Cambrésis 1869 – Nice 1954

Seated Woman, Back Turned to the Open Window

About 1922
Oil on canvas
73.3 × 92.5 cm
Purchase, John W. Tempest Fund
1949.1015

■ Early in his career, Matisse discovered the Mediterranean light that beams out of his first Fauve paintings. He became a regular visitor to the French Riviera, staying mainly in Nice after 1917. Weary of expensive hotel rooms, in 1921 he rented an apartment that he could also use as a studio at 1 Place Charles-Félix, where this canvas was painted. Behind the sitter, the sunlight and the deep blue of the Baie des Anges flood in through the wide-open window. The palm trees and the sailboats strung out opposite the quay suggest the seaside holiday of an artist who has not lost the tourist's sense of wonder. As so often in Matisse's work, the window itself is the main subject of the painting. A bold foreground is provided by the young model, Henriette Daricarrère, a native of Nice and a ballet and music student. The artist has decorated the studio in which she is posing with richly patterned Oriental fabrics.

After the War, Matisse reverted to a more classical-looking style that was in fact extremely decorative: the layout of this scene, hemmed in by emphatic bands, contrasts with the exquisite blue of the sea on the horizon, rendered in graduated shades. This canvas, a fine example of his Nice period, was purchased by Stephen C. Clark, a New York lawyer who was also co-owner of the Singer Manufacturing Company and on the Board of both the Metropolitan Museum of Art and the Museum of Modern Art. Clark had some fifteen of Matisse's Nice paintings hung in a special room in his house, which had been decorated to echo the colours of the artist's studio. N.B.

■ Maillol was born in the countryside and loved the land, endlessly depicting it. He was trained as a painter and learned from the Nabis how to simplify planes; he was also a tireless draftsman, aiming at purity of line. As his eyesight began to fail around the turn of the century, he gave up painting and tapestry to devote himself almost exclusively to sculpture. His work in that field embodies the "return to style", the revival of a classical quality.

Critics often compared Maillol to Rodin: the one tormented, the other calm, and yet both modellers, unabashed lovers of the female body and admirers of ancient Greek sculpture. However, where Rodin fragmented his shapes, contorting and varying them, Maillol constructed, stabilized and refined his material. Always working from the trunk outwards, he pruned the limbs, producing rounded, fruit-like, fecund shapes. There is no story behind the image: it is always the same high-breasted, round-hipped woman and the same *contrapposto* that he reinvents, each figure embodying an ideal of beauty relentlessly repeated. And so Maillol went on sculpting female torsos, named or nameless, after Rodin and in the manner of Antoine Bourdelle and Constantin Brancusi. Thereafter, he would add a head and arms or legs; he might clothe her in a wet chemise. He designed monumental torsos for public monuments and miniature, palm-sized ones.

This sculpture of sand-cast bronze is a single edition by the founder Alexis Rudier. It was made under Maillol's supervision after his plaster model of about 1932 (Indiana University Art Museum, Bloomington.) N.B.

Aristide Maillol
Banyuls-sur-Mer 1861 –
Perpignan 1944

Torso of a Young Woman

1935
Bronze, 1/1
97 × 32.5 × 27.8 cm
Purchase
1949.1016

Alberto Martini
Oderzo 1876 – Milan 1954

Self-portrait

1929
Oil on canvas
65 × 54 cm
Purchase, Horsley and Annie Townsend Bequest
2001.5

■ Martini stands at the crossroads of Symbolism, *pittura metafisica* and Surrealism. He was already a recognized name at the Venice Biennale of 1907. His work, like that of Alberto Savinio and Giorgio De Chirico, was at first "proto-Surrealist". His grotesque, dramatic images demonstrate a visionary's sensibility and a taste for macabre eroticism, as can be seen in this self-portrait.

In 1928, Martini moved to Paris, where he stayed until 1934. In his studio on Boulevard du Montparnasse, he entertained many well-known figures of the day. When André Breton invited him to join the Surrealist group in 1929, Martini refused, preferring independence and solitude. And yet, he was friends with Francis Picabia, Max Ernst, René Magritte and Joan Miró.

He was the inventor of a "black style" that informs so many of his self-portraits. This one is characteristic of his original "teleplastic" and "psychoplastic" approach, executed with a deliberate absence of restraint and a creative intensity that he himself likened to hypnosis or clairvoyance. The hallucinatory power of this canvas is comparable to contemporary experiments by Surrealist photographers (*Portrait of the Marquise Casati* by Man Ray, 1922). It is almost an X-ray portrait. Its stamp of strangeness reveals the artist's soul, his perception of his self – a self obsessed with erotic visions that fire the senses of sight and touch, expressing voyeuristic, even murderous, impulses. N.B.

Georges Rouault

Paris 1871 – Paris 1958

The Circus

1936
Oil on canvas
70 × 107.8 cm

A Millenium Gift of Sara Lee Corporation

2000.10

■ Rouault, a favourite pupil of the Symbolist master Gustave Moreau, lived a solitary life, creating an oeuvre unique in its mystic Expressionism (he was a devout Catholic). Throughout his career, but particularly in the 1930s, he was fascinated by circus people. He painted clowns and acrobats, alone or in small groups, often backstage. One day, he wrote of an old clown he had seen: "I saw clearly that the 'Clown' was me, was us . . . almost all of us . . . This *rich, sequinned* costume is given us by *life*, we are all *more or less Clowns*, we all wear a *sequinned costume*, but if someone takes us by surprise, as I surprised the old clown, oh who will then dare to claim he is not shaken to the marrow by immeasurable pity?"

The Circus is remarkable for its subject, since Rouault rarely painted circus artists in performance, and this is the largest of such canvases. In the ring, a lady equestrian and other acrobats are doing their number; in the background, an athlete, hands on hips, dominates the centre of the composition. The upper corners of the canvas are set off, evoking the big top, as though we viewers were spectators in the seats. The thick black outlines around the shapes and areas of colour are characteristic of his style, which recalls stained glass (Rouault had been an apprentice in that craft). The depiction of the circus thus becomes for the artist as solemn as a religious rite, a metaphorical, disenchanted vision of life's trivialities. N.B.

Alberto Giacometti

Borgonovo, Switzerland, 1901 – Chur, Switzerland, 1966

Portrait of the Artist's Mother

1947
Oil on canvas
43.3 × 30.7 cm
Gift of Mr. and Mrs. Ira Young
1983.30

■ Throughout his career the painter and sculptor Giacometti persisted in using the people he was closest to for models. In an odd case of namesakes, his life's course moved from his mother, Annetta Stampa (1871-1964) and the village of his childhood in the Swiss canton of Les Grisons to which he remained attached, to his wife Annette, who in her turn was to be his favourite sitter. By her husband Giovanni Giacometti, a well-known Neo-Impressionist painter, Annetta had three gifted sons: Alberto, the most famous; Diego, an ornamentalist craftsman; and Bruno, an architect. Alberto was devoted to his mother, corresponding with her at length and visiting her regularly. "She personified the presence and permanence of the inward flame that illuminated the sculptor's work and life", as poet Jacques Dupin wrote. Unwavering in his devotion and always speaking to her in the local dialect, Giacometti remained quite submissive to her strong will when in her company, as witnesses recall. Those who knew her said she seemed a rock-solid being.

The hieratic quality of her personality was completely in tune with the style of Alberto's portraits and his quest to render features that always seemed to elude him, to achieve an impossible likeness. He required absolute immobility from his model, whom he seated in a chair positioned with extreme precision. Thus the images of his mother with head high and intense gaze, captured full-length or half-length in a web of lines, trace the advance of years into old age. N.B.

Ansel Adams
San Francisco 1902 – San Francisco 1984

Clouds above Golden Canyon, Death Valley, California
Portfolio I, pl. 12
1946
Silver print, 43/75
35.6 × 45.6 cm
Anonymous gift
1989(Gr.1950.61).Ph.1l

White Stump, Sierra Nevada, California
Portfolio V, pl. 9
1936
Silver print, 19/110
49.1 × 33.4 cm
Purchase, Mrs. J. Michael G. Scott Funds and Horsley and Annie Townsend Bequest
1989(Gr.1975.41).Ph.2i

■ Ansel Adams tirelessly photographed the landscape of the American West and Southwest in all their immutable grandeur. Ever faithful to his ideal of nature and an unspoiled America, he produced black-and-white images of memorable clarity, monumentality and sublimity. Adams was a promoter and defender of strict photography, allowing no room for camera tricks or darkroom manipulations. Yet, while his photographs truthfully represent reality, he never considered them merely environmental records. He created his images through visualization, calculating the end result before exposure to create prints that express his ideas and emotions.

Sensitive to natural arrangements, Adams constantly counterbalanced dramatic masses with subtle forms and exploited the instantaneous interpretation of the play of light on the landscape. There is a pronounced cohesion to his geometric compositions, ruled by rationalism and repetition: foreground mountain peaks and sky in harmoniously balanced dark, light and lighter shades of grey, with only rarely an impenetrable black.

Adams was also fascinated by perspective, horizon and patterns of horizontal and diagonal lines or strong verticals and repeated triangular forms, as can be seen in *Clouds above Golden Canyon*. The appeal of other compositions – particularly close-ups of vegetation and rocks, like *White Stump* – lies in their almost abstract quality. D.C.

Milton Avery

Altmar, New York, 1885 – New York 1965

Trees against the Sea

1959
Oil on canvas
50.6 × 61.1 cm

Purchase, Horsley and Annie Townsend Bequest
1961.1281

■ This canvas was the first by a contemporary American artist to be purchased by the Museum. Avery had already visited Canada, spending a holiday in the Gaspé in 1938 and staying with a Toronto collector in 1947. In 1961, when the work was acquired, he was a famous and respected painter. The year before, a retrospective of his work had been held at the Whitney Museum of American Art. Clement Greenberg published a study of his oeuvre, and through his friendship with Mark Rothko and Adolf Gottlieb, the artist had considerable influence on the emergence of Abstract Art in post-war New York. And yet he himself never went beyond the limits of figurative art, allusive but always real.

After his first heart attack in 1949, Avery's style changed to one of extreme simplicity and quiet restraint. In 1959, when he painted *Trees against the Sea*, he was in failing health, obliged to take nitroglycerine daily for chest pain. His painting, however, was still airy, like a breath of colour on the canvas's surface. In a commemorative essay on Avery, Rothko wrote, "Avery is first a great poet. He is the poetry of sheer loveliness, of sheer beauty," and further on, "What was Avery's repertoire? His living room, Central Park, his wife Sally, his daughter March, the beaches and mountains where they summered; cows, fish heads, the flight of birds; his friends and whatever world strayed through his studio: a domestic, unheroic cast." N.B.

Henry Moore

Castleford 1898 – Much Hadham 1986

Two Draped Reclining Figures

1961

Watercolour, black ink, white, black and coloured chalk on paper

29.1 × 23.9 cm

Gift of Dr. Sean B. Murphy

2000.134

■ The drawings of British-born Moore, recognized as one of the twentieth century's greatest sculptors, are not only preparatory sketches for sculptures but works of art in themselves. Drawing to Moore was an essential activity, a reservoir of ideas that do not necessarily have anything to do with sculpture. He even exhibited his drawings alongside his sculpture.

Moore started his career drawing and ended it the same way. During World War II, he had no materials for sculpture. He was appointed an official war artist and during the Blitz, he depicted the world of the people sheltering themselves from the bombs in the London underground stations. From 1955 to 1970, he made fewer drawings, concentrating on sculptured models. Towards the end of his life, however, he was particularly interested in drawing, as well as copper engraving.

Influenced by Surrealism, the vitality of the organic shapes found in nature informed Moore's human figures. This watercolour demonstrates his interest in bones, which at this period he would assemble so as to compose a body out of several blocks (*Two Reclining Figures*, 1961). By making the heads smaller, he emphasizes the monumentality of the group, while the lines of bust and legs suggest mountains. The recumbent figures, a constant in his work, were initially inspired by an ancient Mayan sculptural type known as *chacmool* (Rain Spirit). For Moore, the position expressed both stability and freedom.

The Museum also possesses thirteen sculptures by Moore, which are small for the most part, except for two monumental pieces – *Parze* (1977.43) and *Large Totem Head*. N.B.

Karel Appel
Born in Amsterdam
in 1921

Portrait of Sir Herbert Read

1962
Oil on canvas
115.9 × 89.2 cm
Purchase, Horsley and Annie Townsend Bequest
1962.1367

■ When the distinguished English poet and essayist Sir Herbert Read (1893-1968) came upon his portrait at the Museum, he exclaimed, "It's a fine picture. I suppose there is a traits resemblance. But he might have given me more brains." Read had come to Montreal to make the opening address as honorary president at the Fourth International Conference of the International Society for Education through Art, and agreed to be photographed in front of his recent portrait, "if only in self-defence". After missing several sittings with Sir Herbert, Appel decided to paint him from memory. Looking at the red face, the writer remarked, "Its strength lies in its calligraphic dynamism, its violence of colour, its direct-ness, whatever its value as a portrait. It is a powerful image and that is the artist's intention." He added, "I admit I feel like [that] sometimes. Rather hot under the collar. But I would say that is a subjective memory of the artist rather than a representational portrait. Some people might feel insulted by what they would regard as caricature but I have too much respect for the art of Appel to feel any resentment. In other words, I am a very willing victim."

In 1948, Appel, who had been trained at the Amsterdam Academy of Fine Arts, took part in the launching of the Experimental Group. With the support of the periodical *Reflex*, he was opposed to the geometric abstraction then dominant in the art of the Netherlands. In 1949, he was a founding member of the Cobra movement (COpenhagen / BRussels /Amsterdam), citing van Gogh and Expressionist figuration; he defended ges-tural, primitive, childlike art. Dividing his time between Paris and New York, he won distinguished international awards. His voluminous and monumental oeuvre includes graphically explosive portraits in cheerful, loud colours. N.B.

Joan Miró
Barcelona 1893 – Palma de Mallorca 1983

Head

1976
Oil on canvas
91.8 × 72.4 cm
Gift in memory of Barry Seymour Boyd
2002.107

■ Miró, a leading exponent of Surrealism, discovered modern art in Barcelona with Francis Picabia. He went to join Picasso in Paris, where he took part in Dadaist events before joining the Surrealists in 1924. As a fervent Republican during the Civil War, he did not return to Spain in the years 1936-1940. The Museum of Modern Art in New York presented his first retrospective in 1941. In 1960, he was awarded the Grand Prize of the Guggenheim Foundation. The Miró Foundation, built in 1974 in Barcelona by Josep Lluis Sert, holds a major collection of his works.

Towards the end of his life, Miró, who said he was wary of discussions of his work, took no care to keep his painting "clean"; in this regard, his late work might be compared to Picasso's and to contemporary "bad painting". Such blatant carelessness with his working materials reflect the new effects he was trying out, which included burns, for example. That is why drips, smears and uneven areas are so often seen in the later work. This poetic canvas is characteristic of the output of his old age. The black background, crescent moon and fish-shaped heads rendered in vibrant warm tones signal Miró's painterly world appeal to the imagination. In its extreme simplicity of form and technique, this canvas is a fine example of the artist's creative vigour in the twilight of his days. N.B.

Pablo Ruiz Picasso

Málaga 1881 –
Mougins 1973

Embrace

1971
Oil on canvas
195 × 130 cm
Gift of Jacqueline Picasso
1985.5

■ The erotic art of the twentieth century's most famous painter is copious. Picasso put down his loves on paper and canvas, from his experiences in Barcelona to the imaginings of his riper years. Beyond his own life, it is painting that he celebrates throughout the long "copulatory" movement of his work: "I can't help myself when it comes to painting – it makes me do whatever it likes," he said. Scenes of bodies entwined in love or violence – or both – recur continually in the work of this artist who never abandoned the power of figuration.

When Picasso executed this painting, he was ninety years old, working with "dirty language" and rapidly. That time was of the essence in this struggle with painting is evident from the vehemence of the rendering. The quick manner and sloppy handling manifest his wish to identify things quickly, painting and drawing at the same time: "I want to say the nude, I don't want to make just a nude as a nude; I want to say just breast, say foot, say hand, belly . . ." This is less an embrace than the portrait of a couple, side by side and identified by their genitals. Here, Picasso does not make use of masks and disguises as elsewhere: there is no characteristic here but sexuality. In their nobleness and monumental nudity, this couple come closer to great art than to graffiti.

When he exhibited at the papal palace in Avignon in 1970, it caused a furor: he was considered nothing more than a disgraceful old man, an artistic has-been, before being properly re-appraised by artists and art history. N.B.

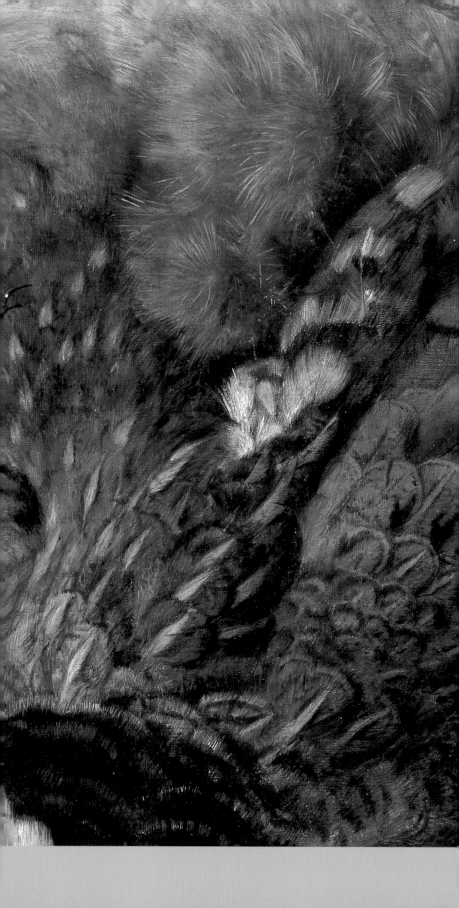

Workshop of Louis-Amable Quévillon
Saint-Vincent-de-Paul

Death of Saint Francis Xavier

About 1811-1816
Polychrome wood
93.5 × 74.8 cm
Gift of Samuel Breitman
1964.Df.17

■ In the first quarter of the nineteenth century, noteworthy changes occurred in the methods of sculpture in the Montreal region, where Louis-Amable Quévillon directed a workshop that operated on a factory-style division of labour. The workshop employed many apprentices and workers, and its production of ornamental elements was distributed not only around Montreal, but throughout Quebec.

Consisting of carved elements that have been nailed and glued to an assemblage of wooden slats, the whole then painted, this relief tableau clearly illustrates the new sculptural practice. Executed about 1811-1816, the panel is probably from the Church of Saint-Rose de Laval. The subject is based directly on a small engraved pious image that is in turn a schematic version of a more sophisticated engraving executed by the French artist François de Poilly. It depicts the death of Jesuit missionary Francis Xavier (1506-1552), laid low by fever and abandoned on the small island of Sancion, off the coast of China, where he was going to preach. He has been depicted with the only objects he kept in his possession – a breviary, rosary and crucifix (although the latter, visible in an old photograph, has since disappeared). Devotion to Saint Francis Xavier, who was canonized in 1622, reminds us how important the presence of the Jesuits in the colony had been. Many paintings depict this subject, but this piece is the only sculpted version remaining today; it was created at the time of a revival of popular fervour associated with the novena of Saint Francis. J.D.R.

Antoine Plamondon
Ancienne-Lorette 1804 – Neuville 1895
The Arrest of Christ
1839
Oil on canvas
154.3 × 239.4 cm
Purchase, Horsley and Annie Townsend Bequest
1961.1321

■ After studying painting with Joseph Légaré, Antoine Plamondon made the most of a stay in France from 1826 to 1830 to perfect his art in the workshop of Paulin-Guérin. Back in Canada, he embarked on a brilliant career as a portraitist. He also produced a large body of religious work, like the fourteen-canvas Way of the Cross intended for Notre-Dame Church in Montreal. The cycle was executed between 1836 and 1839 with the assistance of two apprentices, François Matte and Théophile Hamel. For obscure reasons of religious orthodoxy, the Sulpicians responsible for the parish rejected six of the paintings, including this *Arrest of Christ*. They made their way finally to the Museum in 1961.

Plamondon based his religious paintings on known works. This practice, in no way viewed as a defect, remained a constant in Canadian painting through the first half of the nineteenth century; very seldom did painters execute original compositions. Plamondon's Way of the Cross is no exception: *The Arrest of Christ* is derived from an engraving, the source of which was in turn a painting by French artist Jacques Stella. Of course, the transfer from one medium to another precludes making an exact replica, for the painter must at the very least invent his own colour palette. J.P.L.

William Berczy

Wallerstein, Bavaria, 1744 – New York 1813
Active in Canada 1794-1812

Still Life with Flowers

Oil on cardboard
28 × 23 cm

Purchase, Horsley and Annie Townsend Bequest
1970.1647

■ William Berczy arrived in Canada with his family and a group of settlers after a failed attempt to settle in the United States. They started out in the region of York (now Toronto); Berczy can be considered a founder. After many problems with the government of Upper Canada, he then alternated residences, according to circumstance, between Quebec City and Montreal. With art training in Europe that was far superior to that of his Canadian contemporaries, Berczy was sought after to paint portraits as well as religious paintings for Quebec churches.

This still life – a rarity for the artist – was probably painted on a book cover. The flowers it depicts (nasturtium, rose, carnation, sweet william, delphinium, sweetpea, marigold) were common varieties in both Europe and North America at the time, and thus far, research has not determined whether the artist brought this work from Europe or whether he painted it in this country. The only other known flower painting by Berczy, of dimensions similar to this one, is likewise undated. Otherwise, flowers appear as decorative elements in two of his portraits: a vase (about 1782-87) and a corsage (1803-04). Whenever it may have been painted, this still life attests to Berczy's fondness for traditional models as well as his skill with small formats. J.P.L.

Jean-Baptiste Roy-Audy
Quebec City 1778 – died before 1848

Louis Léandre Lemaître-Auger
About 1838
Oil on canvas
66 × 55.8 cm
Purchase, gift of F. Cleveland Morgan
1936.1259

Madame Louis Léandre Lemaître-Auger
About 1838
Oil on canvas
67 × 56.5 cm
Purchase, gift of F. Cleveland Morgan
1936.1260

▨ The son of a craftsman, Jean-Baptiste Roy-Audy first worked as a carpenter, coach builder, gilder and sign painter. Like Joseph Légaré and Antoine Plamondon, among others, his initiation to painting came by way of "restoring" some European canvases from the collection assembled by Abbé Philippe-Jean-Louis Desjardins in the early nineteenth century. Thereafter, Roy-Audy painted portraits and religious paintings, often going from city to town according to demand.

This pair of portraits reflects the rise of the Quebec bourgeoisie at that period. The sitters' pose, costume and accessories, which reveal their social rank, are as important as the likeness. The couple portrayed are Louis Léandre Lemaître-Auger of Louiseville, a notary, and the woman he married in 1828, Élisabeth Ranvoyzé, granddaughter of the silversmith François Ranvoyzé.

The portraits expose the weaknesses of these self-taught painters. Lacking a firm grasp of the laws of perspective and anatomy, they distract the beholder's attention by bringing out the details. The drawing is linear to the point of stylization, as in the folds of the cravat, and the colour is simplified, while the clothing and accessories, such as the jewellery, belt buckle and fine embroidered lace along the neckline, are depicted meticulously. This approach is characteristic of the work of various Canadian and American painters sometimes referred to as "primitives". J.P.L.

Joseph Légaré
Quebec City 1795 – Quebec City 1855

View of Quebec City from Pointe Lévis
About 1840-1842
Oil on canvas
90 × 120 cm

Purchase, gift of the Succession J.A. DeSève and Horsley and Annie Townsend Bequest
1980.3

■ Joseph Légaré apprenticed as a painter-glazer under Moses Pierce, which prepared him for accomplishing tasks as diverse as painting carriages, signs and apartment decorations, as well as retouching paintings. He had the opportunity to try his hand at restoration in 1817, with the arrival of the first lot of paintings sent from France to Quebec by Abbé Philippe-Jean-Louis Desjardins. The lessons Légaré acquired from this contact with European painting consequently enabled him to turn his hand to portraiture, history painting and landscape.

Légaré was the first Canadian artist to show an interest in the representation of nature, a genre then dominated by the topographical painters of the British army. For *View of Quebec City from Pointe Lévis*, Légaré no doubt drew his inspiration from a similarly framed view in a watercolour by Robert Coulson, an officer of the Grenadier Guards stationed in Quebec City between 1839 and 1842. In this carefully ordered composition, Quebec City, the "Gibraltar of North America", as writers of the period called it, is presented in a panorama that includes Cap Diamant, bordered by the Saint Lawrence and the mouth of the Saint-Charles River, with the Beauport coast in the distance. In the foreground, dense vegetation frames the scene, while the Laurentian Mountains melt into the hazy background. J.P.L.

Théophile Hamel
Sainte-Foy 1817 – Quebec City 1870

Madame Charles-Hilaire Têtu and Her Son Eugène

1841
Oil on canvas
115.1 × 97.2 cm
Anonymous gift
1968.1585

■ At the age of sixteen Théophile Hamel was apprenticed to Antoine Plamondon, and he completed his training in Europe from 1843 to 1846. Back in his homeland, he became an admired portraitist. The culmination of his career came in 1853, when the government commissioned him to paint the portraits of former and new presidents of the Assembly, a commission that would later be extended to include the presidents of the Legislative Council. The prestige attached to these offices attracted a clientele of notables and clergy.

This portrait, dating from 1841, was commissioned by Charles-Hilaire Têtu, a rich merchant from Rivière-Ouelle, in Kamouraska county. It depicts his wife, Elizabeth O'Brien, with their son Eugène. In keeping with the nineteenth-century fashion for children, the three-year-old boy has long hair and wears a light-coloured embroidered dress that, like the mother's attire, indicates their social status. Behind them, a parted curtain reveals a landscape evocative of the Lower Saint Lawrence. Every element is painted with care and the conventional arrangement of the scene confers upon it a somewhat solemn air, the only diversion from which is in the way the child plays with the chain of his mother's watch. Although this painting, executed two years before Hamel's European sojourn, does not display the ease and cheerful description of sitters that some years later were to signal his originality and spell his success, it is a fine example of his early work. J.P.L.

Homer Ransford Watson
Doon, Ontario, 1855 – Doon 1936

A Coming Storm in the Adirondacks

1879
Oil on canvas
85.7 × 118.3 cm
Gift of George Hague
1887.203

■ Homer Watson was one of the most prominent Canadian landscape painters of the late nineteenth century. Although he is considered self-taught, he benefited from the advice of artists he met while working at photographer William Notman's Toronto studio. In the United States in 1876 and 1877, Watson discovered the painters of the Hudson River School. Their landscapes, realistic yet suffused with spirituality, proved a source of inspiration, as did those of Gainsborough and Constable, two British painters he admired.

Painted in 1879, *A Coming Storm in the Adirondacks* is one of Watson's first important canvases. Nature's majesty, signalled by the monumentality of the mountain, is presented in the spirit of Romanticism. The bear in the left foreground recalls the untamed state of the still largely unexplored wilderness. Contrasting with the brightness of the rock-strewn stream, the sky filled with threatening dark clouds heralds the imminent storm. To heighten the dramatic effect, Watson has lit the crest of the mountain from behind, a technique often employed by the Hudson River School. J.P.L.

Cornelius Krieghoff
Amsterdam 1815 – Chicago 1872

Still Life with Game

1860
Oil on canvas
61.6 × 51.8 cm

Purchase, estates of Serge Desroches, Hermina Thau, David R. Morrice,
Mary Eccles, Jean Agnes Reid Fleming, G. C. Chisholm, Margaret
A. Reid, F. Eleanore Morrice

2001.33

■ Cornelius Krieghoff – a painter of Dutch-German background who greatly admired Brueghel the Elder and Jan Steen – is best known for his depictions of country dwellers and Native people intended to satisfy a public with a taste for the picturesque. Krieghoff was an enthusiastic hunter and made a number of paintings that portray him hunting with friends and patrons accompanied by a Native guide. While hunting scenes are frequent in his oeuvre, still lifes like this are atypical.

Still Life with Game depicts, counter-clockwise from the left, a common snipe, a ruffed grouse, a bufflehead and an American woodcock. The birds, arranged in a lozenge shape and hung on a rough plaster wall, are represented according to the conventions of European painting at the time. The remarkable quality of the treatment contrasts with the hasty execution one often notices in the artist's genre scenes. He approaches this subject with greater gusto, and the composition provides him with the opportunity to demonstrate his talent, especially in the minute care required by the subtleties of colour and texture. This is particularly true of the rendering of the varied smooth and downy plumages. A patch of red brick showing through the plaster seems to echo the colour of the duck's webbed foot. J.P.L.

Allan Edson
Stanbridge, Quebec, 1846 – Glen Sutton, Quebec, 1888

Giant Falls

1872
Watercolour
55.7 × 45 cm
Purchase, Dr. Francis J. Shepherd Bequest
1963.1434

▓ Allan Edson went to London in 1864 to finish up his art training. In 1867 he was one of the founding members of the Society of Canadian Artists, whose first exhibition he took part in the following year. He was also one of the earliest members of the Ontario Society of Artists (1872) and a founding member of the Royal Canadian Academy of Arts (1880). When Edson painted *Giant Falls* in 1872, he was one of the most prominent landscape painters in Canada. Described by his contemporaries as an extremely modest man, Edson lived the greater part of his life in the Eastern Townships, where, in the area around Lake Memphremagog, he derived the majority of his subjects.

The artist was a part of one of the most important trends in Canadian painting of the second half of the nineteenth century, Luminism, following in a similar direction to the American landscape painters of the Hudson River School, who attached particular importance to the treatment of light. The waterfall in this watercolour of Edson's divides the composition in two. While at the right, the foreground depicts foliage and vegetation in precise detail, the background disappears into a haze of aerial perspective. The artist evinces great skill in representing the mist from the falls, which veils the mountains silhouetted beyond, heightening their distance. J.P.L.

Paul Kane

Mallow, Ireland, 1810 – Toronto 1871

Caw-Wacham

About 1848
Oil on canvas
75.7 × 63.2 cm
Purchase, William Gilman Cheney Bequest
1947.991

■ With the support of Hudson's Bay Company, Paul Kane undertook a journey across the Prairies in May 1846. It stretched out over nearly three years and took him all the way to Fort Vancouver (today Portland, Oregon). He brought back more than five hundred sketches, which served as studies for oil paintings. Kane's attention to detail and the ethnographic nature of his observation of Amerindians contrasts with the picturesque approach of Cornelius Krieghoff and gives a more accurate idea of their way of life. Although the setting and pose in Kane's compositions remain subject to the painting conventions of the time, his depictions are for the most part quite credible; they are also very similar to those of the American painter George Catlin, who turned his attention to the same subjects.

According to Kane, *Caw-Wacham* was a woman of the Flathead tribe, who lived along the Cowlitz River, a tributary of the Columbia. The descriptive name of this tribe affirms that she is of the Salishan tribe, which lived in the same region. The representation of the child gives an idea of how the cranial deformation seen in the adults results from the constant pressure exerted on the head of infants by the headboard of their portable cradle. J.P.L.

Henry Sandham

Montreal 1842 – London, England, 1910

Evening on the Wharf, or *Montreal Harbour*

1868
Oil on canvas
44.5 × 55.9 cm
Gift of Mrs. J. Campbell Merret
1999.10

Henry Sandham acquired his training in drawing, watercolour and painting from John Arthur Fraser, Otto Reinhold Jacobi, Adolf Vogt and Charles Jones Way – artists who developed in the circle of photographer William Notman. Apprenticed to Notman, Sandham also became a leading artist-photographer.

He made his first oil paintings on canvas in 1868. *Evening on the Wharf* reuses a subject he had previously done in watercolour. Full of anecdotal detail, this colourful painting illustrates the activities at the Montreal harbour, which was rapidly expanding at the time. The composition is livened by the many oblique lines of the bowsprits and rigging of the ship partly visible at the right edge of the picture. At the same time, these lines serve as a repoussoir, leading the eye towards the green-hulled ship at the centre bathed in intense late-afternoon light. In the same patch of light, three figures stand conversing on the wharf in front of the ship. At the left, in the distance, is the outline of a row of harbourfront houses. The style of this canvas recalls the presence of the picturesque in Canadian painting of the time, as well as the artist's talent as an illustrator, which surpassed that of most of his Canadian contemporaries. J.P.L.

William Brymner
Greenock, Scotland, 1855 – Wallasey, England, 1925

Champ-de-Mars, Winter

1892
Oil on canvas
74.9 × 101.6 cm
Mrs. R. MacD. Paterson Bequest (R. B. Angus Collection)
1949.1008

This winter scene depicts the esplanade behind Montreal's city hall, where military parades and drills used to be held. In the peaceful day's end, strollers gradually vacate the square; beyond the houses, the sky glows pink-orange, and in the foreground, the snow gives off a bluish reflection as the shadows deepen. In the windows can barely be discerned the glimmer of newly lit lamps. A sensitive and attentive landscape painter, Brymner has captured the exact moment when day gives way to night.

The Brymner family arrived in Canada from Scotland in 1857, when William was just two. In 1878, after studying architecture in Ottawa, Brymner went to Paris to finish his training with drawing and painting courses. There, he decided to devote himself entirely to painting and enrolled at the Académie Julian where, for five years, he worked under William Bouguereau, among others.

Brymner holds a special place in the Museum's history because he was the director of its art school for thirty-five years, from 1886 to 1921. Although Brymner's work remained true to his conservative training, he encouraged his students, especially the Beaver Hall Group, to explore new artistic avenues. J.P.L.

James Macdonald Barnsley
West Flamboro, Ontario, 1861 – Verdun, Quebec, 1929

High Tide at Dieppe
1886
Oil on canvas
111.7 × 152.2 cm
Gift of David Morrice
1911.4

■ In 1879, James Macdonald Barnsley entered the Saint Louis School of Fine Arts, Missouri. He then travelled to Europe, where he developed a style influenced by the Barbizon School and Impressionism. In his early thirties, Barnsley, was stricken with schizophrenia and discontinued painting. He might have been completely forgotten had his mother and the Montreal gallery W. Scott & Sons not persevered in frequently presenting his work in numerous exhibitions until 1921.

A discreet painter with a sure technique, Barnsley excelled at rendering seaside atmospheres influenced by Eugène Boudin, as can be seen in *High Tide at Dieppe* (previously exhibited as *La Jetée du Pollet, Dieppe*). Having set up his easel at one end of the pier, the artist organized his composition around two docked boats with sails unfurled. The heavily clouded sky modulates the light, as it conditions the tonalities of the entire canvas. In the foreground, passersby are going about their activities, while at the far right, a steamboat is entering the harbour. J.P.L.

Paul Peel
London, Ontario, 1860 – Paris 1892

The Spinner

1881
Oil on canvas
119.6 × 91.4 cm
Gift of William G. Murray
1882.138

■ Paul Peel entered the Pennsylvania Academy of Fine Arts, Philadelphia, in October 1877, and his contact with American artists had a decisive influence on him. A few years later, Peel travelled to Europe, visiting England and subsequently settling in France. From 1881, he made several trips to Pont-Aven, surrounded by the American artists who were among the first foreigners to "discover" Brittany, founding artists' colonies in Pont-Aven and Concarneau.

The Spinner was painted by the young Peel in his Paris studio. It is also one of the first Canadian works to enter the collection of the Art Association of Montreal. Applying the principles of his academic training, the artist has structured the composition around a central figure and treated the modelling with precision. The spinner, probably a professional model, is dressed in Breton costume, with the small headdress typical of the Rosporden region, in the south of the Finistère. She holds a distaff in her left hand; behind her, a child is sleeping in a box bed. Many elements of this painting reveal Peel's more idyllic than naturalist view of peasant life. J.P.L.

Ozias Leduc
Saint-Hilaire 1864 – Saint-Hyacinthe 1955

Still Life with Open Book

1894
Oil on canvas
38.5 × 48 cm

Purchase, grant from the Government of Canada under the terms of the Cultural Property Export and Import Act, and by a gift of The Montreal Museum of Fine Arts' Volunteer Association
1985.7

■ The work of Ozias Leduc is divided between church decoration, portraiture and a more personal symbolist production, where still lifes and landscapes predominate. *Still Life with Open Book* is an inquiry into art and its relationship to sources, models and imitation. On the left page of the book, Leduc has represented the central group of Botticelli's so-called *Madonna of the Rosary*, and in the background a grisaille inspired by Rubens's *Presentation in the Temple*. These images, in combination with the pile of books (among them a history of art), candle holder and violin and bow protruding from behind either edge of the open book, compose a tribute to knowledge and the arts. The painting emanates a feeling of introspection and contemplation.

During his long life, Leduc witnessed many changes in Canada's artistic scene: the creation of the first museums and art schools, increased contact with Europe through travel and imported books and periodicals, and the development of the Royal Canadian Academy of Arts and the Art Association of Montreal, both of which often exhibited his works. Through his teachers Adolphe Rho and Luigi Capello, Leduc was rooted in traditional mural painting, which he later taught to his student Paul-Émile Borduas before the latter turned to abstract art. This connection shows how Quebec modernity, which at first appears to be the result of ruptures, can reveal surprising continuities. J.P.L.

Marc-Aurèle de Foy Suzor-Coté

Arthabaska, Quebec, 1869 –
Daytona Beach, Florida, 1937

Shepherdess at Vallangoujard, Seine-et-Oise

1898
Oil on canvas
235.5 × 100.5 cm

Gift of the Graziella Timmins Raymond Estate
1985.10

■ Born in the Bois-Francs region, Marc-Aurèle de Foy Suzor-Coté first studied painting with Maxime Rousseau, a church decorator. Between 1891 and 1912, he travelled in Canada, the United States and Europe. He studied at the École des Beaux-Arts in Paris, then at the Julian and Colarossi academies. From 1894, he exhibited regularly at the Salons of the Société des artistes français.

An idealized illustration of peasant life, this *Pastourelle* falls in line with the Academic French painters of the second half of the nineteenth century, like Jules Breton. Depicted life-size, the peasant girl is lit from behind, standing amid minutely detailed plants, set off from the background by a brilliant light stretching across the meadow bordered by a woods. The format and careful execution of this painting make it a suitable Salon piece, and in fact, it was shown in 1899 under the title *"Pastourelle"; vallon Goujard (Seine et Oise)*. The place name appears to be a misspelling for the more probable Vallangoujard, a village located near Pontoise and Auvers-sur-Oise, a region then frequented by many artists. Favourably received by the critics, the work was acquired by Sir Rodolphe Forget and exhibited the following year, 1900, at the Art Association of Montreal's annual Spring Exhibition. J.P.L.

■ Louis-Philippe Hébert is doubtless the most important Canadian sculptor of his generation, who by modelling marked a break with the local tradition of wood sculpture. This technique enabled him to execute in bronze the fifty commemorative and funerary monuments, as well as medallions and busts, that he created throughout his career. He also produced a significant number of statuettes, some of which, like this one, were cast in bronze editions.

Only a few copies were made of *The Nicotine Sprite*, also called *Le rêve du fumeur* [The Smoker's Dream]. Its style and narrative content set it apart from the majority of Hébert's compositions and illustrate the presence of Symbolism in his work. A female nude rises from the bowl of a pipe grasped firmly in a man's hand. Supple and sinuous, entwined in vine-like curls of smoke, she is a lascivious creature who intoxicates the smoker. The tangle of arabesques and the sensual aestheticism conjure the inaccessible beauty typical of Symbolist reveries. This allegorical figure gives the artist the opportunity to make a close study of the female form; and if the female nude is common in Hébert's work, this piece does not share the moralizing intent of his more monumental compositions. E.A.P.

Louis-Philippe Hébert
Sainte-Sophie-de-Mégantic
1850 – Westmount 1917

The Nicotine Sprite

1902
Bronze, marble base
53.2 × 26.4 × 15.3 cm
(with base)

Purchase, Horsley and
Annie Townsend Bequest
1994.10

Robert Harris
Tyn-y-groes, Wales, 1849 – Montreal 1919

The Countess of Minto

1903
Oil on canvas
132 × 96.5 cm
Purchase, John W. Tempest Fund
1903.66

■ Born in Wales, Robert Harris was only seven years old when his parents emigrated to Canada and settled in Charlottetown. He received solid art training, which he completed with studies in Boston, London and Paris before coming to Montreal. From 1883 to 1886, he directed the art school of the Art Association of Montreal. In his teaching as in his art, he applied the principles of the French academic tradition, with its focus based on the study of form. He was a member of the Royal Canadian Academy of Arts and served as its president for thirteen years, until 1906.

This portrait of the Countess of Minto was painted in 1903 at the request of members of the Art Association of Montreal, of which she was a benefactress. Born Marie-Caroline Grey, she was the wife of Canada's Governor General, the Earl of Minto, and the sister of Earl Grey, who would occupy the post as of 1904. Psychological intensity is subtly conveyed in the young woman's averted gaze and faint smile. Although the painting was executed in the ballroom at Rideau Hall, the Governor General's official Ottawa residence, an ethereal space puts the focus on the subject. The sculpture-like pose of the Countess, and the richness of her clothes, particularly the turquoise-blue fabric, point to her nobility and rank. E.A.P.

Clarence Gagnon

Sainte-Rose, Laval, 1881 – Montreal 1942

Moonlight, Venice

1906
Etching
19.5 × 13.1 cm

Purchase, Dr. Francis J. Shepherd and
Dr. and Mrs. Charles Francis Martin funds
Gr.1938.542

Copper printing plate
17 × 10 cm

Purchase, Horsley and Annie Townsend Bequest
Gr.1989(1967.1562).5i

■ Clarence Gagnon studied with William Brymner at the Art Association of Montreal, and in 1904 a patron's generosity enabled him to spend a long sojourn studying in Europe. There, he learned the technique of etching and executed a large corpus of more than forty prints that made him one of only a few Canadian printmakers recognized on the Continent. Except for his book illustrations, such as *Maria Chapdelaine*, his prints depict mainly European scenes. As part of the etching revival, Gagnon, like a number of his contemporaries, was influenced by the prints of Americans James McNeill Whistler and Joseph Pennell.

The somewhat enigmatic *Moonlight, Venice* shows Gagnon's talent as a draftsman and his ability to structure his image with subtle effects of black and white. The fine, light strokes judiciously obtained from the copperplate etching process are clearly visible in the variations of the patterns on the wall in the foreground, the barely suggested rippling of the water, and the shimmer of the sky. The six etchings he sent to the Salon des Artistes français the year this print was executed earned him an honourable mention. The Museum has a large collection of Gagnon's prints and many of his printing plates. E.A.P.

James Wilson Morrice
Montreal 1865 – Tunis 1924

Venice, Looking Out over the Lagoon

About 1904
Oil on canvas
60.6 × 73.9 cm
Gift of the estate of James Wilson Morrice
1925.334

■ James Wilson Morrice, from a well-to-do Montreal family, studied law to appease his father. Recognizing Morrice's talent, Sir William Van Horne convinced the family to let him go to Paris to study painting. Morrice left Canada in 1890, and though he returned several times, he remained abroad for the rest of his life. Travelling constantly, he saw Brittany, Normandy, Corsica, Venice and spent time in Algiers, Tangier, Cuba and Jamaica. He became friends with various painters, among them Maurice Prendergast and Henri Matisse. Fond of the atmosphere of public places, Morrice would settle in at a café to observe the passersby, draw and make oil sketches.

About 1900, he became interested in Whistler's ideas about the relationship between painting and music, establishing an analogy between the key that gives a piece of music its particular character and the colours of a painting that awaken a range of emotions. In *Venice, Looking Out over the Lagoon*, Morrice, attentive to the effects of light, creates a colourful atmosphere where the arrangement of areas of colour is more important than narrative, and the summarily drawn figures become accessories to the space occupied by the sky and the canal, both bathed in pink.

Through a number of bequests from the Morrice family, among them those of the artist's niece Eleanore and nephew David, the Museum today possesses one of the most important collections of Morrice's work in Canada. E.A.P.

Alfred Laliberté

Arthabaska, Quebec, 1878 – Montreal 1953

Fishing by Torchlight, Île d'Orléans

1928-1932
Plaster
51.5 × 49 × 32.5 cm
Gift of David and Claire Molson
1989.34

■ From 1909 to 1922, after studying modelling at the Council of Arts and Manufactures in Montreal and attending the École des Beaux-Arts in Paris, Alfred Laliberté participated in the sculptural programme for the provincial parliament building in Quebec City and created many of the commemorative monuments that ensured his reputation. From 1928 to 1932, a major commission from the provincial museum in Quebec City turned his attention to the customs, legends and trades of bygone days. A number of the preparatory plasters for the resulting 214 small bronzes came to the Montreal Museum of Fine Art's collection after long remaining in the artist's studio. "My intention", he said, "was that these bronze groups should serve as a basis or as a source of information for those who might one day need to create something to do with Canada's past, before the machine age."

The sculpture *Fishing by Torchlight, Île d'Orléans* depicts traditional nighttime eel fishing and evokes the legends attached to it. According to the nineteenth-century author Hubert Larue, the inhabitants of the shores neighbouring the island must have found it "a curious and enchanting sight, to see rise up at nearly the same instant and at a fairly advanced hour of the night all those flames coming and going, crisscrossing, sometimes coming together only to move apart and scatter again." These practices lie at the root of fabulous legends like that of the witches of the island. E.A.P.

Helen Galloway McNicoll
Toronto 1879 – Swanage, England, 1915

Under the Shadow of the Tent

1914
Oil on canvas
83.5 × 101.2 cm

Gift of Mr. and Mrs. David McNicoll
1915.122

■ Helen McNicoll lost her hearing in childhood, becoming deeply introspective, which marked her work. She studied painting with William Brymner in Montreal and then at the Slade School of Art in London and in Saint Ives, Cornwall. She achieved considerable recognition in her career, winning the Jessie Dow Prize in 1908 and the Women's Art Society Prize in 1914. McNicoll became a member of the Royal Society of British Artists in 1913 and an associate member of the Royal Canadian Academy of Arts the following year. In 1925, the Art Association of Montreal organized a memorial exhibition with 141 of her works.

She painted landscapes, seaside views and genre scenes, and numerous figure studies, which demonstrate her sensitivity and her art's affinity with Impressionist painting. This painting shows McNicoll's predilection for depicting the play of light and colour in unexpected reflections. In the foreground, filtered by the canvas sides and top of a tent, the sunlight reflects off the sand, outspread tablecloth and figures. The brilliant sun-drenched beach fills the background, creating a contrast that emphasizes the main subject. Executed one year before the artist's death, this is one of her finest paintings. J.P.L.

Emily Carr
Victoria 1871 – Victoria 1945

Indian War Canoe, Alert Bay

1912
Oil on panel
65 × 95.5 cm
Gift of A. Sidney Dawes
1948.995

■ Emily Carr, who was born in Victoria, British Columbia, had a keen interest in the life and ways of the Northwest Coast Native peoples. Between 1907 and 1913, she visited many villages, bringing back more than two hundred paintings that document the art and activities of their inhabitants and illustrate her desire to grasp their "spirit". Within the same period, in 1910 and 1911, while studying at the Académie Colarossi in Paris and taking courses with foreign painters, she discovered Post-Impressionism and Fauvism. With its bright colours, *Indian War Canoe,* painted over the summer of 1912, approaches Fauvist painting.

According to an annotation on the back of this panel, it depicts an "Indian War Canoe taken at Alert Bay during a Potlatch". It is one of the three canoes commemorating the history of the Kwakwaka'wakw nation, who lived around Alert Bay on an island between the mainland and the north of Vancouver Island. In 1908, when Carr made the watercolour this painting is based on, the canoe was displayed in the public square at the entrance to the village. Always at pains to be accurate and faithful in her descriptions, Carr was never insensitive to her position as an observer or unconscious of the fact that her transposition of these vanishing traditions represented a personal vision. E.A.P.

Tom Thomson
Claremont, Ontario, 1877 – Canoe Lake, Ontario, 1917

In the Northland

1915
Oil on canvas
101.7 × 114.5 cm
Purchase, subscription
1922.179

■ Despite the brevity of his painting career, Tom Thomson was a decisive figure in Canadian art during the second decade of the twentieth century. He was a photoengraver at Grip Engraving in Toronto when he met J.E.H. MacDonald, Arthur Lismer and Franz Johnston, future members of the Group of Seven. Thomson, who also worked as a forest ranger, organized canoe trips in Algonquin Park, to which he introduced his painter friends Lismer and two other painter friends, A. Y. Jackson and Fred Varley. It was in the heart of the woods and lakes of this region that he drew the best of his inspiration.

In the manner of the new Scandinavian landscape painters, Thomson used undulating impastos and pure colours to convey the dense ruggedness of the Canadian forest. The critics of the time reproached his heavy-handed brushstroke and what they perceived as a brash display of paint combining ugly colours in bizarre landscapes. Some considered it nothing less than a form of moral degeneracy. This painting, modern though not radical, attests to a new interest in the landscape, far different from the studio conventions that then held favour with the public. Thomson disappeared under circumstances considered mysterious – he was found drowned in Algonquin Park – three years before his friends formed the Group of Seven. In their view, his painting embodied the ideal of the modern Canadian landscape. E.A.P.

Lawren S. Harris
Brantford, Ontario, 1885 – Vancouver 1970

Morning, Lake Superior
About 1921-1928
Oil on canvas
86.3 × 101.6 cm

Purchase, William Gilman Cheney Bequest
1939.686

Lawren Harris, the only member of the Group of Seven to have attended university, was in some measure the group's theoretician. He subscribed to the ideas of Irish poet George Russell on the artist's social role in his ability to denounce injustice and disseminate the nation's higher ideals. In 1914, with the support of a patron, Dr. James MacCallum, Harris founded the Studio Building in Toronto, creating a space for artists' studios where young painters who shared his vision and convictions gathered. Painter Bertram R. Brooker thought Harris's painting contributed to restoring the nation's soul, showing how strongly landscapes then resonated with a national identity founded upon the land.

In the forests of the Algoma and Algonquin Park, Harris preferred the stark immensity of the Arctic landscape and the austere shores of Lake Superior, which he visited in the 1920s. The smooth brushstroke and distant viewpoint of *Morning, Lake Superior* convey the sublime grandeur of nature, bathed in the light of dawn. The spiritual connotations of this vision are in keeping with Harris's interest in mysticism; he did not think twice about drawing upon concepts from Eastern religions and philosophies. Furthermore, the contemplation of the northern landscape, with its pure, spare forms, carried him into abstraction. E.A.P.

Frank Carmichael
Orillia, Ontario, 1890 – Toronto 1945

North Shore, Lake Superior

1927
Oil on canvas
101.5 × 121.7 cm
Purchase, Robert Lindsay Fund
1959.1211

▇ Frank Carmichael, a member of the Group of Seven as of their first exhibition in 1920, practised painting, watercolour, drawing and graphic art. Like many members of the group – Tom Thomson, J.E.H. MacDonald, Arthur Lismer and Lawren Harris – Carmichael first worked for Grip Engraving, a Toronto commercial printing firm, but unlike them, he continued to pursue a double career as a painter and a commercial artist. He taught at the Ontario College of Art as well.

In the opinion of the Group of Seven, pastoral scenes – great favourites with Canadian collectors – were too enslaved to European models to truly convey the vitality of the Canadian wilderness. What was needed was a renewal of the painter's vocabulary, daring forms, vivid colours. While the others scoured Canada in search of new landscapes, Carmichael confined himself to the stark Precambrian setting of northern Ontario mining regions. In *North Shore, Lake Superior*, he emphasizes line and contrasts of tone and plane. Playing near against far, he paints a vast panorama of clean, spare forms with dead tree trunks rising before it. Stylistically, the result is not unrelated to the work of Lawren Harris. Some critics at the time suggested that artists' groups like the Group of Seven risked engendering repetition. For others, such paintings provided the desired fresh look at the Canadian landscape. E.A.P.

Alexander Y. Jackson

Montreal 1882 – Woodbridge, Ontario, 1974

Grey Day, Laurentians

About 1931
Oil on canvas
63.5 × 81.6 cm

Purchase, A. Sidney Dawes and Dr. Francis J. Shepherd Funds

1945.944

◾ In 1913, after studying in Europe, Montreal painter A. Y. Jackson moved to Toronto and shared a studio with Tom Thomson. After serving in the army during World War I, he joined the Group of Seven. First decried then acclaimed by the critics, especially following the *British Empire Exhibition* of 1924, the Group of Seven enjoyed a true national celebrity during the 1930s. One of the most influential members, Jackson sought to rally the artists around a common vision based on the desire to make art more democratic and to develop a modern Canadian painting free of European academism. More than all the others, he travelled throughout Canada to absorb its changing features and to expound his ideas. He is considered the group's spokesman and its intermediary with French Canada.

Every spring brought him back to Quebec, to the Laurentian Mountains or the shores of the Saint Lawrence River. *Grey Day, Laurentians* was painted from a study made in Saint-Urbain, Charlevoix county, about 1931. Jackson, who excelled at portraying the physical features of the land in successive planes of colour, unfurls this hilly country landscape, crossed by a little road and dotted with houses and farm buildings. This painting recalls the influence of Scandinavian painters on the Group of Seven. The immensity of the landscape, developed without shading in zones of colour, spills beyond the canvas's frame to evoke the immeasurable. E.A.P.

Arthur Lismer

Sheffield, England, 1885 – Montreal 1969

Cathedral Mountain

1928
Oil on canvas
122 × 142.5 cm
Purchase, A. Sidney Dawes Fund
1959.1219

■ Born in England, Arthur Lismer immigrated to Canada in 1911 and settled in Toronto, where he soon made the acquaintance of the young artists who were to form the Group of Seven. In 1914, he was one of the group of artists to go to Algonquin Park on a trip organized by Tom Thomson. Lismer followed the holistic approach of William Morris, a central figure in the British Arts and Crafts movement, who believed art should be present in every aspect of life as "a kind of awareness that escapes from specialization to accede to the universal." This approach, applied to the teaching Lismer devoted a great part of his life to, would make him a renowned educator, associated most notably with the Montreal Museum of Fine Arts' art school, which he directed from 1940 to 1967.

Fascinated by the geomorphology of the Canadian landscape, Lismer developed a concept of pictorial space very similar to that found in Cézanne's paintings. *Cathedral Mountain,* painted in the studio from sketches made from nature during a summer visit to the area of Lakes Moraine and O'Hara in the Rocky Mountains, incorporates this influence in its arrangement of planes, irregularity of volumes and use of distinct outline. While recognizing the contribution of outside influences on his approach, Lismer still believed, like the others of the Group of Seven, that Canadian art should have, and show, an identity all its own. E.A.P.

■ The son and the brother of artists, Henri Hébert received most of his training at the École des Beaux-Arts in Paris. He returned to Montreal in 1909 and taught modelling at the McGill University School of Architecture. He also taught at the Monument National in Montreal. He created many bas reliefs and monuments for public buildings and squares in Montreal. A proponent of modern sculpture, he was a contributor to Montreal's short-lived literary journal *Le Nigog* (1918) and a founder of the Sculptors' Society of Canada (1928).

The bas relief *Woman* was owned by architect Ernest Cormier, and it decorated the garden of his first studio on Saint-Urbain Street in Montreal. This somewhat provocative androgynous figure is a rarity in Quebec sculpture of the period, which was then more concerned with the land as a subject. The iconography of this sculpture can only be understood in relation to its companion piece, *Love*, which is no longer extant. The latter bas relief represented Cupid, the god of love, drawing his bow. Notwithstanding her resolutely modern curves, *Woman* is a nude nymph attempting to flee Cupid's arrow. The line linking the figure's knee and right shoulder forms an almost uninterrupted curve; the hair divided into eight curls spreads out like a fan. These elements, as well as the refined spareness of the forms, place the work of Henri Hébert in the current of Art Deco. E.A.P.

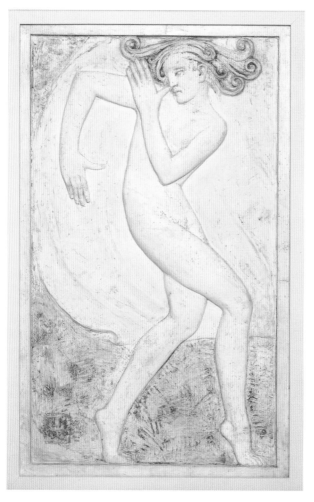

Henri Hébert

Montreal 1884 –
Montreal 1950

Woman

1925
Painted plaster
119 × 74 cm

Purchase, Horsley and
Annie Townsend Bequest
1982.31

Adrien Hébert
Paris 1890 – Montreal 1967

Montreal Harbour

1925
Oil on canvas
101.6 × 81 cm
Purchase, gifts of Maurice Corbeil and Nahum Gelber
1985.6

Louis-Philippe Hébert and his sons Adrien and Henri form a remarkable artistic triumvirate, at the crossroads of tradition and modernity. Adrien, the painter of the family, was born in Paris, his parents having gone to France for his father to supervise the casting of the bronzes for the sculptural programme decorating the facade of the provincial parliament building in Quebec City. Adrien spent his youth and studies moving between Paris and Montreal. In Montreal he attended classes at the Monument National and at the Art Association of Montreal's art school, then went to the École des Beaux-Arts in Paris.

He loved to paint the streets of Montreal teeming with activity: the grain silos – whose architecture Le Corbusier considered an example of formal perfection – the ocean liners and the ceaseless movement of loading and unloading the docked ships. Modernity informed his choice of subject. The composition of Montreal Harbour is animated by the many lines giving shape to the industrial buildings, the grain belts, the deck of the Lakers (Great Lakes freighters), and the ship hulls, masts and stacks. Rejecting the regionalist concept of painting upheld by many of his contemporaries, Hébert became the painter of the city and its harbour: "Is it not preferable", he wrote, "to draw and paint these scenes rather than heeding those who would compel me to be moved by an old woman at her spinning wheel or an old man smoking a pipe?" J.P.L.

Prudence Heward

Montreal 1896 – Los Angeles 1947

At the Theatre

1928
Oil on canvas
101.6 × 101.6 cm

Purchase, Horsley and Annie Townsend Bequest
1964.1497

■ Prudence Heward lived with her family in London during World War I. She then came to Montreal where she studied at the Art Association of Montreal and became associated with the Beaver Hall Group (1920-1921), which was made up mainly of artists who had been students of William Brymner. This short-lived but influential group with modernist leanings was the first in Montreal where women occupied the front rank and could express their point of view on art. Concerned with broadening the domain of Canadian art, Heward was actively involved with the Canadian Group of Painters, serving as its vice-president from 1933 to 1939, and the Contemporary Arts Society (1939), of which she was a founding member. The asthma that affected her all her life prompted her to move to California, where she died in 1947.

Included in the Fifth Annual Exhibition of Canadian Art, *At the Theatre* was praised by critics, who found it a "remarkable" scene. Turning their backs to the beholder, the two spectators dominate the space of the painting. With its simplified forms and strictly defined lines recalling Art Deco, the painting marks a clear departure from Heward's previous work. E.A.P.

Lilias Torrance Newton
Lachine, Quebec, 1896 – Cowansville, Quebec, 1980

Lady in Black

About 1936
Oil on canvas
91.8 × 71.3 cm
Purchase, William Gilman Cheney Bequest
1939.699

■ Along with Prudence Heward, Sarah Robertson, Kathleen Morris and Mabel May, Lilias Torrance Newton belongs to the nucleus of pioneering women artists who, after studying at the Art Association of Montreal's school, made their mark as professional artists. Newton was associated with the Beaver Hall Group (1920-1921), named after the street where Randolph Hewton, Edwin Holgate and Mabel May and Newton shared their studios. Over the course of her career she would paint nearly three hundred portraits, which included the most famous Canadians of her time. Commenting on the genre in 1927, she said, "The impact of the sitter's personality on mine is what I paint . . . There must be sympathy between the subject and the artist for the portrait to be good." Although she painted mainly men, she observed, "There is more colour to work with, and I feel I can paint a more imaginative portrait of a woman, because of her clothes, through which she expresses herself."

The elegant *Lady in Black* of this portrait is Mrs. Albert Henry Steward Gillson, a member of the Montreal bourgeoisie. Using a limited range of colour, Newton plays on the contrasts between the sitter's black dress and the cushions placed behind her. The artist has created an ambivalent work, both distant and intimate, as the young woman is dressed in an evening gown that contrasts peculiarly with her informal pose and relaxed attitude. J.P.L.

David Milne

Near Burgoyne, Ontario, 1882 – Bancroft, Ontario, 1953

Dark Pool, Ti Magami (Temagami)

About 1929-1933
Oil on canvas
50.8 × 63.8 cm
Purchase, Canadian Artworks Acquisition Fund
1958.1198

■ This painting, inspired by Lake Temagami in Northern Ontario, was done in the summer of 1929, when Milne returned to Canada from the Adirondack region in the United States. A native of Ontario, Milne had studied painting with the American artist Maurice Prendergast at the Art Students' League in New York between 1904 and 1906. Five of Milne's works were exhibited at the landmark Armory Show of 1913 in New York.

For Milne, the creative process was more important than the subject painted. He compared his landscapes and still lifes to "compressions", by which he meant they were characterized by a kind of emotional intensity related to a fleeting vision. To capture such moments he often used watercolour, a technique better suited to working quickly and which he favoured until the late 1920s. This technique also enabled him to use the white reserve areas of the paper as zones of light, a method he carried over into his oil paintings. *Dark Pool, Ti Magami* is a fine example of his work in oil. Milne has written of his painting, "This line and this scratchy sparse laying-on of colour comes in part from a feeling that I am often aware of, a desire to set things down with as little expenditure of aesthetic means as possible, just to touch the canvas or paper, even just to wish on them without any material agent, if that were possible!" E.A.P.

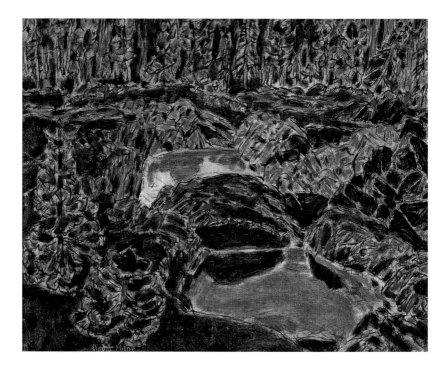

Bertram Richard Brooker
Croydon, England, 1888 – Toronto 1955

Recluse

1939
Oil on canvas
61 × 45.7 cm
Gift of Walter Klinkhoff
1978.3

■ Born in England, Bertram R. Brooker immigrated to Canada in 1905. His interests were wide-ranging: he was a novelist, poet, journalist, actor, playwright, singer and, later, art critic. By attending the Arts and Letters Club, "the centre of living culture in Toronto", he came in contact with many artists, and in 1922, he made his first experiments with painting. His eclectic tendencies led him to explore Figurative Realism and Cubism, Symbolism and Abstraction, of which he was a pioneer in Canada. He was also one of the first Canadian artists to be interested in Kandinsky, and it seems it was his love of music that drew him to the writings of the Russian painter. During a conversation with his friend Lawren Harris, Brooker confessed his desire to "paint music".

In *Recluse*, the subject becomes a pretext for a study in plastic values and their harmonization in the fictive pictorial space of the canvas. The Cubist-inspired geometric forms define the urban setting, the figure's clothing and the square set of his face. The dark tones and artificial lighting produce dramatic chiaroscuro-like effects. Although the painting, which dates from 1939, recalls the figures of unemployed workers being painted by other artists at the time, the solitary man's partially hidden features suffuse the scene with a disturbing, almost menacing strangeness. E.A.P.

Fritz Brandtner
Danzig, Prussia, 1896 – Montreal 1969

The Sunflower

1936
Oil on canvas
53.5 × 63.5 cm

Gift of Marc Régnier and Claudette Picard

2001.119

▨ Taken prisoner in France during World War I, Fritz Brandtner felt a dread of oppression his whole life. Disturbed by the political developments in his homeland, in 1928 he immigrated to Canada, where he was sent to work in Manitoba farms. In 1934 he moved to Montreal, a metropolis better suited to his expectations. Brandtner believed creative energy represented the best means of freeing mankind, and he divided his time between his art and teaching. He became a friend of Dr. Norman Bethune, who purchased one of his sunflower paintings. In 1936, he set up the Children's Art Center with Bethune; reflecting the founders' social commitment, the classes there were for underprivileged children.

Brandtner's work was inspired by both the formal experiences and social concerns of German and French avant-garde artists of the first third of the twentieth century – references that were still foreign to most of his Canadian contemporaries. He was also influenced by the local artistic context, and he vacillated between figurative and abstract art; he was a pioneer in Canada of the latter. From this apparently eclectic mediation, he devised a personal syntax that became his synthetic vision of modern painting, free of dogmatism. *The Sunflower*, with its expressionist tendencies, emphasizes the motifs over the saturated primary colours – the flowers, the fence boards, the sky – that stand out strongly against each other. J.P.L.

Edwin Holgate

Allandale, Ontario, 1892 – Montreal 1976

Bathers

1937
Oil on canvas
81.3 × 81.3 cm
Purchase, Robert Lindsay Fund
1937.664

▨ Known for his portraits, nude studies and landscapes, Edwin Holgate was also one of the great Canadian masters of the woodcut, and it is with this medium that he first established his reputation as an artist in the 1930s. The poet and artist Saint-Denys Garneau stated that in Holgate's work, "nothing is left to chance, nothing is superfluous, everything is controlled by a profound sense of the volumes and forms". Holgate, who spoke French fluently, frequented both anglophone and francophone artistic and literary circles in Montreal. Though he was associated with various artists' groups from time to time, especially the Beaver Hall Group, he never tied himself exclusively to any, not even the Group of Seven, of which he became the "eighth" member in 1930, and the only one who lived in Montreal.

In the 1930s, Holgate undertook a series of female nudes set against northern scenery. He shared the Group of Seven's taste for these vast landscapes, but whereas the others generally represented them uninhabited, Holgate filled his with figures in harmony with nature. Thus, the addition of the nude was an original feature of these works that, with their imposing bathers, solidly formed and robustly modelled, have often been described as "vigorous". Here, the landscape and the figures are linked inextricably through colour relationships and similarities of treatment and rendering of volumes. E.A.P.

Akeeaktashuk
Inukjuak 1898 –
Grise Fiord 1954

Walrus

1952
Serpentine, ivory
9.4 × 18.7 × 19.7 cm
Gift of F. Cleveland Morgan
1953.Aa.1

Sheokjuk Oqutaq
Cape Dorset 1920 –
Cape Dorset 1982

Caribou

1965
Serpentine
15.1 × 6.7 × 17.5 cm
Purchase, gift of
L. Marguerite Vaughan
1966.Aa.3

■ Contemporary Inuit art came to light in 1948, when the Canadian government and the Quebec branch of the Canadian Guild of Crafts encouraged the setting up of carving programmes in the Far North. Later, the Hudson's Bay Company administered the marketing and distribution of the artwork that was produced.

Early carvings from Inukjuak depict carefully rendered hunters and animals expertly carved from local stone, generally serpentine. A distinctive characteristic is the technique of inlaying steatite and ivory to create decorative motifs or to emphasize a particular feature. In this *Walrus*, Akeeaktashuk has exploited the iron oxide and pale green veins in the dark green serpentine to convey the effect of the walrus's sagging folds of skin, thus transforming the massive grey-brown animal into an elegant sea mammal. The inlaid ivory eyes stand out dramatically.

Cape Dorset artists are known for a keen sense of realism in addition to their interest in mythological characters. The sophisticated naturalism of Sheokjuk Oqutaq is evident in this elegantly rendered Caribou – every detail is thoroughly investigated, down to the extended hind leg, the thrown-back ears and the shape of the eyes. As always, Oqutaq has polished the stone to a high lustre, heightening the well-defined musculature of the caribou's legs and abdominal area. N.S.

Joe Talirunili
Puvirnituq 1893 – Puvirnituq 1976
The Migration
1964
Steatite, skin
33 × 19.7 × 30 cm
Purchase, gift of John G. McConnell
1974.Aa.2

■ Puvirnituq artists are renowned for their portrayals of animals and people. More concerned with storytelling, however, Joe Talirunili fills his sculptures, prints and drawings with detailed accounts of traditional Inuit ways and legends, as well as episodes from his own life. He made one such incident famous through his "Migration" series, which used various materials. The story begins one spring when his and other families were changing campsites. Taken by surprise by the melting ice, they found themselves adrift on an ice pan. Fortunately, they were able to construct an *umiak*, or large boat, from the materials at hand – sealskins, caribou sinew, wood from kayaks, and sealskin drying racks – and managed to make their way home to Puvirnituq.

Each time Talirunili was commissioned by a dealer or collector to create a depiction of this "migration", he would give it a slightly different twist, adding or subtracting a detail or two. The Museum's version, for example, includes a rifle and telescope but not the oars found in other renditions. It is a particularly important version because the *umiak*'s underside bears an inscription in Inuktitut listing the names of everyone who experienced this terrifying journey. The artist is represented in the figure of the standing child. N.S.

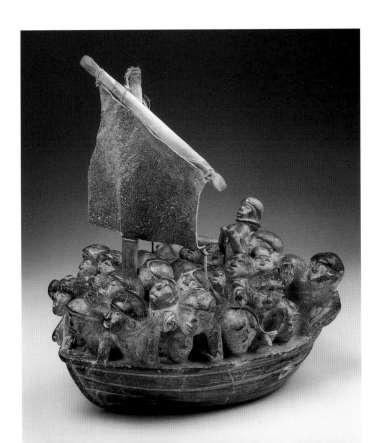

John Pangnark
Windy Lake 1920 – Rankin Inlet 1980

Face

1971
Basalt
12 × 17.4 × 11.7 cm
Gift of Kathy Lippel
1972.Aa.42

■ John Pangnark was a minimalist, almost abstract, sculptor whose work has been compared to Constantin Brancusi's. He was concerned chiefly with the simplification of form, allowing the shape of the stone to determine the subject matter. His works are generalizations and little attention is paid to the kind of detail seen in sculpture from Inukjuak and Puvirnituq. To some extent, the Keewatin stone itself accounts for this lack of detail, as its hardness does not lend itself readily to carving.

Pangnark usually portrayed single figures that can rarely be identified as male or female. Anatomical detail is limited to an indication of a jutting arm or leg at most. More often, simply incised horizontal or diagonal lines represent an eye, mouth or nose.

This carving is one of Pangnark's most minimalist works. N.S.

Alain Iyerak
Igloolik 1920 – Igloolik 1997

Hunter's Story

1971
Whale backbone, caribou antler, sinew
57.8 × 100.7 × 33 cm
Purchase, Horsley and Annie Townsend Bequest
1972.Aa.41

■ This massive yet delicate whale-backbone sculpture of a hunting scene exemplifies the traditional way of life of Nunavut's Iglulingmiut. They hunted marine mammals, like walrus and narwhal, either on foot on the ice, or from kayaks in open waters. Especially large harpoons mounted with large heads were needed to penetrate these animals' thick skins. Hunters in kayaks would also pursue caribou swimming across lakes.

With the complexity and ingenuity characteristic of Igloolik art, Alain Iyerak presents the viewer with a trophy-like arrangement of the animals hunted by kayak. The hunter – perhaps a self-portrait – is carved in great detail, as if to commemorate his prowess. The harpoon is lodged in the narwhal's tail and the left hand holds a plaited rope tied to the sealskin float at one end, and to the harpoon at the other. The narwal – shown leaping out of a wave's crest that is carved into the smooth end of the piece of backbone – was carved separately and then attached to the piece, as was the caribou head at the centre. On the back is a walrus head with tusks, carved directly from the whalebone. N.S.

Niviaksiak

1908-1959
Active in Cape Dorset

Man Hunting at a Seal Hole in the Ice

1959
Stencil with blue, green and black ink on beige Japanese paper
60.9 × 46.5 cm

Purchase, Horsley and Annie Townsend Bequest
Gr.1960.71

■ Over the past fifty years or so, the millennia-old artistic traditions of the Inuit have given rise to a modern production of carvings and prints. Upon contact with European culture, both ritual and everyday objects – amulets, adornments, toys and tools – have become art forms in their own right. The technique of printmaking was first introduced in Cape Dorset during the 1950s by artist James Houston. The earliest methods adopted by the Inuits were – at times in combination – stonecut engraving and stencil printing from walrus skin.

As the traditional Inuit way of life underwent profound change, the introduction of modern artistic techniques enabled Inuit artists to keep the memory of past beliefs, legends and customs alive in their images. Niviaksiak, one of the first Cape Dorset residents to gain recognition as an artist, offers an example of this in *Man Hunting at a Seal Hole in the Ice*. The artist depicts what he knows best: the seal (which provides food, clothing, lamp oil and the wherewithal to fashion tools) and the art of the chase. Patiently lying in wait to harpoon the animal as soon as it surfaces was a familiar occupation to Niviaksiak, both hunter and artist. N.S.

Karoo Ashevak
Taloyoak 1940 – Taloyoak 1974

Drum Beater

About 1973
Whalebone, peridotite
46.5 × 29.5 × 51.2 cm
Purchase, gift of L. Marguerite Vaughan
1973.Aa.6

▪ Although his career was curtailed by a tragic death at the age of thirty-four, the exceptional Nunavut sculptor Karoo Ashevak is considered a major artist of his time. His work was discovered in the early 1970s and its modern aspects have ever since attracted the admiration of many art lovers, especially collectors of Inuit art. His artistic production, limited to the space of a few years, amounts to approximately two hundred and fifty pieces.

He is especially admired for his representations of spirits and shamans. In traditional Inuit culture, the "drum dancer" played an important part in the community's songs and chants as well as in shamanic rituals. The regular beating of the drum helped the shaman enter a trance so that he might communicate with the spirits.

Exaggeration of facial features, at times taken to distortion, is characteristic of Karoo Ashevak's art. Here, the drummer's thrown-back head is proportionally larger than the rest of his body, especially the flaring nostrils and the open mouth. Ashevak's works have contributed considerably to an understanding of the world of the Inuits, through the masterful manipulation of the medium and the rich and detailed subject matter. His style inspired many of his fellow Taloyoak artists, who in turn had an influence on Kitikimeot artists. N.S.

Saggiak
Cape Dorset 1897 –
Cape Dorset 1980

The Sea Spirit Nuliayuk

1961
Serpentine
10 × 13.2 × 28.3 cm

Purchase, Horsley and Annie Townsend
Bequest
1962.Aa.3

Toonoo Sharky
Born in Cape Dorset in 1970

Untitled

1995
Marble
24.3 × 19.5 × 7.5 cm

Purchase, The Montreal Museum of Fine
Arts' Volunteer Association Fund
1995.Aa.10

■ Cape Dorset sculpture has been broadly influenced by traditional Inuit beliefs in spirits and forces that control daily existence. The most powerful of these is the sea spirit Nuliayuk, whose appearance is part human and part sea mammal. The numerous accounts of her origin have some things in common: a girl, or young woman, refuses to marry; her angry father cuts off her fingers one by one, takes her out to sea and throws her overboard; she sinks to the bottom of the sea and becomes the keeper of the sea creatures, which are symbolically thought of as her children. Saggiak ingeniously incorporates the parka hood to depict Nuliayuk's transformation. Her face and hands – fingers intact – are human, while her body has changed into that of a marine animal.

Toonoo Sharky represents the younger generation of Cape Dorset artist. Inspired by the sculpture of his grandfather, Kopapik Ragee, he has a style consistent with previous generations' highly refined and stripped-down work. Though Sharky usually sculpts in the green serpentine common to the region, he has here used local marble to impart a spirit-like quality to this winged head, which imaginatively assimilates human and avian features. Such images are generally interpreted as shamanic flight and transformation rituals, in which the shaman assumes the physical traits of the animals that will take him to the spirit world. N.S.

Kenojuak Ashevak
Born in Ikerrasak in 1927, active in Cape Dorset
Eegyvudluq Pootoogook
Printmaker, born in Cape Dorset in 1931
The Enchanted Owl
1960
Stonecut, 43/50
61.1 × 66 cm
Purchase, Horsley and Annie Townsend Bequest
Gr.1961.100

■ In 1959 Cape Dorset was the first Arctic community to take up the method of stonecut printmaking specially devised for the Inuit by James Houston, who had studied the art of woodcut in Japan. Kenojuak Ashevak, a pioneer printmaker in Cape Dorset, is best known for her stylized representations of birds, especially owls. She created images of fanciful creatures, figurative abstractions of birds, with an overall interest in design. In *The Enchanted Owl*, the plumage fans out, creating a radiating effect of negative and positive space, symbolizing the owl's power to overcome the endless darkness of winter days.

Throughout her career spanning some fifty years, Kenojuak Ashevak has exhibited repeatedly and has received numerous honours. She is a Companion of the Order of Canada, a member of the Royal Canadian Academy of Arts and holds honorary doctorates from Queen's University and the University of Toronto. She came to public attention in 1970, when *The Enchanted Owl* was reproduced on a Canadian stamp to commemorate the Northwest Territories Centennial. N.S.

Northwest Coast, Alaska
Kaigani Haida or Tlingit

Crest Helmet
Late 19th-early 20th c.
Wood, copper, nails, cotton, deerskin, pigment
25 × 23.8 55.5 cm
Purchase, gift of F. Cleveland Morgan
1946.Ab.3

■ The First Nations of the Northwest Coast – the Kaigani Haida, Tlingit and Tsimshian
– are sometimes called the People of the Totem, in reference to the large carved poles found
in their villages. For them, totems symbolize a secret power, the mythic ancestor-guardian
of a family or clan. They are also the visual representation of this power, which is generally
associated with an animal, such as a bear, wolf, whale, raven or a fish, and even a plant.
Interpreting this symbolic pantheon is the domain of the elders and shamans. The figures

must be easily identifiable and so their forms are stylized and symmetrical, as well as punctuated with geometric motifs, like the typical round-cornered rectangles that decorate this helmet. The canoes, masks, utensils and various other objects that bear these emblems and corresponding motifs have a spiritual dimension.

One of the most important of the figures is the raven, creator and benefactor of mankind. It is also the totem of the Tlingit and Haida. Here, the raven sits astride a fish whose hollowed-out form is a wooden helmet, highlighted with colour and applied copper cutouts. A dancer would wear this type of headwear during a ritual ceremony such as a potlatch. Signs of the power and wealth of an individual or group, gifts were central to this tradition, leading to one-upmanship in their exchange between rival clans. H.L.

CONTEMPORARY ART

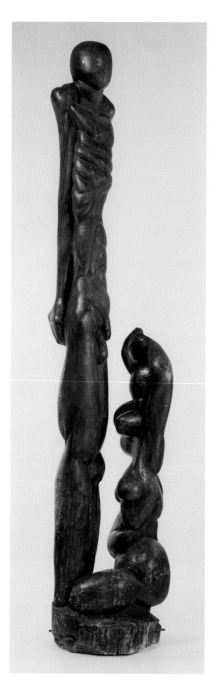

Robert Roussil
Born in Montreal in 1925

The Family

1949
Spruce, red wax coating
318 × 74 × 66 cm
Gift of Bernard Janelle
1990.37

■ Few Canadian works have had as tumultuous a past as *The Family*, by Montreal sculptor Robert Roussil. In 1949, this large totemic sculpture carved from a single tree trunk was impounded by the Montreal police for violating a law prohibiting public nudity. Roussil had in fact left it on the sidewalk outside the Museum of Fine Arts overnight with the intention of including it in an exhibition of the works of students and teachers of the Museum's art school where he taught. Press photographs showing the sculpture being carted away in a "paddy wagon" made the rounds of the country. After some time in France and another scandal in Tourrettes-sur-Loup – the village in the south of France where Roussil had taken up residence in the mid-1950s – *The Family* returned home in 1964. It sparked a new controversy when it was shown at the Musée d'art contemporain de Montréal a year later. This time, however, Roussil came away the winner in a Quebec that was catching up with the times. Poet Gaston Miron commented, "In twenty years, Roussil managed, despite everything and despite the reactions he evoked, to win recognition for his art and works, and for a certain notion of the dignity of the artist in a context in which the latter's existence was seen as inferior and marginal."

Only in 1990 did this historic work, or this "totem of the atomic age" as one critic described it, find its way into the Museum where its creator had always meant it to go. Through its forms derived from primitive art, *The Family* echoes the anti-academic and revolutionary spirit that fuelled Montreal's post-war art scene. S.A.

Alfred Pellan
Quebec City 1906 – Laval 1988

Under the Blue Sun

1946
Oil on canvas
208 × 168 cm

Gift of Power Corporation of Canada

2002.240

■ Art history credits Alfred Pellan, who returned to Montreal in 1940 after a fifteen-year sojourn in Paris, with being the first to introduce Surrealist ideas to Quebec, particularly through the classes he taught at Montreal's École des Beaux-Arts. He introduced his students – who included Jean Benoît, Mimi Parent and Françoise Sullivan – to the practice known as *cadavre exquis*, or exquisite corpse, which involves several people successively contributing to a collective work without being privy to what has been done before. At the start of the 1940s the artist executed a series of large Surrealist compositions that are now considered his masterpieces. *Under the Blue Sun*, painted in 1946, belongs to this group. The composition leans towards the "exquisite corpse" vein. Interlocking geometric and human forms metamorphose into one another in a semblance of dream-like discontinuity. Representing a sort of dream experienced in broad daylight, with its figures and shadows devoid of any weight or solidity, the painting is distinguished by its supersaturated colour scheme, whose orange and red tones constitute a complementary echo to the blue sun prominently placed above the centre of the composition. As an additional sign of the ascendancy of Surrealism in Pellan's work, the title alludes to Éluard's famous poem "The Earth is blue like an orange". S.A.

Jean-Paul Riopelle

Montreal 1923 – L'Isle-aux-Grues, Quebec, 2002

Austria

1954
Oil on canvas
200 × 300.7 cm
Purchase, Horsley and Annie Townsend Bequest
1963.1395

■ Jean-Paul Riopelle, who settled in Paris in 1947, was sponsored first by André Breton and then by the critic Georges Duthuit, and supported by the dealers Pierre Loeb in Paris and Pierre Matisse in New York. Riopelle was one of the leaders of a movement that, under its various designations (Art Informel, Lyrical Abstraction, Hot Abstraction, Abstract Expressionism), predominated in both European and North American post-war abstract painting. This movement emphasized gesture as a personal signature and as a way of constructing pictorial space, and Riopelle's "Mosaic" series from the mid-1950s is one of its most accomplished expressions.

Painted in 1954, the year of his first one-man show in New York, *Austria* aptly illustrates the expressive and formal possibilities inherent in Riopelle's adoption of the palette knife. Veined with many colours, the way the paint is applied highlights the artist's personal energy, and constructs the work as an integrated whole. Moreover, by organizing the surface around a large central white mass, the painter introduces a semblance of composition and, at the same time, an allusion to landscape – also suggested by the title. In a handwritten note, Evan H. Turner, who acquired the painting for the Museum, recalls a conversation with Riopelle in the course of which the artist related how he was struck by the sight of ice fields while on a trip to Austria. S.A.

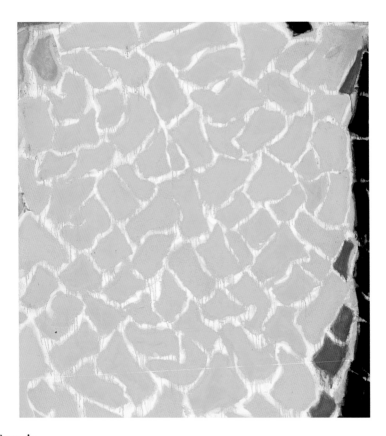

Sam Francis

San Mateo, California, 1923 – Santa Monica 1994

Abstraction

1954
Oil on canvas
197.8 × 185.7 cm
Purchase, Mr. and Mrs. Maurice Corbeil Fund and gift of Gilles Corbeil
1961.1315

■ Sam Francis discovered painting while bedridden in hospital, recovering from a plane crash. This was in 1944. He later moved to Paris (1950-1957) to work on his painting. *Abstraction*, executed in 1954, attests to the cardinal influence of Monet, whom Francis discovered in 1953 when the Musée de l'Orangerie reopened its doors. This work is a superb illustration of the transition – barely hinted at so far by other American painters such as Clyfford Still, Morris Louis and Kenneth Noland – from Abstract Expressionism to a lighter form of painting characterized by broad forms and bright, luminous colours. Exhibited in 1956 at Montreal's Galerie L'Actuelle, *Abstraction* was to have a decisive influence on several young Montreal painters, who saw it steer an unprecedented path between Automatisme and Plasticisme. This was an odd turn of events, since it was a young painter from Montreal, Jean-Paul Riopelle, who in Paris introduced Francis to Parisian art circles and put him in contact with critic Georges Duthuit, "a guide to French culture." At Duthuit's house in Provence, Francis' palette grew lighter. Riopelle also introduced the American artist to Nina Dausset, who gave Francis his first one-man show at her Galerie La Dragonne in 1952. S.A.

Paul-Émile Borduas

Saint-Hilaire 1905 – Paris 1960

The Black Star

1957
Oil on canvas
162.5 × 129.5 cm
Gift of Mr. and Mrs. Gérard Lortie
1960.1238

■ The artistic path of Paul-Émile Borduas – from church decoration to monochrome abstraction – has, through its successive interpretations, come to exemplify the modernization of Quebec society. However, before becoming a prophet of the Quiet Revolution, Borduas, from 1942 on, drew out all the artistic and philosophic implications of the Surrealist notion of automatic writing. Based on the principle of inner necessity, Automatisme required the rejection of preconceived ideas, and called for the free association of forms and colours. Borduas's manifesto *Refus global* [*Global Refusal*], launched in 1948, expressed the "savage need for liberation" felt by the members of the Automatiste group: "Within a foreseeable future, men will cast off their useless chains. They will realize their full individual potential according to the unpredictable, necessary order of spontaneity – in splendid anarchy."

The Museum possesses a remarkable group of forty-eight works by Borduas. One of these, *The Black Star*, which came into the collection in 1960, the year of the painter's death in Paris, has always been considered his masterpiece. This canvas, with its inverted reality – it is the night that is white, and the stars that are black – and its triangular composition, strives for a balance between modernism and classicism. S.A.

Jean Mc Ewen
Montreal 1923 – Montreal 1999

Black Cell

1959
Oil on canvas
152.3 × 152.3 cm
Purchase, Mr. and Mrs. Gérard O. Beaulieu Fund
1960.1247

A pharmacist by profession, Jean Mc Ewen was self-taught as a painter. He began his painting career under the influence first of Paul-Émile Borduas, whom he saw regularly from 1949 to 1951, and then of Jean-Paul Riopelle, with whom he struck up a friendship during a year-long stay in Paris. There, in 1952, he also became acquainted with the work of Sam Francis and Mark Rothko, who would have a tremendous impact on the development of his work. After returning to Montreal, Mc Ewen gradually moved away from Automatisme and worked instead towards an aesthetic based on a quasi-monochromatic colour field, to which he strove to impart a tactile depth. The results of these new experiments were shown in the exhibition *Espace 55,* at the Montreal Museum of Fine Arts in 1955.

Black Cell, from the "Cell" series executed at the start of the 1950s, admirably illustrates Mc Ewen's desire to free colour from its expressive function without reducing it to a single picture plane in the process. The stratification of colour, visible through the brushstrokes, and the use of plum-coloured borders to surround the black and blue cells and define the bottom portion of the piece, combine to produce a double effect of floating and depth that Mc Ewen would continue to explore throughout a long and productive career that never broke with Abstraction. In 1960, Mc Ewen was elected president of the Non-figurative Artists Association of Montreal, dedicated to promoting the cause of abstract art to the public. S.A.

Guido Molinari
Born in Montreal in 1933

Violet Mutation

1964
Acrylic on canvas
213.8 × 183 cm

Gift in memory of Irwin Gliserman, Q.C., given by his wife,
Rosalind, and sons Howard, John and Michael Gliserman
1995.34

■ The young Guido Molinari quickly made a name as one of the leaders of the Montreal-based Plasticisme movement, which challenged Automatisme on behalf of a strictly formalist aesthetic. In 1955 during the debate that surrounded the *Espace 55* exhibition held at the Montreal Museum of Fine Arts (which signalled the transition from one of these opposing systems to the other), Molinari made his aesthetic position known in the following terms: "Regardless of the literary or plastic vocabulary with which an art form may seek to define itself, it will be valid only as a function of the spatial structure it creates. And that space will be conditioned by the solution to the colour-light problem that is adopted."

Executed in 1964, *Violet Mutation* gave shape to this vision: by repeating a chromatically precise sequence, the painter imparted a rhythm of contraction and dilation to the space. The hard-edge look, the commercial colours, the formalist rejection of all composition, in fact everything about this painting, clearly stresses the primacy of the retinal experience. The year after this painting was made, Guido Molinari and Claude Tousignant took part in the exhibition *The Responsive Eye*, which New York's Museum of Modern Art devoted to the various manifestations of Op Art. S.A.

Jack Bush

Toronto 1909 – Toronto 1977

Sea Deep

1965
Oil on canvas
223.4 × 145 cm

Purchase, grant from Communications Canada, through the Cultural Property
Export and Import Act, and funds donated by Elca, Jonas and Mark London
1990.27

■ Abstraction found its roots in Toronto with the founding in 1953 of the Painters Eleven. Even though the group had no defined aesthetic programme, it did initially draw its influences from Abstract Expressionism, which was all the rage in New York. Painters Eleven's contacts with the American metropolis were such that Clement Greenberg paid them a visit in 1957. This visit would be followed by several others that would have far-reaching effects in Canada.

Jack Bush particularly benefited from this contact, and his work, bogged down until then in a sombre and heavy style, underwent a profound transformation. "Try painting simpler, and thinner, as you have done in these watercolours", was the advice of the American critic.

Painted in 1965, a year after Bush took part in *Post-painterly Abstraction,* the historic exhibition organized by Greenberg at the Los Angeles County Museum of Art, *Sea Deep* attests to this inspiration. Freed from the heavy gestural quality of Bush's previous work, this painting, composed of thinly applied diluted colour in a loose geometric arrangement, approximates watercolour to such an extent that it suggests an underwater landscape – indeed, its title says as much. S.A.

Josef Albers
Bottrop, Germany, 1888 – New Haven, Connecticut, 1976

Homage to the Square: Saturation

1967
Oil on hardboard
121.9 × 121.9 cm

Purchase, Horsley and Annie Townsend Bequest
1969.1617

■ Josef Albers was a great master of twentieth-century abstract art. At the Bauhaus, where he enrolled as a student in 1922 and became a teacher four years later, he shaped his thought through a rigorous analysis of the properties of different visual vocabularies. When the Nazis closed the school in 1933, Albers emigrated to the United States with his wife, Anni, also an artist. A professor at Black Mountain College in North Carolina (1933-1949) and then at Yale University (1950-1959), he had a major influence on several generations of North American artists. Inspired by a universalist conception of abstraction, his art sought to transcend the contingencies of style and expression. "When I paint, I construct", Albers wrote. "I try to develop visual articulation."

In 1949, Albers embarked on the "Homage to the Square" series, one of the most accomplished bodies of abstract art, and by far the most widely disseminated. Using subtle colour variations, in this case different shades of green, Albers imparts a high degree of dynamism to the square, one of the most static of all geometric forms. By the same token, he demonstrates the relativity and instability of colour, the quality of which varies in accordance with adjacent colours. These discoveries of Albers had a decisive influence on the development of such art movements as Op Art and Kinetic Art. S.A.

Alex Colville
Born in Toronto in 1920

Church and Horse

1964
Acrylic on hardboard
55.5 × 68.7 cm

Purchase, Horsley and Annie Townsend Bequest and anonymous donor
1966.1529

■ A seasoned practitioner of high realism since his return from World War II, when he served the Canadian army as a war artist, Alex Colville, in his capacity as a teacher at Mount Allison University in New Brunswick, has done much to promote this style in the Maritimes.

Executed in 1964, a year after Colville quit teaching following his long-awaited commercial success, *Church and Horse* is a fine example of his mature work. Enhanced by the lightness of acrylic, which the artist took up in 1963, the painting is technically flawless. The composition, with its cadenced succession of planes, is skilfully orchestrated; consistently refusing to rely on photographs, Colville would instead produce a host of preparatory drawings for each of his paintings. The scene's striking realism coexists with an intense symbolism accentuated by certain details: the church is closed, and the gate through which the horse is about to flee seems to have been left open. In a lecture at the Art Gallery of Hamilton in 1973, Colville stated that, "Realists are, primarily or initially, concerned with content." *Church and Horse* can be understood as a metaphor for secularization in Canada and the breaking away from the bonds of worship. S.A.

Leon Golub

Born in Chicago in 1922

Mercenaries II

1979
Acrylic on canvas
305 × 366 cm

Purchase, Horsley and Annie Townsend Bequest
1983.1

■ Leon Golub is one of the masters of political realism, and one of the few American painters of his generation to have steered away from abstraction. Several complex artistic currents come together in his sensibility, which was forged during a stay in Italy (1956-1957), where he discovered Hellenistic, Etruscan and Roman art. Golub lived in Paris from 1959 to 1964, exhibiting with artists under the banner of New Figuration, a movement that sought a third way between Abstraction and New Realism, advocating a critical examination of contemporary social conditions. Golub, for his part, had already developed a grim vision of the brutality of power, which he dubbed "brutal realism". He fully engages in political current events with the "Napalm" series, which evoked the horrors of the Vietnam War. This was followed by a series devoted to the world of mercenaries, paramilitaries and interrogations under torture. Critic Donald Kuspit has described the artist as "the Jacques-Louis David of the reactionary American empire, showing it defending its outposts through mercenaries . . . affecting every life in the world."

Painted in 1979, *Mercenaries II* is characteristic of the other works in the same-titled series. Against a background of red oxide inspired by the murals of Pompeii, Golub imparts a heroic dimension to a scene that is anything but heroic – mercenaries horsing around. The artist says of them: "they may be brutes, but . . . they're not that different from everybody else . . . they are part of a system of domination and control." S.A.

Serge Lemoyne
Acton Vale, Quebec, 1941 – Saint-Hyacinthe 1998

Dryden

1975
Acrylic on canvas
224 × 346 cm
Purchase, The Montreal Museum of Fine Arts' Volunteer Association Fund
2000.8.1-2

◼ During the 1960s, Quebec saw the emergence of a new avant-garde, one that adopted the paths of performance, happenings and urban action. Serge Lemoyne played a key role among these artists (who carried out their activities under such names as Semaine A, Groupe L'Horloge and Groupe Zirmate), giving "live" painting performances. "After *Global Refusal*, total art!" he proclaimed, referring to the emancipatory project of Paul-Émile Borduas.

It was during a 1969 painting performance in London, Ontario – during which Lemoyne converted Gallery 20-20 into a skating rink – that the "Red, White, Blue" cycle (the colours of the Montreal Canadians) was born. "To me, hockey is more than a sport", the artist explained. "It's the phenomenon par excellence, the one that touches the most people, whatever their background: intellectual, working class, red, white or blue collar, or the Brothers of the Sacred Heart."

Dryden represents an icon that is immediately recognizable to the Canadian public – the mask of goaltender Ken Dryden in the thick of the game. A populist artist and skilled painter, Lemoyne, in this masterful work that remained in his personal collection until his death, combines a Pop Art vocabulary taken from newspaper images with a syntax inherited from modernist abstract painting. S.A.

Paterson Ewen
Montreal 1925 – London, Ontario, 2002

Solar Eruption

1982
Acrylic on gouged plywood
243.8 × 228.6 cm
Purchase, Horsley and Annie Townsend Bequest
1987.4

■ The work of Paterson Ewen divides into two major periods – abstract, during his Montreal years, and figurative, after he moved to London, Ontario at the end of the 1960s. It was there, following a profound personal crisis that led him to reject all the pictorial conventions he had subscribed to so far, that he embarked on the "Phenomena" series, to which *Solar Eruption* belongs.

Having reimmersed himself in his youthful enthusiasm for geography and astronomy, Ewen set out to depict an atmospheric phenomenon through engraving. He proceeded by gouging out the surface of a large sheet of plywood and applying paint to it with a roller in preparation for printing. With the realization that this plywood printing block was a work in itself, Ewen's art was transformed; his decision to let the block stand on its own gave rise to one of the most remarkable chapters in the history of Canadian painting. With the outline of its subject hacked into its surface and its colours stripped of any hint of mannerism, *Solar Eruption* suggests a forceful and primitive vision of the solar landscape. The critics, moreover, saw Ewen's "Phenomena" as a continuation of the Canadian landscape tradition and its attraction to the Sublime. S.A.

Norval Morrisseau

Born Fort William (Thunder Bay) in 1931

Untitled

1950
Oil on birchbark
84 × 90.5 × 3 cm
Gift of Rya Levitt
2002.14

■ The discovery of the work of Norval Morrisseau in 1962 and its presentation to the Toronto public by dealer Jack Pollock were landmarks in the history of Canadian art. For the first time, a Native Nation artist was recognized by the art market. Born in northern Ontario of Ojibwa parents, Morrisseau was trained in the shamanic tradition of illustrating his ancestral tales on large pieces of birchbark. "I am being taught what to put down on the bark, for only the shamans made the scrolls. You could say that through history, the shamans were the artists; they were the only members in the tribe allowed to do this. So all my painting and drawing is really a continuation of the shamans' scrolls", he explained. Most of Morrisseau's work on bark has been lost or destroyed; the few known examples date mainly from the late 1950s, that is, not long before he achieved public recognition.

Painted on a piece of bark stretched by a frame made of branches, this untitled composition depicts a dialogue between a bird and a creature that is half man, half bird and resembles the artist being transformed into a Thunderbird, Morrisseau's life-long symbol. Towards the start of the 1960s, Morrisseau began working on paper and canvas, and his previously somewhat rustic formal language took on a stylized manner that opened the way for modernity in Amerindian art in Canada. S.A.

A. R. Penck
Born in Dresden in 1939

The Start of the Lion Hunt

1982
Synthetic resin on canvas
290.2 × 500.4 cm
Gift of Nahum Gelber, Q.C.
1995.8

■ A. R. Penck, whose real name is Ralph Winkler, is one of the key figures in the post-war generation of German painters who adopted figuration; others include Georg Baselitz, Markus Lüpertz, Jörg Immendorff and Anselm Kiefer. A sculptor and musician as well as a painter, Penck – who took his name from Albrecht Penck, a geologist who studied the ice age – initiated, with his *Weltbilder* (Pictures of the World) from the early 1960s, a sort of "physics of human society" that sought to codify the interaction between the individual and the system. Coming out of a primitivist vision of the human condition, at odds with the contemporary technological environment, and marked by memories of the scorched landscapes of his childhood, Penck's work sets out an extremely simplified iconography composed of spindly silhouettes, shapes and symbols reduced to the state of signs and primitive scenes.

The Start of the Lion Hunt was executed in 1982, two years after Penck left East Germany to settle in Cologne. In its monumental format and the extreme schematization of its signs, this piece shows the strong influence of cave painting, and establishes a parallel between the real and symbolic violence of human society and that of the natural order. S.A.

Betty Goodwin
Born in Montreal in 1923

Carbon

1986
Charcoal powder, wax, oil pastel, pastel, graphite, oil and gesso on dimpled galvanized aluminum
275 × 975.6 cm

Purchase, Horsley and Annie Townsend Bequest
1987.13 a-h

■ Although a late bloomer to art, Betty Goodwin had become a prominent figure on the Canadian art scene by the end of the 1960s. A student of painter and printmaker Yves Gaucher, she distinguished herself initially through her prints. In an homage to German artist Joseph Beuys, a pivotal figure, she ran various pieces of clothing – vests, hats, shirts – through a printing press. An extremely talented draftsman, faithful to the shapes of reality and spurred on by a tragic sense that places her within the great tradition of Symbolist art, Goodwin met success in painting, sculpture and installation.

With her "Swimmers" series, begun in 1982, she brought a sensitive treatment to the study of the human condition, which she depicted as a ballet of bodies floating in an indefinite space. Executed in 1986, *Carbon*, a formally varied work of monumental proportions, shows humanity lost in a sort of gymnastics that evokes the hybrid figures of love and death. As Yolande Racine noted in the catalogue that accompanied the Museum's 1987 Goodwin retrospective, Goodwin's work expresses "the fragility of humans in their own being and in their relation with others." S.A.

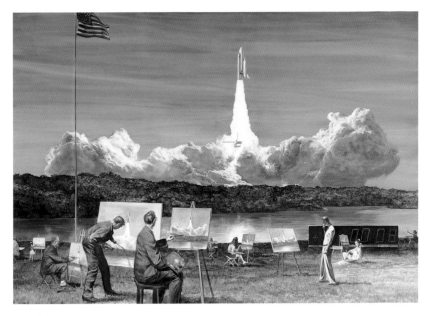

Mark Tansey

Born in San José, California, in 1949

Action Painting II

1984
Oil on canvas
193 × 279,4 cm
Gift of Nahum Gelber, Q.C.
1984.18

■ The New York scene of the late 1970s witnessed the appearance of a new generation of artists eager to have done with the orthodoxy of modernist abstraction and bent on putting images and subjects back into pictorial space. As a recent graduate of New York's Hunter College, Mark Tansey, one of the figureheads of this movement, painted *A Short History of Modernist Painting* (1979-1980), a paradoxical and figurative allegory of painting's evolution towards abstraction. "Pictures should be able to function across the fullest range of content", the artist stated.

The critique of the history and ideology of modern American pictorial art, a key element in Tansey's work, is also evident in *Action Painting II*, which provides a second, radical interpretation of the expression originated by critic Harold Rosenberg who, in reference to Jackson Pollock and other New York painters working with gestural abstraction, described the physical involvement of the artist in the act of painting. The artists depicted here – whose poses conjure up a compendium of artistic practice imagery – are attempting to represent an unrepresentable action: a rocket's blastoff. Ironically, Tansey actually does work in the manner of action painters: he too applies paint quickly but removes the freshly-applied paint from the canvas to arrive at the final representational element he seeks. S.A.

Roland Poulin
Born in Saint Thomas, Ontario, in 1940

Sombre, dans l'étendue

1989
Painted wood
127 × 160 × 430 cm

Purchase, Serge Desroches, Hermina Thau, David R. Morrice, Mary Eccles, Jean Agnes
Reid Fleming, G. C. Chisholm, Margaret A. Reid and F. Eleanore Morrice Estates
1990.31a-c

■ Roland Poulin discovered his artistic vocation in 1964 standing before *The Black Star*, a painting by Paul-Émile Borduas. That same year, he enrolled in the École des Beaux-Arts de Montréal, graduating in 1969. His sculpted work, with its precariously balanced volumes and its sombre and dramatic tonality, shows the influence of Borduas's painting.

Sombre, dans l'étendue was executed in 1989, four years after the artist had given up cement for wood. Minimalist in appearance, the work conveys the artist's fascination with funerary architecture – particularly that of the Père Lachaise cemetery in Paris, which he discovered in 1985 – and with the nocturnal world he encountered in *Hymns to the Night*, by the German Romantic poet Novalis. The scene of a strange nighttime secret meeting, the three volumes of *Sombre, dans l'étendue* evoke a setting of altars, tombs, doors or stelae hovering momentarily between two worlds. As the artist explained, "I see my sculptures somewhat as the site of an encounter between the very material, carnal and sensual on the one hand, and the sacred, spiritual and poetic on the other." S.A.

Gerhard Richter

Born in Dresden in 1932

AB Mediation

1986
Oil on canvas (diptych)
320 × 400 cm

Purchase, Horsley and Annie Townsend Bequest and
The Montreal Museum of Fine Arts' Volunteer Association Fund

1987.8

■ In 1961, the year the Berlin Wall went up, Gerhard Richter left Dresden to settle in Düsseldorf, West Germany. There he met artists Sigmar Polke and Konrad Fischer-Lueg with whom he founded Capitalist Realism. He brought to painting such images of the banality of the contemporary world as were found in numerous iconic sources, such as advertising flyers, magazines and family photographs. Throughout his long and prolific career, Richter has displayed a critical fascination for the ways in which images are constructed, an interest that led him to explore abstraction and figuration in like measure, giving him a unique position in the history of twentieth-century painting. "Since there is no such thing as absolute rightness and truth, we always pursue the artificial, leading, human truth", he noted in 1962.

AB Mediation belongs to the group of "Free Abstracts" that the artist worked on in the mid-1980s. An apparent offshoot of the gestural abstraction Richter had admired during his years of academic training, this magnificent diptych is in fact the result of the artist's analytical approach. Its violent explosion of colours is attenuated by the mechanical application of paint, while certain methodically brushed-on areas of the surface suggest the effects of a landscape viewed through an out-of-focus camera lens – a sign of the preponderance of photography in Richter's work. S.A.

Royden Rabinowitch
Born in Toronto in 1943

Grease Cone

About 1970
Steel, heavy industrial grease
182 cm (h.); 202 cm (diam.)

Gift of Gilles Gheerbrant
1986.34

■ Royden Rabinowitch, like his brother David, is considered to be one of the key figures in the Minimalist movement. Heavily influenced by the writings of French mathematician Henri Poincaré on the situational nature of geometry, he sought to impart a complex emotional content to the geometrical language of Minimalism without relying on the familiar means of Expressionism or including figurative elements.

From 1965 to 1970, he made a set of conical grease-covered sculptures that were well received when presented at the Carmen Lamanna Gallery in Toronto. The geometric purity of these historic pieces is tempered by the soft, viscous coating, whose connotations refer to the world of industry as well as to that of human emotions. The critic Gary Michael Dault has put forward the idea of a "transcendence . . . of the mechanical alienating world of the measured, the formal, the styled, the tasteful and [the] ambitious". Also, the manual application of the grease in broad vertical streaks confers upon this sculpture a singular painterliness previously unknown in Minimalism.

Royden Rabinowitch has also contributed to the development of contemporary sculpture through his work as a teacher at the Ontario College of Art in Toronto, at Yale University (where he began teaching in 1975), and at Oxford (where he now occupies the chair formerly filled by Henry Moore). S.A.

Giuseppe Penone
Born in Garessio (Turin) in 1947

Path

1983
Bronze
180 × 400 × 45 cm
Purchase, Horsley and Annie Townsend Bequest
1983.36

■ Giuseppe Penone is, along with Mario Merz and Jannis Kounellis, one of the driving forces behind Arte Povera, an art movement that took shape in Italy in the late 1960s. Inspired by the theory of critic Germano Celant, and very much in the spirit of the cultural liberation movements of the time, Arte Povera advocated a return to "the real man" who throws off the heavy burden of history.

Path illustrates the deep-seated desire for a closer bond between human beings and nature that pervades all Penone's art. The title itself refers to this goal and suggests how to achieve it. Reproducing traces of the artist's hands left in the ground, this large cast-bronze piece shows a creature composed of leaves and branches in which close scrutiny reveals a human face. "The path follows the man," wrote the artist. "It is the moment between man's passing and the instant in which the effect of his passing vanishes. Finding the path, walking along it, charting it by clearing it of nettles – this is what the sculpture is about." In his search for the quintessential image of humans in motion, Penone, with *Path*, joins the ranks of the great classics of sculptural history. This piece evokes the spirit of the *Nike of Samothrace*, the transformation of the nymph into a laurel tree depicted in Bernini's *Apollo and Daphne*, as well as the force of Rodin's *The Walking Man* and Boccioni's Futurist version of the same subject. S.A.

Stephan Balkenhol
Born in Fritzlar, Germany, in 1957

Large Pair: Head of a Man and a Woman

1990
Painted wood
220 cm (total h.)

Purchase, Camil Tremblay Estate
1991.8a-b

■ Stephan Balkenhol was born near Kassel, where Documenta (perhaps Europe's biggest international art event) takes place every five years. After seeing the 1972 edition Balkenhol decided to become an artist. In 1976 he entered the Fine Arts Academy in Hamburg, where he studied under sculptor Ulrich Rückriem. Resisting the then predominant trends of Minimalist and Conceptual Art, Balkenhol decided to seek his niche in the fold of figurative art. Drawing upon the history of sculpture, he sought to reinvent the elementary statuary of the human figure and animals by playing with theme, scale and mode of representation.

The colossal dimensions and frontality of *Large Pair: Head of a Man and a Woman*, from 1990, hark back to Roman sculpture from the time of Constantine. The colour and hairstyle, nonetheless, give these figures with ordinary but inexpressive features a contemporary allure. The modernity of the group is further accentuated by setting them upon table-like stools rather than pedestals, and the artist's ethical concern for transparency led him to leave signs of his labour by keeping the surface rough and unfinished. S.A.

Christian Boltanski

Born in Paris in 1944

Reliquary

1990
Metal boxes, wire mesh, electric lamps, fabric, photographs
218.4 × 134.6 × 66 cm

Purchase, Horsley and Annie Townsend Bequest

1991.1a-e

■ Born in the conceptual climate of the late 1960s and intended, according to the artist, for the widest possible audience, the work of Christian Boltanski, the most celebrated French artist of his generation, is purposely autobiographical from the outset. Thus, in 1974, in his "Comic Sketches", he reconstructed moments of his childhood by playing himself against a backdrop of crudely painted sets. Boltanski's fascination with childhood memories extended through the work he did based on group photographs. Enlarging photographic reproductions of unidentified children's faces, he executed various series, such as "Monuments" (1985), which uses lamplight to impart a funereal quality to the images. According to critic Adam Gopnik, "perhaps Boltanski has simply discovered something latent in ordinary photographs that can make them, in special circumstances, elegiac." With the "Reliquary" series, created from 1987 to 1990, Boltanski's work took on a particular historical dimension when the artist, who is of Jewish origin, began using photographs of groups of Jewish children.

Dramatically lit, posed atop piles of tin boxes – some containing pieces of fabric – the four faces that make up the Museum's *Reliquary* come from a photograph taken of the children at the Yiddish Language School in Paris during the Festival of Purim in 1939. S.A.

George Segal
New York 1924 – South Brunswick, New Jersey, 2000

Woman Sitting on a Bed

1993
Plaster, wood, acrylic paint, various materials
244 × 363 × 217 cm
Purchase, Horsley and Annie Townsend Bequest
1994.1a-j

■ Although its earliest phases have been associated with the Pop Art movement, the work of the American artist George Segal actually falls within a humanist tradition. His casts of people in everyday environments are intended as a moving commentary on the alienation experienced by human beings.

In the early 1980s, Segal dropped colour and realist props from his compositions and began to paint his backgrounds black. "I am looking a lot at Rembrandt, I am looking at Old Master paintings that are really a flat canvas that magically has been painted to resemble a three-dimensional sculpture. And I am trying the reverse. I am making a three-dimensional sculpture to see what happens if I can indicate some of those strange lights and darks that are purely imaginative."

First exhibited in 1993 at the Sidney Janis Gallery in New York, *Woman Sitting on a Bed* belongs to this new body of work and presents itself simultaneously as a realist scene and as an allegory. Seated in harsh light in a world completely black, her slightly bent back turned towards the viewer, this women is shown at a mundane moment of the day – in her extreme exhaustion, she embodies the weariness of the world. S.A.

Joël-Peter Witkin
Born in Brooklyn in 1939

Still Life with Mirror

1998-1999
Silver print, 3/12
62.4 × 77.4 cm

Purchase, Horsley and Annie Townsend Bequest
2000.9

■ First and foremost, Joël-Peter Witkin is a man haunted – by his own inner turmoil and by the human condition. His photographs provoke overpowering emotions from the viewer, who, caught between horror and seduction, is often repulsed. Yet, for those who can sense the compassion inherent in Witkin's quest for wonder and beauty in the disfigured, the dismembered, the deranged and the dead, his photographs are stunning. Witkin exploits themes from Roman and Greek mythology as well as the Judeo-Christian tradition, particularly its cycle of sin, expiation and redemption as it relates to sexuality and power. The foot pierced with nails in *Still Life with Mirror* alludes openly to the Crucifixion.

Proceeding like a painter, Witkin works out his grotesque tableaus in preparatory sketches. He then stages them in his studio, recomposing the world as he perceives it. He exalts his deviant subjects by setting them up in a high art context, deliberately borrowed from well-known images in the history of Western art and photography. His ambivalent vision is enhanced by the silvery antique quality of his prints, achieved through an elaborate aging process that involves scratches, tissue veils, drips and chemical stains. The result is a work, where the abject is iconized and fetishized through most powerful and haunting images. D.C.

Angela Grauerholz
Born in Hamburg in 1952

Interior

1988
Colour print, 1/3
125 × 165 cm

Purchase, Horsley and Annie Townsend Bequest
1989.Ph.6

■ Angela Grauerholz has been photographing urban scenes, public and private interiors, portraits, nudes, landscapes, windows and details of paintings for many years. Her photographs, strangely distanced and melancholic yet highly alluring, capture the imagination while evoking a sense of déjà vu. Preoccupied with the nature of photography and its role in personal and collective memory, Grauerholz sheds light on the status of the image in the contemporary world. In photographs that are suffused with a kind of supernatural aura, she summons forth a multitude of reminiscences while suggesting a narrative left open to interpretation.

Interior belongs to a series of soft-focus fragments of interiors from the late 1980s and early 1990s. It presents an angled view of the Pompeian gallery at the Metropolitan Museum of Art, New York. The left side of the composition is dominated by frescoes; the right shows a Roman bed under a window that, rather than illuminating the scene, creates a void. The large format, typical for Grauerholz, invites the viewer into this particular room, where, hovering between a sense of identity and a feeling of exclusion, he or she is faced with the ambiguity of time and space. D.C.

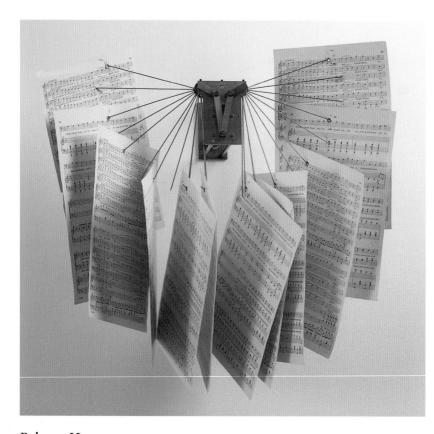

Rebecca Horn

Born in Michelstadt, Germany, in 1944

Lenny Silver's Dream

1990
Sheet music, brass, electric motor
43.1 × 44.4 × 27.9 cm
Purchase, Horsley and Annie Townsend Bequest
1991.2a-b

■ Trained at the Fine Arts Academy in Hamburg in the highly political context of the late 1960s, German artist Rebecca Horn made her mark with an original multidisciplinary approach, particularly through her participation in the Kassel Documenta of 1972 and 1977. Comprising performances, drawings, films and symbolically-charged objects, her work sometimes takes the shape of fictions through which she explores the imaginary overlapping of natural and cultural forms. Made up of music sheets that unfold like birds' wings, *Lenny Silver's Dream* belongs to a group of works that illustrate the fantasies of the characters in *Buster's Bedroom*, a film Horn made in 1990. In this eccentric fable about Buster Keaton, the musician Lenny Silver sees passing by him pages from the score of *H.M.S. Pinafore* by the British operetta-writing team of Gilbert and Sullivan, with the lyrics: "His foot should stamp and his throat should growl, / His hair should twirl and his face should scowl, / His eyes should flash and his breast protrude, / And this should be his customary attitude." S.A.

Geneviève Cadieux

Born in Montreal in 1955

Hear Me with Your Eyes

1989
Cibachrome and black-and-white prints, 1/3
244.8 × 305.3 cm

Purchase, Art Sales and Rental Gallery Fund
1989.40a-c

■ Since the early 1980s Geneviève Cadieux has been making original contributions to the re-evaluation of photography as a tool of contemporary art practice. With *Hear Me with Your Eyes*, the Montreal artist enriches this language by borrowing some of her effects from other art forms: the overall design and sequenced images from film; the monumentality from painting; and the use of space from theatre set design. The work's title and inspiration are taken from literature, more specifically from an English translation of a poem by Sor Juana Inés de la Cruz (1651-1695), a Mexican nun condemned to silence by the Church for having spoken out on the right of women to have an education and to interpret the Scriptures.

Hear Me with Your Eyes gives expression to Sor Juana's mute sorrow, so recognizable to women throughout history. The work also demonstrates the dominant power of the gaze, illustrating the artist's reiterated desire to "embody vision".

Hear me with your eyes
now that distant ears cannot attend,
and, in absent sights,
hear reproaches sobbing from this pen.
and as you cannot hear a voice so faint,
then hear me deaf, for mute is my complaint.

S.A.

Pipilotti Rist

Born in Rheinthal, Switzerland, in 1962

Rainwoman (I Am Called A Plant)

1999
Video installation (projector, player, audio system, kitchen), 3/3
Variable dimensions

Purchase, William Gilman Cheney Bequest and gift of Ann and Barrie Birks

2000.12.1-56

■ Pipilotti Rist studied at the Vienna Institute of Applied Arts and the Basel School of Design. She began her career as a video artist before making her mark as one of the key figures in the realm of video installation. Her work, which comes out of the "expanded cinema" tradition, seeks to reformulate the relationship between the electronic image and the screen by creating a sort of *tableau mouvant*, or moving picture, whose contours are adapted to the site where they are presented. As the artist herself puts it, "I create poems in motion."

In *Rainwoman (I Am Called A Plant)*, an image of a naked woman lying in a puddle in the rain is projected onto a large kitchen wall. The noise of the rain constitutes the soundtrack. The camera moves around the body, switching between close-ups and long shots, picking up the details of the flesh and the specific pose of the subject, who happens to be the artist. In this work, the viewer is presented an inverted image of women's domestic "power", an attitude consistent with the criticism of sexual stereotypes that was current in the artistic production of the 1990s. Above and beyond such critical commentary, however, Pipilotti Rist seems to want to advance a more encompassing, almost cosmic conception of sexuality, one in which there is a fusion of the individual with the natural order. S.A.

Raymonde April

Born in Moncton, New Brunswick, in 1953

Portrait of Michèle

1993
Silver print on coloured paper mounted on cotton canvas
182.4 × 159 cm
Purchase, Petromont Collection of the Montreal Museum of Fine Arts
1994.Ph.1

■ Since the late 1970s, Raymonde April has established herself as one of the most original photographers of her generation, with work that is a cross between a personal diary and a reflection on iconography. Autobiographical, filled with friends and relatives and inspired by a poetics of the memory of the moment, April's photographs are also informed by the codes that painting has used down through its history.

This portrait of April's friend, Quebec artist Michèle Waquant, evokes the history of painting in its scale and composition. With its side lighting, the woman deep in thought elegantly seated at the foot of bookshelves, and the curtain in the foreground, the image is reminiscent of interior scenes belonging to certain pictorial traditions. Displayed on the shelves are books on Hubert Robert and Paul-Émile Borduas, exhibition catalogues and old photos of April herself, enhancing the symbolic content of the image, which combines an anthology of painting and the memory of its own photographic genesis. "I want to work on the shortest distance between life and art, between water and the eye," the artist wrote in 1992. "My images have to be recognizable in their specific ordinariness, yet also resolved and compact like art objects." S.A.

Holly King
Born in Montreal in 1957

Lament

1999
Colour print, 2/3
158.8 × 189.1 cm

Purchase, The Canada Council for the Arts' Acquisition Assistance Program and
The Montreal Museum of Fine Arts' Volunteer Association Fund
2000.59

■ The photography of Holly King is an exploration of the theme of landscape through the medium of set design. King's magnificent tableaus with an air of fantasy transform an entirely constructed reality into a more or less credible, but always manifestly artificial, landscape. With each photograph, the viewer enters a world that evokes psychological and emotional states as well as physical signs, conjuring up his or her own personal experience of landscape.

King's procedure is always approximately the same: calling up a number of types of representation, like film and literature, she constructs the various elements of her landscapes – rocks, bodies of water, terraces, forests, skies – out of everyday materials and natural elements. Once lit, photographed and enlarged, her models become phantasmagorical spaces, where epic combat and intimate struggles rage.

King works in cycles, each having its own character and references: "The Waters" (1985), "The Rivers of Hades" (1986), "The Gardens" (1990-1992), "Imprisoned in the Viewless Winds" (1995). *Lament* is from a more recent cycle, "The Forest of Enchantment". Moving away from the drama of her preceding photos, here King comes back to colours that are more saturated than ever. Black scrolls – signs of the artist's intervention directly on the negative – create obstacles for the gaze while making this a most mysterious landscape, at the boundary between the real and the imaginary. D.C.

Jeff Wall

Born in Vancouver in 1946

A Sunflower

1995
Transparency in a light box (acrylic, metal, fluorescent tubes), 3/4
72.9 × 90.5 cm
Purchase, The Canada Council for the Arts' Acquisition Assistance Program and William Gilman Cheney Bequest
1997.14.1-6

■ Since the 1970s, Jeff Wall has been using backlit transparencies, a medium borrowed from the world of advertising, to create monumental works that fall somewhere between cinema, photography and painting. In carefully arranged scenes where nothing is left to chance, Wall looks at a variety of themes – such as feminism, landscape and street scenes – introducing his personal concerns in the process: narrative, quotation and social criticism. In the 1990s, Wall put his social questioning aside and turned to more conventional photography, dealing with aesthetic matters such as the compositional complexity of the image and its colours.

A Sunflower was taken in Wall's kitchen. The household objects it shows sitting on the counter draw attention to the tastes and habits of the people who use them. This photograph attests to the artist's interest in still life, particularly the seventeenth-century *vanitas*. In keeping with that tradition, he juxtaposes objects evoking daily life with others evoking death, inviting reflection on the passage of time. The composition intentionally refers to other painting traditions as well – the artist's faint reflection on the silver fruit bowl and the choice of the sunflower call to mind the luminous paintings of van Gogh. D.C.

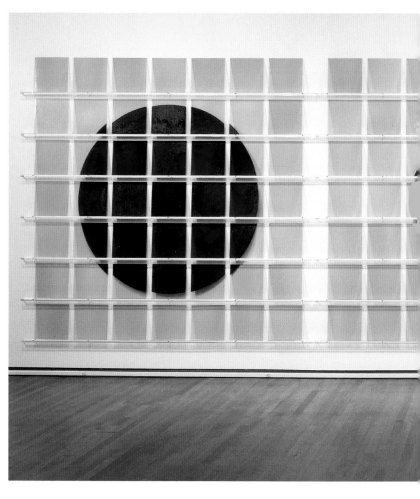

Kiki Smith
Born in Nuremberg in 1954

Red Moons

1998
Glass, acrylic, Plexiglas
226 × 732 × 4.5 cm
Purchase, Horsley and Annie Townsend Bequest
1999.2.1-170

■ Kiki Smith was born into a family of artists – her father is painter, sculptor and architect Tony Smith, and her mother is singer-actress Jane Smith. Kiki Smith began her career as a member of Collaborative Projects, Inc. (Colab), a collective of socially engaged American artists, and first came to prominence through exhibitions held mainly at The Kitchen and P.S.1 in New York. Her ability to breathe new life into traditional art forms via an original and striking vision of the human body and femininity, together with a sensibility highly attentive to materials, eventually made her in the early 1990s one of the most important American artists of her generation.

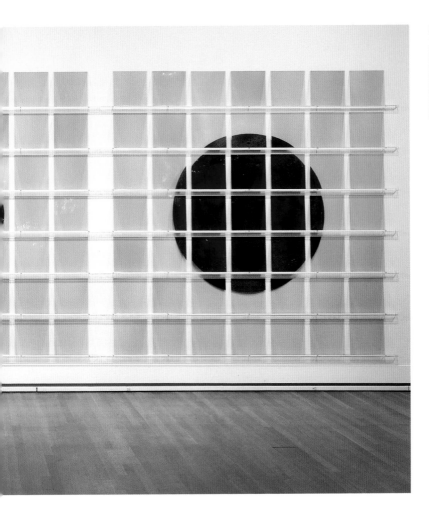

Executed in 1998, two years after she abandoned the direct representation of the body in order to explore its cosmological metaphors and resonances, *Red Moons* is the third and most impressive of the pieces the artist devoted to the theme of the moon. Combining the classic monumentality of the triptych and the fragility of glass, Kiki Smith celebrates the fluid nuptials of the cosmos and the body; these blood moons symbolize the imaginary and immemorial alliance that connects the female body with the order of the cosmos. S.A.

Barbara Steinman
Born in Montreal in 1950

Lux

2000
Steel chain chandelier, crystal chain, shadows
Chandelier: 102 cm (h.); 86 cm (diam.)

Purchase, The Montreal Museum of Fine Arts' Volunteer Association Fund
2001.10.1-55

■ Arising from the conceptual tradition, the work of Montreal artist Barbara Steinman stands at the crossroads of various modes of expression. *Lux* combines the vocabulary of sculpture and installation in an elegant setting where light plays a leading role. The circle of fallen crystal and the cross-shaped shadows cast on the floor correspond to the hanging chandelier's chains. Another characteristic of Steinman's work is the relationship to place, which the artist, who is sensitive to various forms of oppression, most often expresses in a critical vein. Conceived for an exhibition in Prague that never took place, *Lux* refers to its intended destination through the use of Bohemian crystal and by using the chandelier chains as a metaphor for power. "To me, it's as if the chandelier had shed its skin, revealing the toughness beneath the facade of beauty," she explained in an interview. "Originally, I had in mind all the historical layering of different regimes that invaded and dominated Prague and the chandelier became for me an icon of resistance, of a tentative balance between force and fragility." S.A.

Michael Snow
Born in Toronto in 1929

Place des peaux

1998
Plastic-film windows, projectors
15.5 × 5.8 m

Purchase, The Canada Council for the Arts' Acquisition Assistance Program, Aéroports de Montréal Fund,
Harold Lawson, Marjorie Caverhill and Harry W. Thorpe Bequests, Mona Prentice Fund

2001.63.1-42

■ A multidisciplinary artist *par excellence*, with connections to the international conceptual art movement, Michael Snow has distinguished himself in experimental filmmaking (*Wavelength*, 1967), painting and sculpture (notably with the ubiquitous "Walking Woman" series, from 1961 to 1967), photography, holograms, public art, audiovisual installation and music (as a pianist and trumpet player with various jazz ensembles, including the CCMC trio). In 1967 he wrote, "My paintings are made by a filmmaker, my sculptures by a musician, my films by a painter, my music by a filmmaker, my paintings by a sculptor, my sculptures by a filmmaker, my films by a musician, my music by a sculptor who sometimes all work together." His prolific and protean output displays quite a high degree of formal reflection on various art forms with a particular sensitivity to the phenomena of perception and movement. As he once put it, "The nature of art is to direct the gaze."

Place des peaux presents itself as a vast abstract set composed of pure colour and light, which is composed and recomposed as the viewer wanders at will. With its great formal simplicity – the legacy of the Minimalist aesthetic in Snow's work – *Place des peaux* proposes a subtle synthesis of sculpture, painting and cinema. The latter is present in its rudimentary form by way of the light projected through a plastic film – the *peaux*, or skins, of the title. S.A.

Duane Michals

Born in McKeesport, Pennsylvania, in 1932

From the series "Salute, Walt Whitman"
Once Paumanuk
The Body Sluggish

1995
Silver prints, ink inscriptions, 3/25
50.5 × 40.4 cm
Purchase, Horsley and Annie Townsend Bequest
1997.4-5

■ Reluctant to abide by the prescribed rules of the medium of photography and its practitioners, American photographer Duane Michals makes innovative use of narrative sequence by adding handwritten texts directly onto his prints. The result is an intimate form of expression reminiscent of storytelling, in which he raises issues about life and death, desire and memory. Michals conveys his ideas through staged images that vary in tone from serious and melancholic to humorous. His inspiration is drawn from literature, philosophy, cinema and the history of painting. Two sources in particular appear to have influenced Michals's creative approach: René Magritte, whose paintings often incorporate verbal "imagery", and Walt Whitman's poems. *The Body Sluggish* and *Once Paumanuk* belong to a series in which Michals interpreted the nineteenth-century American poet's masterpiece, *Leaves of Grass*, in images juxtaposed with fragments of the poems. A single model and props like flowers, a match and an oversize book displaying the poet's words, give form to the ideas and concerns of Whitman, which Michals held dear. D.C.

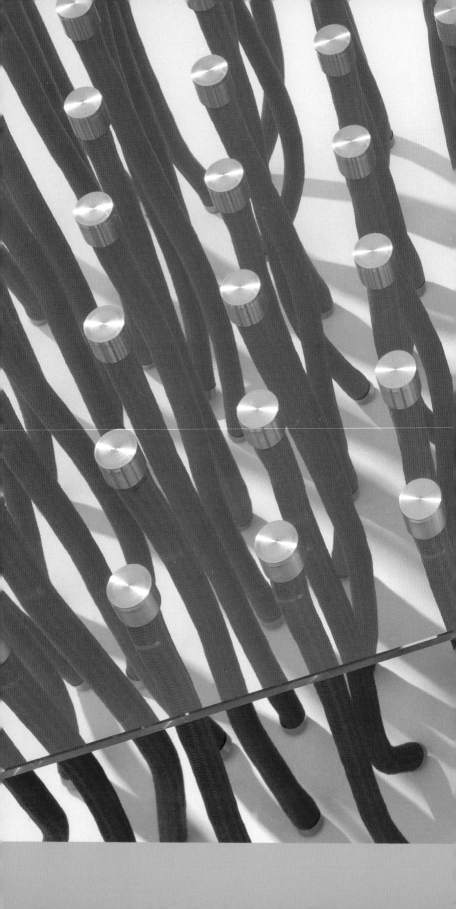

DECORATIVE ARTS

France (?)

Scenes from the Passion of Christ

Diptych
About 1350
Ivory, traces of polychrome and gilt
21.6 × 20.5 cm (open)

Purchase, gift of Miss Olive Hosmer
1950.51.Dv.6

■ This portable diptych for private devotion is typical of luxury products from fourteenth-century Western European ivory workshops. The two panels would have been closed when not in use, and therefore significant traces of the gilt and pigment that originally highlighted the carvings survive. Set within open five-arched Gothic tracery, six scenes of Christ's Passion run up the left panel, beginning with the Entry into Jerusalem, then the Flagellation and culminating in the Crucifixion, and then down the right panel, from the Deposition and the Entombment through the Harrowing of Hell – note the devil's head and monsters devouring the damned at the lower right corner – when Christ released Adam and Eve. The unusual latter scene may reflect the request of a patron.

It is difficult to say with certainty where this diptych comes from. It has usually been considered the work of a French workshop, possibly the school of Paris, but Germany, Spain and England have also been proposed as places of origin. Because Paris was the major centre of production, with a variety of workshops and artists of diverse nationalities, an attribution to France seems quite plausible, though the piece may have been made by an English artisan trained in France. H.T.G.

Italy

Cassone (Chest)

About 1460
Cedar or cypress, traces of pigment, iron
56.5 × 206.5 × 64 cm
Gift of Roberto Ferretti di Castelferretto
1998.46

■ The cassone, or storage chest, remained an essential piece of furniture until the late sixteenth century, when it was gradually superseded by the chest of drawers. Often made for an impending marriage, a cassone might contain the bride's trousseau: sometimes, they were made in pairs bearing the armorial devices of the families to be united. Cassoni were arranged along the walls of private rooms, such as a study or bedroom, and some were built into the sides of large beds. Utilitarian and decorative objects could be placed on their flat tops, and fitted with cushions, they served as seating.

Reflecting the sense of style or social status of the owners, cassoni provided an ideal ground for a variety of decorative techniques: inlay, carving, incised and moulded gilt plasterwork, and painted images, often executed by important artists. The pictorial elements of this piece were delineated by fine lines engraved in the wood in flat relief on a punched background, which was filled in with a coloured paste. The Fountain of Life, an appropriate subject for a marriage chest, is depicted here in a courtly style, whose details, compressed space and composition reflect the influence of Veronese artist Antonio Pisanello and Venetian artists working in the first half of the fifteenth century. These various elements are found in a group of stylistically related cassoni attributed to the area of northeastern Italy delimited by Verona, Venice and the Adige River. R.L.

Italy, Sulmona

Processional Cross

1468-1483
Silver, gilded silver,
gilded copper, enamel,
iron, wood
51.7 × 48.2 × 7.5 cm

Gift of the John Main Prayer
Association, by prior gift of
The J. W. McConnell Family
Foundation

1994.Ds.1

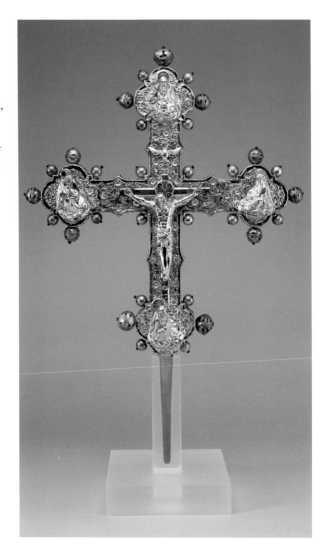

■ The main body of this processional cross is made of wood, with thin plaques of silver nailed to it. The silver figure of Christ, cast in the round, is attached to the centre. At the end of each arm of the cross are figures in high relief: at the top, God the Father; to the left, Saint John; to the right, the Virgin Mary; and at the bottom, Mary Magdalene. The reverse displays bas-relief figures of the four Evangelists and small enamel roundels with engraved images of the Archangel Gabriel, the Virgin Mary and Saint Anthony Abbot. The edges are decorated with gilded copper bells and spheres nailed into the wood.

Each silver plaque bears the punch mark of the town of Sulmona for the period from 1468 to 1483. Sulmona was the centre of goldwork in the Abruzzi region of Italy, and this art reached a peak there in the fifteenth century with the presence of master goldsmith Nicola da Guardiagrele. The cross does not bear a goldsmith's mark, but each figure's pose, the naturalism of the facial features, and the fluid drapery resemble da Guardiagrele's work. The volume of the figures suggests the influence of the great Florentine sculptor Lorenzo Ghiberti, who Guardiagrele had worked with. The processional cross is an especially fine example of the Early Renaissance sculptural tradition in a commission by a Sulmona goldsmith. R.P.

Mattia di Nanni
Siena 1403 – Siena 1433

Curius Dentatus, Pompey and Mettus Curtius

1424-1429
Intarsia of walnut, oak, bog oak, various fruitwoods, bone
63.8 × 41.6 cm
63.6 × 41.7 cm
62.2 × 41.4 cm

Gift of the John Main Prayer Association, by prior gift of The J. W. McConnell Family Foundation
1994.Df.2a-c

■ Intarsia is the art of inlaying pieces of wood into a solid wood ground to create patterns and pictures through the juxtaposition of a varied range of dark and light tones. In the fifteenth century, the Italian city of Siena was a recognized centre of this art form. The Museum has three intarsia panels attributed to Mattia di Nanni, a young pupil of one of the most famous Sienese specialists of the art, Domenico di Niccolò. The panels are among ten commissioned by the city fathers in 1424 for a bench in the council chamber of the Palazzo Pubblico. Outstanding examples of the technique, they depict Curius Dentatus, Pompey and Mettus Curtius, all ancient Romans called upon to sacrifice personal ambition for the common good. The choice of subject reflects Siena's admiration for the ideals of Republican Rome.

In his short life, di Nanni surpassed his master at creating fluid lines of drapery and modelling figures with his expert handling of the intricate arrangement of strips of wood often no larger than a sliver. The Museum's panels vary in composition and draftsmanship, probably because di Nanni would have worked from cartoons by other artists.

For almost a century, scholars believed these panels were lost, until they turned up in a Montreal residence and were given to the Museum in 1994. R.P.

MAGNVS · PONPEVS ·

England, probably Hereford

York School artist or workshop

Saint Anne Teaching the Virgin to Read, Saint Winifred and Saint Thomas Becket

About 1435
Coloured and clear glass with silver stain, lead latticing
92 × 163.5 cm

Gift of John Main Prayer Association, by prior gift of the J. W. McConnell Family Foundation
1995.Dg.15-17

■ These three lancet windows, exceptional examples of fifteenth-century English painted stained glass, have been attributed to an artist working in the region of Hereford. They have been traced to the domestic chapel of Hampton Court, near Leominster, Herefordshire, whence they were removed in 1924. All three depict saints: Saint Anne teaching her daughter, the Virgin Mary, to read; Saint Winifred, a Welsh saint who was admired in medieval Britain; and Thomas Becket, Archbishop of Canterbury, who was murdered by Henry II in 1170.

The placement of the figures under an architectural canopy against a ground of vegetal motifs or textile patterns was a common feature of fifteenth-century English stained glass. At some point, the canopies in these windows were cut down and the lower parts recomposed from assorted fragments. The colours of the glass are restricted to red and blue, with yellow highlights that resulted from the application of a silver stain to the white glass. The emphasis is on painted line rather than pure colour, and the draftsmanship, modelling of the figures and fluid lines of the drapery are extremely skillful. Similar characteristics are seen in windows at Great Malvern Priory, 30 kilometres from Hampton Court, and in the Saint William window at York Minster. The technique may also reflect Continental influence. R.P.

Nicholas Hilliard
Exeter 1547 – London 1619

Queen Elizabeth I

About 1590
Gouache on vellum
4.9 × 3.9 cm

Gift of Mrs. F. Cleveland Morgan
1955. Dv.6

■ Nicholas Hilliard was the master of his age in the art of the portrait miniature. His *Treatise on the Arte of Limning* (about 1600) forms the basis of understanding the techniques and development of miniature painting in England from its inception in the sixteenth century. These delicately painted portraits were offered as gifts and mementos. Because they were intended to be worn as jewellery or carried on one's person, they ranged in height from about four to no more than nine centimetres. Having developed from the art of manuscript illumination, portrait miniatures were at first painted on very fine parchment, or vellum. In the mid-eighteenth century, paper-thin ivory was introduced as a ground. The art form flourished across Europe until about the 1820s.

As court artist to Queen Elizabeth I, Hilliard painted many portraits of his sovereign, each differing in dress and facial expression. Here, the sitter's coiffure, lace ruff and necklace are bedecked with jewels meticulously rendered. Trained as a goldsmith and jeweller, Hilliard was renowned for his ability to capture the brilliance and texture of precious metals and gems in his miniatures by burnishing the metallic pigments so they gleamed like real jewels. Over time, oxidation has blackened the silver highlights in this miniature. The frame complements the painting's jewel-like quality. R.P.

France

Two-tiered Cabinet

About 1590-1600
Walnut, marble, brass
223.5 × 104.5 × 43 cm
Gift of Mrs. Charles F. Martin
1956.Df.6a-e

■ Two-tiered cabinets illustrate the flowering of the French Renaissance in the decorative arts. Their form reflects the architecture of the period in the incorporation of pediments, cornices, friezes, consoles and columns. Many such pieces originated in sixteenth-century Parisian workshops on the Île-de-France. The strong Italian influence, evident in the design of works from the School of Fontainebleau region in the early sixteenth century, is still to be found in the decoration of this later example, with its inlaid marble plaques and panels elaborately carved in low relief. The wood used is walnut, as was common for quality furniture of that time. Walnut is easy to carve, and its grain, colour and sheen when polished are pleasing to the eye.

The front of this piece is a display of allegorical sculpture, characteristic of sixteenth-century French cabinets. The female figures of the upper door panels symbolize Summer and Autumn. The lower panels' depictions of the elements Water and Fire are based on engravings by Hendrick Goltzius from 1586. The smaller panels are finely carved with animal motifs, masks, reclining nymphs, sphinxes and other fantastic creatures. This model of cabinet remained in fashion into the first years of the seventeenth century. R.P.

Master "R. B."

Active in London about 1610-1640

Tankard

About 1630-1640
Silver
21.3 × 19.2 × 14 cm

Gift of Miss Barbara B. Buchanan
1996.Ds.88

■ One of the earliest and rarest examples of English domestic silver in the Museum's collection, this tankard dates from the reign of Charles I (1625-1649). Little English silverware from this period survives because, owing to difficult economic times, much of it was melted down for coinage. The tankard's tapered cylindrical body, hinged lid and S-shaped handle are typical of this type of drinking vessel, although the spreading base and domed cover with finial are more characteristic of earlier silver tankards. In the time of Charles I, elaborately decorated silverware gave way to more restrained ornament in the form of a matt effect created by repeatedly striking the metal's surface with a small round-headed punch. This tankard's matt areas of silver contrast impressively with the smooth, brightly polished surfaces. The coat of arms on the side is that of the Irish branch of the Beresford family. R.P.

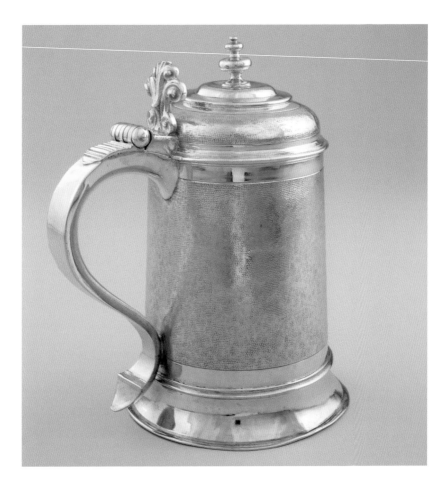

Italy, Urbino

Tazza
The Gathering of Manna

About 1550
Tin-glazed earthenware (maiolica)
7.6 cm (h.); 33.2 cm (diam.)

Purchase, Horsley and Annie Townsend Bequest
1972.Dp.27

■ Maiolica wares are admired for the lively portraits and narrative scenes painted in vivid colours over their whole surface. The term "maiolica" refers to the tin-glazed earthenwares that were first exported to Italy from the Spanish island of Majorca. Italian potters learned the technique, and Florence, Faenza, Deruta and Urbino became major centres of the art in the sixteenth century. The decoration was painted directly on the powdered surface of the glaze, which immediately absorbed the pigment. The artists, many of whom remain anonymous, had to work with a sure hand, as there was no leeway for mistakes.

Urbino was especially known for its istoriato, or narrative wares, depicting scenes from the Bible and mythology. This tazza illustrates an Old Testament subject (Exodus 16). Fleeing from Egypt to the Promised Land, Moses and the people of Israel wandered in the desert for forty years. Because they had nothing to eat, the Lord sent manna raining from heaven for them to gather every morning. The manna is shown in the form of small clumps of white flakes on the ground; the man with a staff seen from the back is probably Moses.

Maiolica artists copied their subjects from woodcuts and engravings, and this scene was probably inspired by a Bible published in Lyons with illustrations by Bernard Salomon, whose work was a major source of imagery in the late sixteenth century. R.P.

LEFT: **Attributed to Giuseppe Nepoti**

Rocca Contrada, Italy, 1677 – Rome 1753

Chalice

About 1735
Silver gilt
30 cm (h.); 15.1 cm (diam.)

Gift of the Honourable Serge Joyal, P.C., O.C.

1996.Ds.16a

RIGHT: **Attributed to Johannes Lutma II**

Amsterdam 1624 – Amsterdam 1689

Ciborium

1671
Silver, silver gilt
65.4 cm (h.); 23.3 cm (diam.)

Purchase, special replacement fund

1975.Ds.1a-b

■ The maker's mark on this chalice was used from 1703 to 1774 by three successive goldsmiths. This tour de force of late Baroque art was most likely made by the first of them, Giuseppe Nepoti, who was active in Rome from 1702 to 1753.

The chalice is replete with scenes and symbols depicting the Passion of Christ. The triangular plan, an allusion to the Holy Trinity, is embodied in a complex interplay of convex and concave elements that owes much to the Baroque architecture of Francesco Borromini. Other details, such as the half-shell framing devices and the C-scroll pediments over blind panels, show the influence of Pietro da Cortona. More immediate influences can be found in the designs of Roman goldsmith Giovanni Giardini. His highly influential pattern book, *Disegni Diversi* (1714), translated the architectural vocabulary of Borromini into that of the metalworker. Nepoti incorporated features from Giardini's design for a hanging lamp into the base and central knop of this chalice. R.L.

■ The abundance of silverware in seventeenth-century Holland was due to the prosperous times and a flourishing of the arts in general. The main centres were the Hague and Amsterdam, where Johannes Lutma II worked with his father Johannes Lutma I, and used the same heart-shaped maker's mark. According to the date letter stamped on this ciborium, it was created in 1671, during a period known for the appearance of profuse naturalistic ornament and an ordered balance of forms. The ciborium is an exceptional display of intricate chasing and embossing. On the foot, three scenes from the life of Christ are set in cartouches, and around the lower cup are three putti holding symbols of the harvest. Surmounting the cover is a crown of acanthus leaves held aloft by three putti. The finial, originally in the form of a putto, has been replaced. R.P.

Bohemia
Goblet

About 1725
Glass, wheel-engraved and cut,
metal threads
20 cm (h.); 10.7 cm (diam.)
David R. Morrice Bequest
1981.Dg.24

Attributed to the Verrerie royale d'Orléans

Orléans, founded in 1662

Trick Drinking Vessel

About 1700
Glass
21.4 × 13.5 × 9.9 cm
Purchase, Decorative Arts Fund
1954.Dg.1

■ In the late seventeenth and early eighteenth century, Bohemia (now part of the Czech Republic) was a leading European centre of glass-making and engraving, rivalling even Venice. Its wares were exported all over Europe. The discovery of potash glass in Bohemia led to the production of a clear, hard glass with a surface ideal for engraving. Wheel engraving, which traditionally had been used on gems and crystals, could now be done on glass. Here, loosely engraved foliate scrolls cover the sides and foot of the cup, which is otherwise plain but for an aristocrat's monogram on one side and an unidentified Polish coat of arms on the other. The twisting red and gold glass threads encased in the turned and faceted stem add a touch of colour. R.P.

■ Greatly admired in Europe, Venetian glass was exported north of the Alps as early as the fifteenth century. European glass-making centres lured Italian craftsmen away to create glass in the Venetian style. One of the most famous Italian glassmakers who immigrated to Nevers and then to Orléans in 1662 was Bernardo Perroto, or Perot as he was called, who received royal patronage and made Orléans the most important centre in France for the production of glass *façon de Venise* in the seventeenth century. He developed new forms and production methods and invented the use of translucent red glass to give touches of colour to clear glass vessels. With this trick drinking vessel, one can only drink from the base of the handle, which acts as a siphon, drawing all the liquid rapidly upward to pour out onto the surprised drinker. R.P.

William Spackman

Active in London after 1714

Teapot and Warming Stand

1716-1717
Silver, wood
22.7 × 26.1 × 13.6 cm
Gift of Mr. and Mrs. Neil B. Ivory
1983.Ds.1a-d

■ A splendour of curved lines and unadorned brilliant surfaces, this teapot is a quintessential piece of early eighteenth-century silver. English silver teapots had only been introduced at the end of the previous century, inspired by Chinese stoneware teapots. As tea was expensive, teapots of the period were small. This one has its own tripod stand, supporting a circular spirit lamp for keeping the tea warm. The teapot's octagonal pear-shaped body is undecorated except for a coat of arms finely engraved within a scrolled cartouche. The simplicity of form and decoration in this work represents a reaction to the excessive ornament of Baroque silver, and also shows the influence of the restrained designs of the Huguenot silversmiths who had fled to England in the late seventeenth century. Little is known of William Spackman except that, after serving an apprenticeship from 1703 to 1712, he was active in London from 1714 until 1726. R.P.

China
Yung Cheng period

Plate (Chinese Export)

About 1730-1735
Hard-paste porcelain
3.5 cm (h.); 25 cm (diam.)

Gift of Mrs. Neil B. Ivory
219.2002

■ This rare plate is an exceptional example of the thriving trade in Chinese porcelain that reached a peak in the mid-eighteenth century. At this time, European porcelain manufacture was still in its infancy, and so the whiteness and translucence of hard-paste, or true, porcelain from China were greatly admired. The European market for these Chinese wares developed out of the established trade in silk, spices and tea. Portugal and Holland had long engaged in trade with the Orient, but in the early eighteenth century, England held a monopoly on trade with China.

Ordered through a London dealer, this plate would have been part of a large dinner service. The armorial in the centre is that of the Lee of Coton family from Shropshire, quartered with the Astley family of Staffordshire. The client would have provided a drawing of the armorial with colour notations. The plate was probably made at Jingdezhen, an inland porcelain-manufacturing centre, and then decorated in Canton. The hand-painted grisaille views on the border depict the place of origin and destination in the plate's journey from maker to client. Canton, on the Pearl River, was one of the most populous cities in China and the thriving centre of the porcelain trade. The finely painted scene shows the walled town and its waterfront of warehouses, factories and shops. The London view shows the old London Bridge, Saint Paul's Cathedral and numerous spires rising above rows of houses. Though otherwise accurate, this decoration shows junks sailing on the Thames instead of barges. R.P.

Lotbinière, Quebec
Two-tiered Buffet

Late 18th c.
Pine
255 × 155 × 65.1 cm
Gift of Miss Mabel Molson
1938.Df.13a-b

■ North America's interest in old furniture was spawned in the 1920s. This sensitivity was shared by F. Cleveland Morgan, a connoisseur who was a great benefactor of the Montreal Museum of Fine Arts, which accounts for the Museum's considerable holdings of early Quebec furniture.

Early Quebec furniture like this piece was made by rural artisans who based their designs on French provincial models and craft traditions. This two-tiered pine buffet is a good example of what would have been found in the home of a well-to-do family in Quebec in the late eighteenth century. Its large size confers an air of monumentality, which is tempered by the simple decoration and rococo-style scrolling curves on the door panels. Their supple lines, as well as the fruit baskets in carved relief decorating the centre of the upper doors, soften the overall severity of the piece. The heart motif in the middle of each basket suggests that this buffet may have been a wedding present. For the most part, furniture of this type was originally painted, but ironically, out of a misled desire to return them to their original state, the collectors who ensured their preservation stripped the finish from most of them. J.P.L.

Laurent Amiot
Quebec City 1764 – Quebec City 1839

Teapot
About 1805
Silver, wood
15.1 × 28.4 × 12.1 cm
Ramsay Traquair Bequest
1952.Ds.41

■ Along with sculpture, metalwork was one of the first forms of art to have developed in New France. By the seventeenth century, silversmiths working in the colony were creating both liturgical and domestic silver. Canadian silverwork reached a high point in the early nineteenth century, when there was a great number of craftsmen producing silverware of high quality. One of the most talented of them was Laurent Amiot, who renewed the medium's ornamental vocabulary. Amiot spent five years in France to perfect his training. When he returned to his native Quebec City in 1787, his work marked a transition from Rococo to Neoclassicism, attesting to both his training and his contact with British silver, which had come into wide circulation at this period.

An assemblage of relatively simple forms with smooth, soberly ornamented surfaces, this teapot from about 1805 is a good example of Neoclassicism in Canadian silverwork. For practical reasons, the knob and handle are made of wood. Amiot has skilfully taken advantage of the contrasting textures and colours of the two materials.

This teapot is one of forty pieces bequeathed by Ramsay Traquair to the Museum from his silver collection in 1952. Traquair, a famous historian of Canadian architecture, directed McGill University's school of architecture for twenty-five years. J.P.L.

Derby factory

Derby, England, about 1750–1848

Pair of Vases

About 1820
Porcelain, bone ash added
33.5 × 28 × 19 cm; 34.1 × 28 × 20 cm
Gift of Lucile E. Pillow
1964.Lp.185-186

■ The Derby porcelain works, founded about 1750, were among the earliest in England and gained a reputation for their porcelain figures and painted floral decorations. About 1811, the original Derby factory was taken over by Robert Bloor, who continued the tradition of flower-painted wares and produced showy display pieces like these vases.

Many talented artists painted Derby porcelain and trained succeeding generations. However, it is difficult to attribute wares to specific artists, as they often moved from one factory to another and did not usually sign their work. Rather than the painted decoration of floral sprays scattered against the white porcelain ground typical of eighteenth-century Derby wares, these vases display a variety of flowers massed closely together over the main body. The painter has used the porcelain surface like a canvas for the naturalistic depiction of flowers and plants; such decoration was usually copied from botanical illustrations in magazines and books. The fine quality of the enamelling is revealed in the shading, highlights and range of colour. The remaining decoration of scroll and leaf gilding is also done by hand. The urn shape and scrolled loop handles reflect the fashion for Neoclassical forms and motifs.

These vases are part of the extensive English porcelain collection amassed by Lucile E. Pillow and given to the Museum in 1964. R.P.

Workshop of François Gourdeau
Active in Quebec City from 1864 to 1916

Sofa

About 1870
Varnished walnut, upholstery
144 × 38 × 180 cm

Gift of the Succession J.A. DeSève
1986.Df.1

■ Furniture-making was a thriving industry in late nineteenth-century Quebec. Workshops and factories prospered in Montreal, with William Drum and William Hilton, and Quebec City, with Philippe Vallière. This sofa, typical of the Victorian era (1837-1901), is from the workshop of François Gourdeau of Quebec City; it is part of a twelve-piece set that belonged to the notary Théophile Levasseur in that city.

Whereas the evolution of styles in previous centuries corresponded closely with historical periods, decorative arts in the nineteenth century intentionally reinterpreted all that had come before, leading to the coexistence of the Neo-Egyptian, Neo-Baroque, Rococo Revival, Neoclassical and Gothic Revival trends. The structure of the sofa seen here, with its straight base and the figure in the medallion in the upper crosspiece of the back, suggests the furniture of the Renaissance. According to the common practice of the time, the design may be based on a plate from *Le garde-meuble ancien et moderne*, a magazine then in circulation in Quebec. Most often, the carved figures represent British writers and poets, but these have not been identified. When this set was acquired, it came with bolts of fabric from the period, which made it possible to restore the seats to their original appearance. J.P.L.

William Morris

Walthamstow, England, 1834 – Kelmscott 1896

Minstrel Figures

1882
Coloured and painted glass, lead
Made by Morris & Co., Merton Abbey
64.7 × 78.7 cm

Gift of the family of David A. P. Watt
1918.Dg.3

■ William Morris was the central figure in a renewal of the arts and crafts based on traditions handed down from the Middle Ages. His firm, from its beginning in 1861, contributed greatly to the English stained glass revival that resulted from a reawakened interest in Gothic architecture and medieval design. While the main clients for large pictorial stained glass windows were churches, transoms decorated with geometric patterns and painted designs became fashionable in homes.

The chief designer for the company's stained glass was Morris's friend and associate Edward Burne-Jones; however, Morris himself designed over a hundred windows, including this one depicting two figures holding a portative organ and a mandolin. It is characteristic of Morris & Co. domestic windows of the period, with its separate figures in richly coloured robes silhouetted against square glass panes painted with sprigs of flowers and leaves. The facial features, details of the instruments and modelling of the drapery are also painted, in brown pigment fired onto the glass.

This is one of a pair of panels in the Museum's collection ordered from the Morris firm in 1882 by the Scottish merchant David Allan Poe Watt for his Montreal home. Watt, who had come to Canada in the mid-1840s, was an active member of the Art Association of Montreal. These panels, and another he had ordered earlier, are the first stained glass to have been commissioned directly from Morris & Co. for Canada. R.P.

William De Morgan
London 1839 – London 1917

Dish

1888-1897
Glazed earthenware, lustre decoration
Painted by Charles Passenger
4.9 cm (h.); 26.5 cm (diam.)
Gift of Graham Drinkwater
1921.Dp.4

■ William De Morgan embodies the British Arts and Crafts movement's ideal of the decorative artist who both designs and handcrafts his works. He was a friend of William Morris, the movement's main proponent, to whom he supplied tiles and pottery wares. De Morgan opened his first factory in 1872 and worked out of a number of successive locations in and around London until 1907, when he closed the business. He conducted many experiments to perfect his ceramic wares, and was especially inspired by the techniques, colours and decoration of Islamic pottery. Although hand-decorated tiles were his firm's mainstay, De Morgan was also known for his lustreware. The lustre technique, invented in the Near East, involves covering earthenware with a metallic film to impart an iridescent finish to the glazed surface. This dish, with the rich palette of reds and brown enhanced by the application of copper and silver lustre, is an excellent example.

The decoration was painted after De Morgan's design by Charles Passenger, who began working with De Morgan in 1877 and became a partner in 1898. The eagle sinking its claws into its prey was conceived to fill the whole dish, and follows its circular shape. The white ground is used to great effect to emphasize the strong, flat colours. This piece was made at De Morgan's Sands End pottery in Fulham, which he opened in 1888. R.P.

Léon Kann

Dombach, Alsace, 1859 – Paris (?) 1925

Fenouil Coffee Service

About 1898
Hard-paste porcelain
Produced by Manufacture Nationale de Sèvres

Liliane and David M. Stewart Collection
D94.300.1-7

■ The organic shapes and sinuous lines of this coffee service epitomize the Art Nouveau style. Produced by the Sèvres porcelain factory between 1898 and 1912, it represents an effort on the part of the company to create more original and varied designs than the historical styles its reputation was based on. The designer, sculptor Léon Kann, drew inspiration from a close observation of nature in his realistic depiction of the insects decorating the lids and in the overlapping leaves of the fennel plant, from which emerge the main bodies of the wares. The curving forms are further accentuated in the undulations of the tray and the sweeping line of the coffee pot handle.

Each piece bears the date and the modeller's initials. There are records indicating that a cream jug was made in the "Fenouil" pattern, but complete sets of this coffee service are very rare. R.P.

Louis Comfort Tiffany
New York 1848 – New York 1933

Pond Lily Table Lamp
About 1900
Bronze, iridescent glass (Favrile glass)
54.5 × 28.5 × 28.5 cm
Produced by Tiffany Studios, New York

Liliane and David M. Stewart Collection
D94.177.1a-m

■ Although Louis Comfort Tiffany was involved in many aspects of interior decoration, he is especially renowned for his glass. Tiffany lamps, produced during an age when electricity was making gas lighting obsolete, are among the best-known and most popular works by Tiffany Studios.

The *Pond Lily* table lamp is a fine example of the sinuous and fluid forms of Art Nouveau design modelled after nature. A series of flat bronze-cast lily pads forms the base, from which a cluster of twelve tall stems rises to terminate in light shades of iridescent glass. The mould-blown pendant flowers are marked Favrile, a term derived from a seventeenth-century English word meaning "handcrafted". It became the trade name for the lustrous multicolour glass that was a Tiffany specialty. R.P.

■ Carlo Zen had been operating a successful furniture factory in Milan since 1881 when he participated in the Italian section of the Paris Exposition Universelle of 1900 and responded instantly to the Art Nouveau movement that predominated there. In the ensuing decade, the spread of Art Nouveau design through the furniture centres of northern Italy was largely due to manufacturers like Zen, who aimed to please the rising industrial class by offering high-quality furniture in the new style, referred to in Italy as the Stile Floreale or Stile Liberty. As with Art Nouveau in France, emphasis on nature as a source of decoration was a key element.

Zen exhibited this solid mahogany cabinet with an ensemble of furniture at the Turin International Exhibition of Modern Decorative Art in 1902. It exemplifies the designer's wish to break from a reliance on historical furniture styles and become part of the international design movement in Europe. The flat surfaces are decorated with intricately inlaid meandering filaments of brass and silver, and floral patterns of mother-of-pearl; these were characteristic of Italian work and of Zen's furniture in particular. R.P.

Carlo Zen

Verona 1851 – Milan (?) 1918

Cabinet

1902
Mahogany, inlay of mother-of-pearl, silver, brass
198 × 94.5 × 31.8 cm

Purchase, estates of Serge Desroches, Hermina Thau, David R. Morrice, Mary Eccles, Jean Agnes Reid Fleming, G. C. Chisholm, Margaret A. Reid, F. Eleanore Morrice

2001.73.1-5

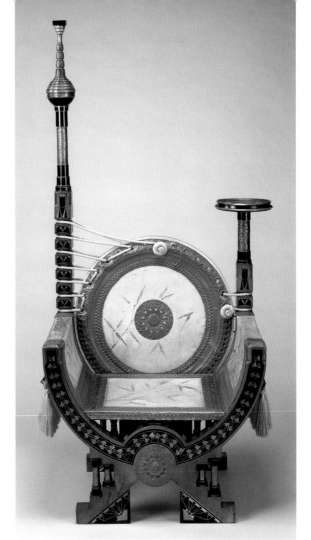

Carlo Bugatti
Milan 1856 – Molsheim,
France, 1940

Armchair

About 1895
Mahogany, parchment, brass, white metal, silk
149 × 75 × 58 cm
Purchase, Deutsche Bank Fund
2002.9.1-2

■ Carlo Bugatti – father of animal sculptor Rembrandt Bugatti and famous car designer Ettore Bugatti – was one of the most original Italian designers working at the end of the nineteenth century. The 1890s was a fruitful period in his career, as exhibited to great acclaim at many international expositions. In 1900 he won a silver medal at the Paris Exposition Universelle, and in 1902 he reached the apogee of his career with his award-winning ensembles at the Turin International Exhibition of Modern Decorative Art.

This chair combines all the features of his work from the 1890s. It reflects the designer's various sources of inspiration, from the curule chair of ancient Rome to Middle Eastern and North African Islamic design. Bugatti's interest in architecture is evident in the playful use of columnar elements and especially in the tall, turned finial that rises above the back of the chair like a minaret. Characteristic of Bugatti's furniture is the parchment decorated with painted Japanese-style brushwork, and the stylized geometric patterns of metal inlaid into the wood. R.P.

Paul Follot
Paris 1877 –
Sainte-Maxime 1941

Piano and Stool

About 1908
Satinwood and ivory marquetry, inlay of various woods, gilded bronze, brass
98.2 × 142 × 162 cm (piano); 57.7 × 46.5 × 46.5 cm (stool)
Cabinetry: Dumontier, Paris
Action: Pleyel, Wolff, Lyon et cie, Paris

Gift from Raymonde Marchand in memory of her father, J. Omer Marchand, architect, from the Montreal Museum of Decorative Arts and from an anonymous donor
1992.Df.9a-b

■ Paul Follot created luxurious, one-of-a-kind pieces of furniture, their rich wood veneers and decorative details far removed from the concerns of mass production. Follot was in charge of the Atelier Pomone, the interior design studio of the Parisian department store Bon Marché. He was also a principal figure of the Société des Artistes Décorateurs, at whose annual Paris Salon he exhibited this piano in 1908.

Though traditional in overall shape, this piano and stool reflect the stylized organic

forms of Art Nouveau, which was prevalent with French designers from the 1890s. However, the ordered placement of the mounts and the attenuated lines of the ivory and wood marquetry represent a more sober, rectilinear version of the style, after the Scottish and Viennese models. The work seems to herald the transition to the classically oriented geometry of Art Deco design that Follot was to pursue in his later career.

The piano belonged to Montreal architect Joseph-Omer Marchand, who studied at the École des Beaux-Arts in Paris from 1893 to 1902 before setting up a practice in Montreal. A proponent of Beaux-Arts architecture, Marchand would have kept in touch with developments in design and architecture in France. R.P.

Gerrit Thomas Rietveld
Utrecht 1888 – Utrecht 1964

Sideboard

1919
Beechwood
104 × 200 × 45 cm
Executed by Gerard van de Groenekan in the 1960s

Purchase, gift of the Lake St. Louis Historical Society

2003.32.1-5

■ The Dutch architect and furniture designer, Gerrit Rietveld, is most readily associated with the De Stijl group of artists and architects in Holland. *De Stijl* was the name of a journal founded in 1917 by this group, whose most famous member was Piet Mondrian. The De Stijl group invented a radical, highly abstract form of expression based on planes of primary colours and an equilibrium of line and form. Rietveld's furniture and his most celebrated architectural commission, the Schröder House (1924) in Utrecht, epitomized De Stijl principles.

The original Rietveld sideboard, designed in 1919, was destroyed in a fire, and so this piece is a reconstruction by Gerard van de Groenekan, after Rietveld's drawings. Van de Groenekan worked as Rietveld's assistant in the furniture-making workshop from its earliest days in 1917, and he took it over in 1924 when Rietveld became more involved in his architecture practice.

The frame of the sideboard is made up of criss-crossed horizontal and vertical rails. There are no corner joints; instead the rails bypass each other and extend out into space like lines that have been severed. To emphasize their independence from each other, the cut-off endgrains have been painted white. The openness of construction allows space to pass around and through the work, creating separate geometric elements that appear to float. The sideboard becomes an abstract composition; its function becomes secondary to the visual effect Rietveld was trying to achieve. R.P.

Josef Hoffmann
Pirnitz, Austria, 1870 –
Vienna 1956

Sitzmaschine
Reclining Chair

About 1908
Beechwood, laminated
wood
112 × 68 × 123 cm
Produced by Jacob &
Josef Kohn, Vienna

Purchase, Deutsche
Bank Fund

2002.51.1-2

■ This celebrated example of modern design was created by architect Josef Hoffmann, a leading figure of the arts in Vienna in the early twentieth century. His architectural masterworks were the Purkersdorf sanatorium (1904-1905) and the Palais Stoclet in Brussels (1905-1911), but he also designed furniture, glass, metalwares, ceramics and textiles. Hoffmann taught at the Vienna School of Applied Arts and was closely associated with the Viennese Secessionist group headed by Gustav Klimt. In 1903, Hoffmann and his colleague Koloman Moser founded the Wiener Werkstätte, workshops dedicated to raising the standard of design and combining the talents of architects, artists and designers in the creation of a total work of art, or *Gesamtkunstwerk.*

Manufactured by Jacob & Josef Kohn, a firm renowned for its bentwood furniture, this reclining chair was first exhibited at the 1908 Vienna *Kunstschau* in Kohn's display for a small country house. Easily mass-produced and assembled, the chair is based on the geometric forms of the rectangle, square and sphere. The sweeping backward curve of the side arms, each made from a single piece, shows a skilful use of the bentwood technique. The chair, with all its nuts and bolts visible, is called *Sitzmaschine*, or "sitting machine", implying that the primary concerns are function and technology. In its radical simplicity and straightforward use of materials, it anticipates the revolutionary plywood chair designs of Alvar Aalto and Marcel Breuer from the 1930s. R.P.

Gio Ponti

Milan 1891 – Milan 1979

The Classical Conversation Vase

1926 (form), about 1927 (decoration)
Hard-paste porcelain
19.5 × 19.6 × 15.3 cm
Produced by Richard-Ginori

Purchase
1933.Dp.4

■ Although Gio Ponti was trained as an architect, early in his career he designed ceramics for the Richard Ginori factories in Milan and in Sesto Fiorentino. As the company's artistic director from 1923 until 1930, Ponti revolutionized its output, designing both unique pieces and mass-produced wares. In 1930, he left the firm but continued collaborating with manufacturers and artists to create designs for everything from furniture to glass. He founded *Domus* magazine in 1928, and was its editor for many years, which placed him at the centre of design developments in Italy.

This title of his urn-shaped vase refers to a series of classical figures and motifs that Ponti began using in 1923 and that appear on many of his ceramic wares. The use of gold and white, favoured in Neoclassical design, enhances the vase's elegant refinement. On one side, a draped female torso symbolizes the arts; on the other, an architect carrying a scroll leans against a table on which lie a stick and a cloak, as well as the architectural attributes of books and compasses. The satyr bust added to this particular example gives a vertical accent. The stylized feather pattern running up the sides is a feature of Ponti's wares called "feathered vases". Such was Ponti's reputation that the Museum bought this vase directly from the factory in 1933. R.P.

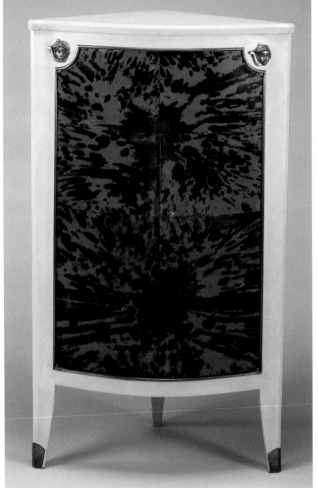

André Arbus
Toulouse 1903 – Paris 1969

Corner Cabinet

1938
Parchment, tortoiseshell, bronze
99.7 × 60.9 × 39 cm
Purchase, Société Générale / Fimat Fund
2001.101.1-2

■ The furniture of André Arbus epitomizes the continuation of the French tradition of fine cabinetmaking in the 1930s and 1940s. It also reflects the classical lines, spare ornament and sober elegance that were fashionable for luxury furnishings of the period. The son of a cabinetmaker, Arbus had a great love of working with wood, and though he included metal detailing in his furniture, he could never give himself over to designing for mass production. In 1937, when he was at the peak of his profession, Arbus was prominently featured at the Paris Exposition Internationale des Arts et Techniques. After the War he was commissioned by the Mobilier National to design furniture for the Élysée Palace and various ministerial offices.

This corner cabinet was part of the interior decoration of a Paris apartment showcased in the October 1938 issue of *Mobilier et Décoration*. It is covered with white parchment, enhancing its luxuriousness and contrasting with the tortoiseshell veneer on the front doors. The veneer's bold abstract pattern enlivens the spare lines of the design, as do the two small bronze heads adorning the upper corners. The heads are the work of Arbus's friend and frequent collaborator, sculptor Vadim Androusov. R.P.

Jean Puiforcat
Paris 1897 – Paris 1945

Soup Tureen

About 1935
Silver, silver gilt
25.4 cm (h.); 27.6 cm (diam.)
Produced by Puiforcat Orfèvre, Paris

Liliane and David M. Stewart Collection
D87.239.1a-b

■ Puiforcat gained an international reputation as one of France's finest goldsmiths in the 1920s. In the next decade, his work moved away from angled and fluted shapes to more rounded and restrained lines, and his attention was directed towards an exploration of the geometry of three-dimensional forms. In this tureen devoid of superfluous ornament, Puiforcat relies on a basic circular shape that appears to swell in bands around the body of the piece. In 1937, Puiforcat exhibited an example of this tureen at the Paris Exposition Internationale des Arts et Techniques, where he had a pavilion devoted to his work.

Puiforcat excelled at setting off the brilliance of silver with materials such as lapis lazuli, jade, dark wood and ivory. Here, it is the warmth and colour of the silver gilt that contrast with the silver's sheen. Although it has the smooth unornamented look of modernist machine-produced work from the 1930s, this tureen was handmade in the tradition of French silverwork. Puiforcat was drawn to the art of sculpture throughout his career, and his understanding of volume and proportion is always apparent. Indeed, this tureen transcends its function to become a piece of sculpture. R.P.

Jean-Marie Gauvreau
Rimouski 1903 – Montreal 1970

Dressing Table and Pouffe

1928-1930
Amboyna, secondary woods, mirror, metal, upholstery
Dressing table: 115 × 149 × 38 cm
Pouffe: 33 cm (h.); 43 cm (diam.)

Purchase, Horsley and Annie Townsend Bequest
1981.Df.5.7; 1981.Df.5.5

■ Jean-Marie Gauvreau was the director of Montreal's École du Meuble for twenty-three years, from the time it was established in 1935. His goal was to promote modern interior design based on traditional principles of quality craftsmanship and materials. Gauvreau designed this dressing table in 1928, during his four years of study at the École Boulle, the famous Parisian cabinetmaking and interior design school. It is part of a seven-piece bedroom set he completed upon his return to Montreal in 1930, and which was acquired from Gauvreau's widow in 1981.

This dressing table is one of the most important pieces of Canadian furniture inspired by the French Art Deco style. It typifies the elegance and glamour of that period, with the choice of amboyna wood reflecting the current French taste for exotic and expensive veneers. Its semicircular handles, chamfered corners and angled edges are also characteristic of French 1920's design. The unembellished geometric form, dominated by a large circular mirror that is echoed in the shape of the pouffe, is based on Art Deco models, notably the work of E. Léon Bouchet, one of Gauvreau's teachers at the École Boulle. Bouchet exhibited a similar bedroom ensemble at the Paris Salon of the Société des Artistes Décorateurs in 1928, and Gauvreau published Bouchet's furniture in his book *Nos intérieurs de demain* the following year. R.P.

Isamu Noguchi

Los Angeles 1904 – New York 1988

Chess Table (model IN 61)

About 1947
Ebonized plywood, aluminum, plastic
48.8 × 86 × 77.6 cm
Produced by Herman Miller Furniture Co., Zeeland, Michigan

Liliane and David M. Stewart Collection, gift of Jay Spectre, by exchange
D85.132.1a-d

■ Although Noguchi is known internationally as a sculptor, he carried out a number of furniture designs and gained a reputation for his paper lamps, which hang like glowing sculptures. This chess table, one of Noguchi's earliest pieces of furniture, was shown in an exhibition on the theme of chess at the Julien Levy Gallery in New York in 1947. Herman Miller began to manufacture the table, but demand for it was limited, and so this is a rare model.

The table is an excellent example of the biomorphic designs that emerged in the late 1940s, inspired by the organic forms in Surrealist works by such artists as Joan Miró and Jean Arp. The interlocking elements and rounded, smooth surfaces refer to Noguchi's own biomorphic sculptures from the 1940s. The way the top of the table appears to balance uncertainly on its base recalls the seemingly precarious arrangement of parts in his sculptures. Here, every element undulates, including the top, which projects downwards in bulbous shapes to meet the curves of the leg supports. The chessboard positions are indicated by yellow and red disks set into saw-cut ebonized plywood. Although in later years Noguchi downplayed the furniture designs from his early career, they reflect his exploration of abstraction in functional objects and his wish to bring sculpture into every aspect of daily life. R.P.

Sven Palmqvist
Lenhovda, Sweden, 1906 – Lenhovda, Sweden, 1984

Ravenna Bowl

About 1948
Blown glass
12.5 cm (h.); 26.7 cm (diam.)
Produced by Orrefors Glasbruk

Liliane and David M. Steward Collection
D95.157.1

■ Sven Palmqvist spent his entire career, from 1930 to 1971, as a designer for the Swedish company Orrefors, whose name is synonymous with Scandinavian glass of outstanding quality and inventive design. Palmqvist's talent lay in the manipulation of the glass medium, and he carried out many successful experiments with innovative techniques.

This bowl is an example of a type of glass Palmqvist invented in 1948, inspired by the Byzantine mosaics of Ravenna, Italy. In this bowl, channels of golden filaments are encased within thick layers of glass to give a mosaic-like pattern of colour. R.P.

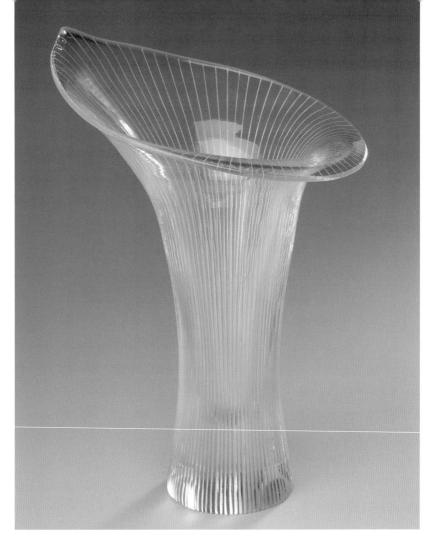

Tapio Wirkkala
Hangö, Finland, 1915 – Espoo 1985

Kanttarelli Vase (model 3280)

1947
Blown glass, machine-engraved
22 × 16.6 × 17.5 cm
Produced by Iittala Lasitehdas, Finland

Liliane and David M. Stewart Collection
D85.134.1

■ Tapio Wirkkala contributed greatly to the success of Scandinavian design in the post-World War II period. In the 1950s, his work in both glass and laminated wood earned him awards and an international reputation, as did his exhibition installations of industrial design. In his later career, Wirkkala continued to experiment with abstract sculptural objects in glass, wood, porcelain and metal.

The organic forms of Wirkkala's work reveal his keen observation of nature. The shape of this vase, flaring gradually upwards and turning outward at the lip in a daring display of technical skill, was inspired by the chanterelle mushroom, after which it is named. The engraved lines that rise up the form of the vase suggest the ridges of the chanterelle's underside. R.P.

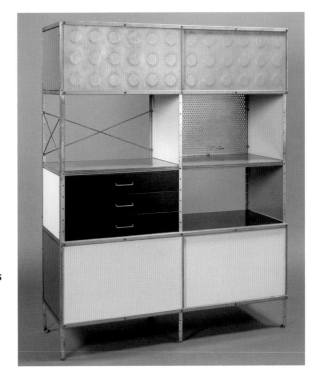

Charles Eames
Saint Louis 1907 –
Saint Louis 1978
Ray Kaiser Eames
Sacramento 1913 –
Los Angeles 1988

Storage Unit
(model ESU 421-C)

About 1949
Zinc-plated steel,
birch-faced plywood,
plastic-coated plywood, lacquered hardboard
148.9 × 119.4 × 42.5 cm
Produced by Herman Miller Furniture Co., Zeeland, Michigan

Liliane and David M. Steward Collection, gift of the American Friends of Canada
through the generosity of Mr. and Mrs. Robert L. Tannenbaum, by exchange
D83.144.1

■ The architect Charles Eames and his wife, Ray, were among the most prominent
American designers of the mid-20th century. They experimented with industrial materials,
in particular plywood and plastics, in order to create furnishings that could be cheaply
mass produced. Function and flexibility were prime features in their furniture, such as this
cabinet. Its design grew out of Charles Eames's experiments in wooden modular furniture in the early 1940s and the couple's success in developing the moulded plywood chair
in 1946. These storage units were designed after the Eames moved to Pacific Palisades,
California, where they built a house in 1948-49, using the same principles of industrial
production of prefabricated, standard parts.

Held together by a steel frame, the cabinet is composed of interchangeable rectangular
units that can be fitted with shelves or drawers. The panels are faced with compressed
plywood or with lacquered hardboard in bright colours. The use of bold primary colours
on the panels recalls the planes of pure colour used by De Stijl architects and designers.
The screws holding the parts together are clearly visible and emphasize the practical construction of this cabinet, which could be enlarged simply by adding units. In its catalogue,
the manufacturer, Herman Millar Furniture Co., illustrated the various options in the size
of the units and in the combination of materials. The flexibility of design and the variety
of surface textures and colours in this modular furniture were intended to make it appeal-
ing not only for the office but also for the home. R.P.

Gio Ponti
Milan 1891 – Milan 1979

Piero Fornasetti
Milan 1913 – Milan 1988

Trumeau Architecture Secretary

1950
Lithographs mounted on hardboard, painted wood,
sheet metal, glass, brass, felt, neon lamp
218 × 80 × 40.5 cm
Produced by Piero Fornasetti

Liliane and David M. Stewart Collection, gift of Senator Alan A. Macnaughton, Sr.
D97.172.1a-k

■ Piero Fornasetti was a master of superimposing two-dimensional decoration onto three-dimensional forms. He delighted in covering everyday objects – whether a porcelain plate, an umbrella stand or a piece of furniture – with designs that he applied as lithographic prints, using black and white for optimal effect.

Fornasetti was attracted to the work of Surrealists like Giorgio De Chirico, Max Ernst and René Magritte, who transformed banal objects into enigmatic forms. Though drawn from many sources, his inspiration was rooted in traditions of Italian mural painting, *trompe-l'oeil* decoration and classical architectural drawing.

A high point of Fornasetti's career was his collaboration with architect Gio Ponti in the 1950s. Together they carried out many interior commissions and furniture designs. The form of the cabinet (called *trumó* in Italian) was designed by Ponti in the spare lines of mid-twentieth-century Italian modernism. Fornasetti, with his skill as a draftsman, eye for fantasy, and sense of graphic design, transformed it into a witty celebration of *trompe-l'oeil*: the doors open out to display, like a theatre set, grand illusionistic spaces of classical Italian architecture. R.P.

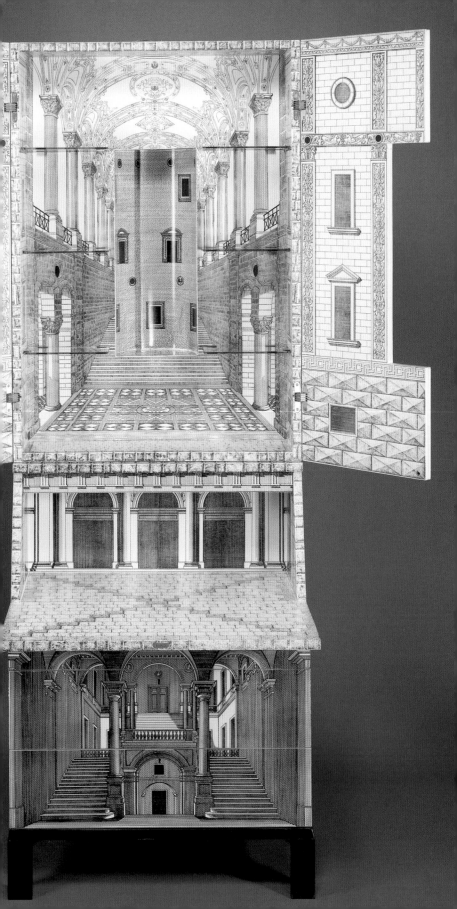

Carl Poul Petersen
Copenhagen 1895 – Montreal 1977

Cigar Box
About 1946-47
Silver
9.3 × 21.8 × 15.8 cm

Gift of the Honourable Serge Joyal, P.C., O.C.

1996.Ds.13

■ Carl Poul Petersen came to Canada in 1929 from his native city, Copenhagen, where he trained under the renowned Danish silversmith Georg Jensen. Upon arriving, Petersen worked for Henry Birks and Sons, the major retailer of silver and jewellery in Canada, but by 1939, he had opened his own studio. Later, Petersen brought his three sons into the business and finally registered his company, C.P. Petersen & Sons Ltd., in 1946. The firm offered a wide range of domestic silverware and flatware in addition to jewellery, presentation pieces and hockey trophies. During the 1950s, the years of his greatest success, Petersen benefited from the international reputation of the Jensen name and also from the popularity of Scandinavian design.

The main body of a Petersen work is sparsely decorated, leaving the lustre and brilliance of the metal to speak for itself. This cigar box is unadorned except for the two magnificent stag beetles, cast in the round, on the cover. The box was probably a special commission, as it represents the only example of this motif in Petersen's production. In addition to the maker's mark, the box is stamped *hand made/sterling* to emphasize the handwork involved in its creation. Silver crafted by Petersen's small workshop was highly prized by clients who wanted something more unique and personal than commercial, mass-produced silver. R.P.

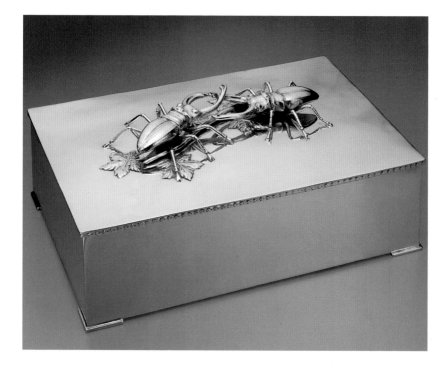

Maurice Brault
Born in Montreal in 1930

Chalice

About 1956
Silver, silver gilt, enamel on copper
10.7 cm (h.); 10.8 cm (diam.)
Gift of the Honourable Serge Joyal, P.C., O.C.
1996.Ds.3

■ Early commissions for silver in Quebec came mainly from religious institutions, and the heritage of ecclesiastical work by Quebec silversmiths from the seventeenth century on is a rich one. In the 1940s, there was a revival of interest in design and craftsmanship of religious applied arts. Maurice Brault's chalice, an outstanding example of the best work that resulted from this revival, is representative of his early domestic and religious silver inspired by modern European design.

After studies in painting at the École des beaux-arts de Montréal, Brault pursued a career as a silversmith. He trained in Belgium, at the École Nationale d'Architecture et d'Art Décoratif, Abbaye de la Cambre, and in 1956, he learned the art of enamelling at the leading Norwegian silver firm Tostrup, in Oslo. This chalice, which was illustrated in the Montreal review *Vie des Arts* in 1956, reflects the emphasis on geometry and simplicity of form that was current in French and Scandinavian silver design. The only decorative element is provided by the juxtaposition of white enamel with the silver-gilt wires and polished silver surfaces. This combination of materials recalls the way the renowned French silversmith Jean Puiforcat introduced ivory and semiprecious stones to contrast their colour and texture with the metal's brilliance.

Brault went on to become a successful goldsmith, and his jewellery has been exhibited both nationally and internationally. R.P.

Verner Panton
Gamtofte, Denmark, 1926 –
Kolding 1998

Chairs (model PA 100)
1960-1967
Luran-S Thermoplastic
83.7 × 49.5 × 56.6 cm (each)
Produced by Vitra for Herman Miller International

Liliane and David M. Stewart Collection, gift of Luc d'Iberville- Moreau
D87.200.1 and D92.209.1

Liliane and David M. Stewart Collection, gift of Herman Miller Furniture Co.
D83.136.1

■ Throughout the twentieth century, designers and manufacturers dreamed of mass-producing a chair made of a single piece that would require no assembly. Moulding a full-size chair in plastic became feasible when synthetic materials like PVC, ABS, vinyl, acrylic and polyurethane foam, which were developed mainly for the aeronautics industry during World War II, were introduced for everyday use. Although it was the Italian designers

who, in the 1960s, paved the way with moulded plastic furniture that was both an engineering achievement and a commercial success, the first single-form chair to reach mass production was the result of collaboration between Danish designer Verner Panton and the Swiss-based firm Vitra.

It took eight years from the time Panton presented his original prototype, in 1960, to find a suitable plastic and a workable one-piece shape sufficiently curved so as to leave room for the sitter's legs and feet while allowing for stacking. The desired bright colouring and smooth, lustrous finish also required considerable experimentation.

The choice of material entailed variations in thickness to create a strong, durable chair that could withstand even prolonged outdoor use. The chair was first made of Baydue, a deformed-and-lacquered rigid polyurethane foam. In 1970, the material was changed to moulded Luran-S thermoplastic. Today, the chair is produced in a structural, integral foam (PUR). It was originally marketed in black, white, blue, green, orange and yellow. D.C.

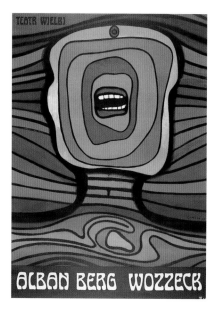

Jan Lenica
Poznan, Poland, 1928 – Berlin 2001

Wozzeck

1964
Poster
98.6 × 72. 6 cm
Produced by WAG

Liliane and David M. Stewart Collection
D90.148.1

■ Posters are beyond question one of the most widely disseminated art form in the world. In Communist Poland, those used for the purpose of publicizing exhibitions, plays and films, often conveyed a metaphorical element that questioned the regime. Created when Poland was under martial law, Jan Lenica's *Wozzeck* poster took on a political dimension and came to symbolize the country's plight. Lenica's style, with its use of vigorous outline and vivid colour, is by turns lyrical, dramatic, expressionist and even surrealistic. Here, the squared mouth set to scream is borrowed from Edvard Munch's *The Scream* (1893). The poster's expressionistic quality echoes the score of Alban Berg's tragic opera about a humble soldier exploited by his superiors. D.C.

■ American graphic designer Milton Glaser also draws inspiration from the history of art to communicate through the medium of graphic design. In *Call for Entries*, a poster announcing the Third National Student Film Festival, Glaser pursues the path of surrealistic imagery and its Pop Art derivative in his use of two disembodied mouths set against a strip of film. The full-lipped mouths, larger than life in imitation of the movie close-up and sequencing animation, function both sensually and as a metonymy. Glaser alludes not only to lip-reading but also to word-of-mouth channels to broadcast the call for entries. D.C.

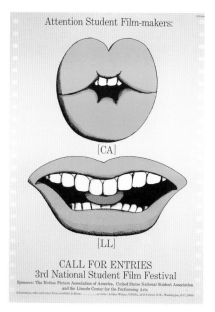

Milton Glaser
Born in New York in 1929

Attention Student Film-makers: Call for Entries

1960s
Poster
86.5 × 60.9 cm
Produced by National Student
Film Association

Liliane and David M. Stewart Collection, gift of
Miljenko and Lucia Horvat
D91.197.1

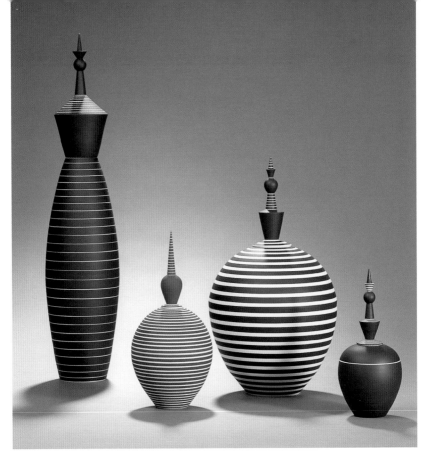

Roseline Delisle
Born in Rimouski in 1952

Covered Jars

Quadruple 9.95	*Triptych 11.95*	*Triptych 12.95*	*Triptych 16.95*
56.3 cm (h.)	27 cm (h.)	37 cm (h.)	21.5 cm (h.)
12.3 cm (diam.)	12.3 cm (diam.)	20.1 cm (diam.)	9 cm (diam.)

1995
Unglazed porcelain, slip

Liliane and David M. Stewart Collection
D95.212-215

■ The cool, mysterious quality of Roseline Delisle's minimalist forms reflects her impeccable craftsmanship. Using a restricted vocabulary, she constantly invents static forms that appear to be imbued with a potential movement. Each vessel balances opposites: symmetry and instability, fragility and strength, seriousness and whimsy. The geometrical forms, based on triangles and spindle shapes, derive from sources as diverse as airplanes, bombs, water towers and the constructivist human figure created by Oskar Schlemmer for the stage in the 1920s. The range of colour is restricted as well, to the white of the clay, and blue and black coloured slips. Delisle's surface decoration is composed of horizontal stripes, rarely of equal width, that set off both an optical play of dark and light and a tension with the vertical shape of each piece. Called "diptych", "triptych" or "quadruple" according to the number of elements, these vessels come apart at sometimes unexpected junctures; a line marks all the joints, some of which fuse during firing. The interiors are also enlivened with colours and striped patterns. D.C.

Frank Gehry
Born in Toronto in 1929

Little Beaver
Armchair and Ottoman
"Experimental Edges" Series

1979
Corrugated cardboard
Armchair: 86.3 × 85.6 × 104.1 cm
Ottoman: 43.2 × 49.5 × 55.9 cm
Produced by New City Editions
Liliane and David M. Stewart Collection, by exchange
D92.132.1a-b

■ Frank Gehry is known for his experiments with rudimentary materials in furniture design, and in the body of work entitled "Experimental Edges" he pursues his investigation of the potential of cardboard. True to his vision, Gehry had chosen this common industrial material in the early 1970s to create the controversial but respected collection "Easy Edges".

Exploiting cardboard's raw look and connotation of cheapness, Gehry created highly spirited furniture. The shaggy, sprawling sculptural forms of the "Experimental Edges" Series have little in common with the taut linearity of their predecessors, however. Here, Gehry works with the versatile material by means of overlapping and removals, taking advantage of its rich texture and varied thickness while retaining its roughness. Surprisingly solid, cardboard can withstand tough treatment and requires little maintenance. Gehry designed a wide range of chairs in a variety of shapes for the "Experimental Edges" Series, frequently in parody of overstuffed chairs.

Contrary to the earlier series, which was a commercial success, "Experimental Edges" was produced in a limited edition, more as a gallery item than a commodity. The *Little Beaver* armchair and ottoman were named after nature's architect. Layer upon layer of cardboard mimic the way beaver lodges are built. D.C.

■ The desire for functionalism and the need for efficient production methods have led twentieth-century silversmiths to depart from traditional methods and forms, and to introduce new techniques and materials like stainless steel and modern alloys. Modern tenets took hold throughout the century, yet a diversity of styles held sway by the century's end. Collaborative ventures between manufacturers, silversmiths, designers and architects also injected a stimulating freshness and vitality into silver design.

Italian silversmith Lino Sabattini represents one of the numerous concurrent trends in post-war modernism. Believing the making of useful objects to be the result of a creative act, he focuses on aesthetic factors rather than the constraints imposed by industrial production. A fine example of Sabattini's elegant classicism and technical mastery, the elliptical cylinder-shaped vase *Inquietante* is characterized by a rhythmic unity that accentuates its formal and functional logic. The vase investigates the notion of transparency, while the columns separating it into two parts emphasize the luminous qualities of the material and the lightness of the form. D.C.

■ Perched on six zigzag legs, the luxury silver fruit dish *Murmansk* is among the first luxury items designed by Ettore Sottsass for the Milan design group Memphis. In harmony with Memphis' pluralistic aesthetics, which allow historical styles and periods to intermingle, Sottsass is interested in popular culture and the traditions of the East and the Third World, as well as being a great admirer of unspoiled nature. This fruit dish, though elegant and functional, nonetheless effectively evokes the cold and isolation of the exotic Russian city from which it takes its name. D.C.

Lino Sabattini
Born in Correggio, Italy, in 1925

Vase
"Inquietante" Series

1988
Silver-plated brass alloy
42 × 13.7 × 10.2 cm
Produced by Sabattini Argenteria

Liliane and David M. Stewart Collection, gift of Lino Sabattini

D90.188.1

Ettore Sottsass
Born in Innsbruck, Austria, in 1971

Murmansk Fruit Dish

1982
Silver-plated brass
30.4 × 35.5 × 35.5 cm
Produced by Rossi e Arcandi for Memphis

Liliane and David M. Stewart Collection, anonymous gift

D91.423.1

Gaetano Pesce

Born in La Spezia, Italy, in 1939

Armchair

"I Feltri" Series

1986

Wool felt soaked with polyester, hemp,
stainless steel, cotton

127.6 × 105.4 × 67.3 cm

Produced by Cassina

Liliane and David M. Stewart Collection
D98.159.1a-b

■ Trained as an architect and industrial designer, Gaetano Pesce is noted as much for the expressive forms of the objects, furniture and interiors he creates as for his experiments and discoveries involving new materials and technological processes. Pesce favours thermosetting plastics, such as resin and unsaturated polyesters, which are ideal for mass production. Yet, even with mass-produced goods, he strives for non-uniformity.

In the "I Feltri" Series, Pesce makes use of felt, an inexpensive, ancient, almost shapeless material composed of fibres bound with glue. The armchairs are easy to manufacture. They consist of a large semicircle cut from a blanket of industrial felt. The felt is soaked with polyester resin in amounts that vary according to the degree of rigidity desired. It is then placed in a mould and subjected to high heat, which hardens it into a solid supporting base and flexible top. The hemp stitching on the exterior helps hold the resin-soaked seat in place while adding a hand-made touch. The brilliantly hued, quilted upholstery is attached with snaps and can be removed for cleaning or replacement. The chair back, also replaceable, can be folded down like a giant collar or wrapped around the sitter like a cloak. A contemporary variation of a traditional wing chair, the "I Feltri" armchair represents the basic values of comfort, warmth and relaxation. D.C.

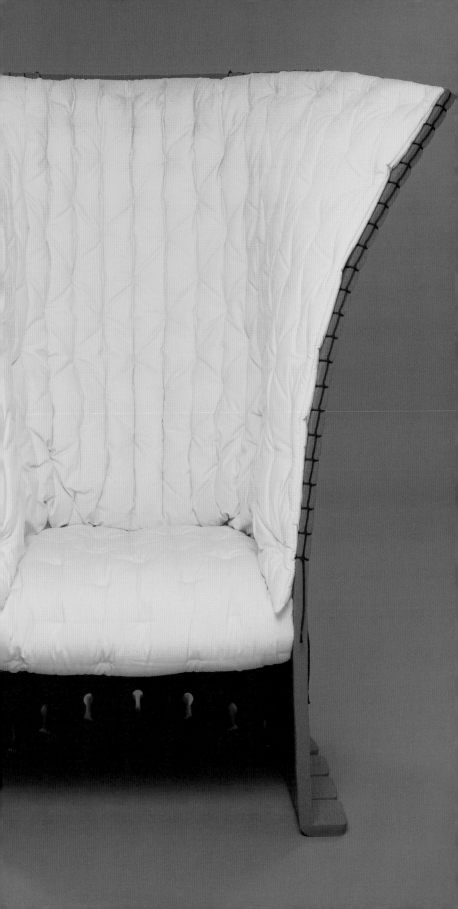

Art Smith
New York 1917 –
New York 1982

Lava Bracelet

About 1946
Silver
5.7 × 14.9 × 7.3 cm
Liliane and David
M. Stewart Collection
D87.213.1

Jan Matthesius
Born in Amstelveen,
Netherlands, in 1950

Not Enough! Brooch

1989
Anodized aluminum, paint
15 × 15.5 × 1.8 cm
Liliane and David
M. Stewart Collection
D98.119.1

Barbara Paganin
Born in Venice in 1961

Bamboo Brooch

1993
Gold-plated silver
2.5 × 12.7 cm
Liliane and David M. Stewart
Collection, gift of Charon
Kransen
D95.218.1

Michael Becker
Born in Paderborn,
Germany, in 1958

Brooch

1993
Gold
4.6 × 8 cm
Liliane and David
M. Stewart Collection
D95.220.1

■ The term "studio jewellery" refers to jewellery created by individual artists, usually working alone in their studio and controlling all stages of production, from design to finished product. The modernist jewellery that developed in the United States after World War II played a significant role in the evolution of the studio jewellery movement. Largely self-taught, American designers explored avenues independent of European silverwork traditions. Finding inspiration in the major currents in modern art, they developed a number of highly innovative techniques. The jewellery of Art Smith combines a primitivist sensibility, associated with his Afro-American roots, and a taste for dramatic effect and biomorphic forms. His *Lava* bracelet is notable not only for its large size but also for its composition, particularly the two undulating amoebic forms hammered on top of one another.

Since the 1950s, studio jewellery has established itself as one of the most dynamic forms of contemporary expression. The 1970s saw a revolution in creative approaches, techniques and the use of both new and recycled materials. A multitude of trends sprang from artistic movements, experimentation and the simple desire for self-expression and story-telling, as in Jan Matthesius' brooch entitled *Not Enough!* Other artists, attracted by the structural and geometric aspects of jewellery, assembled varied elements to produce a coherent three-dimensional whole. The brooches by Barbara Paganin and Michael Becker illustrate this approach. D.C.

Dale Chihuly

Born in Tacoma,
Washington, in 1941

Cadmium Yellow Seaform Set with Red Lip Wraps

"Seaform" Series
1990
Blown glass
43.2 × 61 × 91.5 cm

Liliane and David M. Stewart Collection, gift of the American Friends of Canada
through the generosity of Jay Spectre
D90.219.1a-j

■ The extravagant glass works of Dale Chihuly possess a unique energy and movement.
Their originality arises from Chihuly's belief that glass-making is not bound by any fixed
rules. He therefore constantly extends its limits, spurred on by the spontaneity of the
process and the immediacy of the material. The vessels he creates, hardly utilitarian, play
with form to evoke natural phenomena. Each new series invents works that emphasize
shape, colour and surface.

The "Seaform" Series entails pure movement and lightness of form as well. Its undulating shapes recall the spiral and coil growths found particularly in marine creatures like
molluscs. Chihuly's precariously assembled sculptural forms re-create the fecundity of
nature: smaller bowls and nodules lodge within more expansive vessels, interacting like
living elements momentarily suspended in an ambient fluid. In *Cadmium Yellow Seaform
Set with Red Lip Wraps*, the wavy sides, swirling lips and progressively spaced stripes look
as if they had been shaped by eddying water or gusting wind. D.C.

Masanori Umeda

Born in Kanagawa, Japan, in 1941

Getsuen Armchair [Moonlit Garden Armchair]

1990
Cotton velour, polyurethane foam, Dacron, polyethylene, lacquered iron, steel, wood
83.2 × 100.4 × 92.1 cm
Produced by Edra

Liliane and David M. Stewart Collection, gift of Maurice Forget
D93.259.1

■ From the late 1960s to the early 1980s, Japanese designer Masanori Umeda found himself working in Italy, first at the A. & P. G. Castiglioni Studio, then as a design consultant to Olivetti. He also participated in the Memphis group for which he designed his famous *Tawaraya* boxing-ring (1981) and his *Ginza* bookcase (1982) with its robot-like shape. After founding his Tokyo design studio in 1979, currently known as U-Meda Design, Umeda continues his collaboration with Italian firms. In the early 1990s, in concert with Edra, he designed a series of flower seating, which includes the *Anthurium* coffee table (1990), the *Getsuen* armchair (1990), the *Orchid* chair (1991), the *Rose* chair (1991), and the *Soshun* stool (1992).

The *Getsuen* armchair is particularly comfortable with its wraparound padded petals. A formal and technological feat, the armchair consists of polyurethane foam and Dacron, here upholstered in bright blue cotton velvet. The flower shape conceals a steel structure with sections in shaped wood. Green wheels added to the back enhance its air of frivolity. Yet Umeda's intentions are far from being trivial. He consciously reverts to floral motifs in the hope of recalling his native country, a culture rooted in traditional harmony with the environment, contrary to its recent affluence as a materialistic society. *Getsuen*, with its broad petals springing from a small green stem, is reminiscent of a *Kikyo* flower, a Chinese bellflower that blooms every summer in the designer's own garden. D.C.

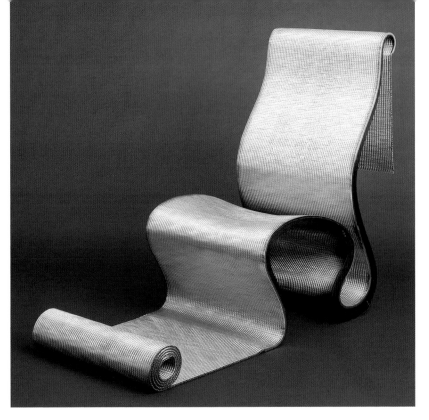

Ron Arad
Born in Tel Aviv in 1951

London Papardelle Chair

1992
Steel, stainless steel
105 × 59.6 × 90 cm (extended: 273 cm)
Produced by One Off Ltd.

■ After attending the Jerusalem Academy of Art, Ron Arad completed architecture stud-ies in England, where he stayed to become Britain's most celebrated designer. Experimenting with various aspects of design in his One Off studio, founded in 1981, Arad draws inspiration from a wide range of influences, from visual artists Marcel Duchamp and Meret Oppenheim to architect-designer Jean Prouvé. His distinctive furniture cre-ations, primarily in steel, are fashioned more like sculpture than furniture; yet, they are entirely functional.

The woven stainless steel used in this chair is the same material used for conveyor belts in the food industry. The seamless fabric, with a soft, light-reflecting quality, provides a robust yet flexible structure. Welded onto partially blackened steel side strips for strength, it unwinds like a ribbon, its undulations creating the seating elements. Excess material at the foot can be either rolled into a footrest or uncoiled like a rug. Thus, the chair is much more comfortable than it would appear from its tough, industrial look. The chair's name, *London Papardelle,* is also a reference to food, based on the smooth, broad variety of pasta served by an Italian restaurant in London.

In 1994, Arad signed an exclusive agreement with the Italian manufacturer Marzorati Ronchetti to produce his furniture. Made prior to this arrangement, the Museum's lim-ited edition example is slightly wider than newer production pieces. D.C.

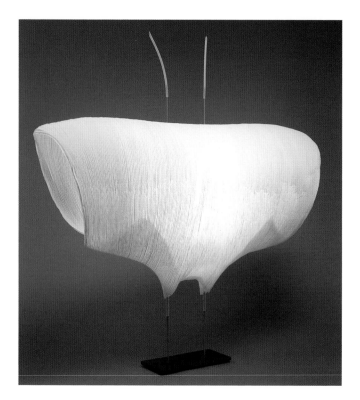

Ingo Maurer
Born in Reichenau,
Germany, in 1932
Dagmar Mombach
and team

Samurai **Table Lamp**

1998
Stainless steel, silicone, paper, glass
82 × 79 × 29 cm
Produced by Ingo Maurer GmbH

Liliane and David M. Stewart Collection
D99.140.1a-b

■ Since the invention of the light bulb around 1880, the formal and functional demands of designing electric lighting have inspired many innovative solutions. Of the handful of designers who shaped the development of lighting, none has had so great an impact as Ingo Maurer. His approach is the result of a highly personal visual and mechanical language. After designing his first lamp in 1966, Maurer went on to build up a unique organization that both designs and manufactures lamps and lighting fixtures. He favours an updated craftsmanship that synthesizes craft skills with industrial techniques, so that his creations display all the qualities of objects customized to the taste of discriminating users. Yet, Maurer's lamps are rich in playful connotations, as shown by their whimsical names – *Ya Ya Ho* and *Bibibibi*, for example.

The *Samurai* lamp's minutely folded paper shade, developed by Dagmar Mombach assisted by Hagne Sezech, was inspired by the traditional Japanese paper lantern as revisited by Isamu Noguchi, but it may also make reference to the upended and pleated dresses of Issey Miyake, for whom Maurer once designed the lighting of an exhibition. *Samurai* is from the "MaMo Nouchies" collection, the name being a compound of MAurer, MOmbach and NOguchi. Each piece represents a perfect harmony of the designers' delicate tactile values and the technical requirements of safe, economical and effective lighting. D.C.

Shiro Kuramata
Tokyo 1934 – Tokyo 1991

Acrylic Stool with Feathers

1990
Acrylic, anodized
aluminum, feathers
54 × 30.9 × 40.5 cm
Produced by
Ishimaru Co.

Liliane and David
M. Stewart Collection
D98.145.1

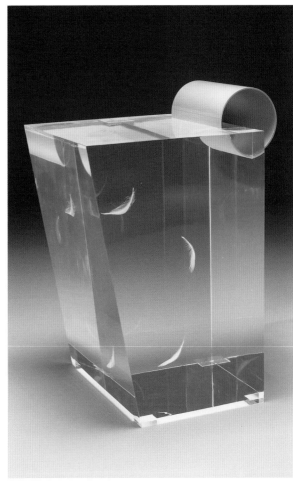

■ From the mid-1960s, Shiro Kuramata's revolutionary approach to furniture and interiors put him at the leading edge of design in Japan. Combining the Japanese concept of the unity of the arts with a fascination for contemporary Western culture – high and low – he invented a design vocabulary at once typically Japanese and highly personal. Kuramata drew inspiration not only from childhood memories but also from Duchamp's mischievous ready-mades, the minimalist sculptures of Dan Flavin and Donald Judd, and his association with the Memphis design group in Milan from 1981 to 1983. He transcended the primary function of everyday objects like tables and chairs to imbue them with Surrealist and Minimalist ideals, and he made ingenious use of industrial materials, particularly steel cable and mesh, glass, aluminum and acrylic.

Kuramata first used acrylic in 1968, but it was not until the late 1980s that he realized the material's full potential. His exploration of the notion of transparency and dematerialization reached its apogee in *Acrylic Stool with Feathers*, whose simple but elegant silhouette – an aluminum cylinder serves as a backrest against the massive acrylic block that forms the seat – is suffused with poetry. The work builds on Kuramata's previous embedding of artificial roses in acrylic for the *Miss Blanche* armchair. Here, the eternally suspended feathers flutter as if swept by the breeze. D.C.

Reiko Sudo
Born in Niihari, Japan, in 1953

Nails **Fabric** "Scrapyard" Series

1994
Rayon
Produced by the
Nuno Corporation

Purchase, Mitsui Canada
Foundation Fund
2001.83

Patched Paper **Fabric**

1997
Polyester, washi paper
Produced by the
Nuno Corporation

Purchase, Mitsui Canada
Foundation Fund
2001.81

Agitfab **Fabric**

1992
Polyester, newsprint
Produced by the
Nuno Corporation

Purchase, Mitsui Canada
Foundation Fund
2001.80

■ Inventive use of new techniques and materials distinguishes the textiles of contemporary Japanese designers like Reiko Sudo. Co-founder and chief designer of Nuno Corporation, Sudo creates fabrics that display the freshness and boldness of her imagination not only as a highly skilled artisan but as an artist. She continually devises astonishing effects that expand the boundaries and possibilities of fabric, such as a process whereby layers are built up and then manually cut or chemically dissolved to reveal each woven surface.

In the "Scrapyard" Series, barbed wire, nails and iron plates are recycled and weathered to become the printing tool. In this example from that series, nails treated with iron oxide until they will leave an imprint are used to create patterns that can be varied according to the placement of the nails and the length of exposure. In *Patched Paper*, Sudo wove thin strips of Mino washi paper into the fabric of polyester organdy. The paper strips were then hand cut to achieve a random pattern. In *Agitfab*, scraps of newspaper were scattered over polyester organdy, portions of which were then heat-sealed under polyurethane. When the fabric was washed, only the polyurethane "pouches" remained as legible design elements. Subsequently, the designer abbreviated the process so that the newspaper scraps are dipped into liquid plastic before being heat-bonded to the fabric. D.C.

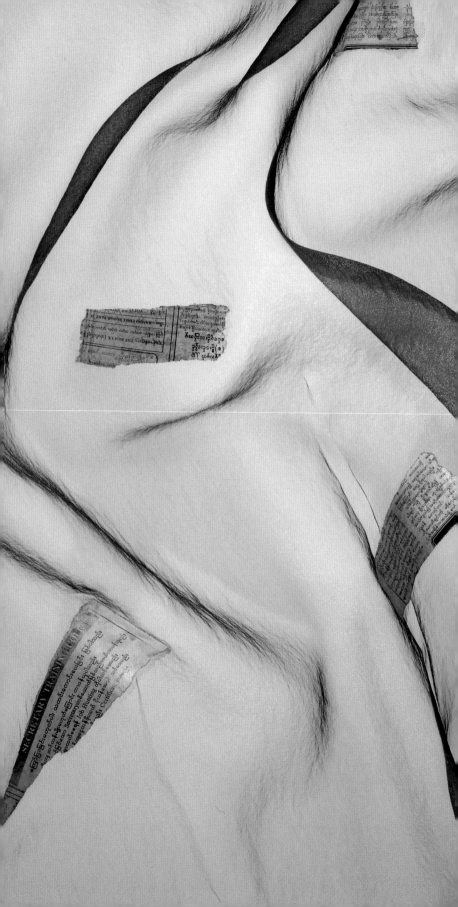

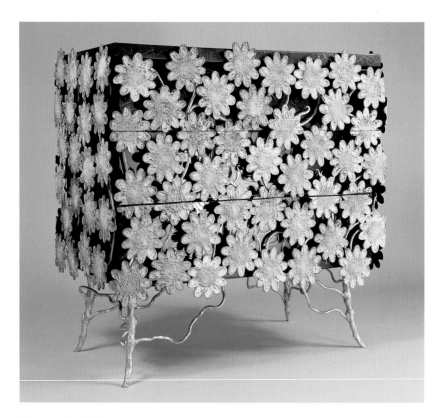

Hubert Le Gall
Born in Lyons in 1961

Anthémis Chest of Drawers

1999
Wood covered with engraved resin, painted bronze and gold-leafed bronze
105 × 110 × 60 cm

Purchase, gift of The Macdonald Stewart Foundation and The Museum Campaign 1988-1993 Fund
2001.79.1-5

■ Hubert Le Gall is a sculptor, painter, decorator and exhibition designer. In his enthusiasm for decorative art, he also creates furniture, rugs, lighting fixtures and so forth, both one-of-a-kind pieces and limited series. His furniture is a hybrid; neither exclusively art nor exclusively utilitarian, partaking of both natures at once. Emphasizing contrasts, Le Gall puts a combination of materials – resin, wood and bronze – to intelligent use. The wooden framework of the *Anthémis* chest of drawers is encased in resin, incised with floral motifs and decorated with patinated bronze flowers. These endow the work with a distinct sculptural force and attest to Le Gall's ingenuity, mastery of the material and a certain poetical whimsy. Evoking a field of spring flowers, the chest returns to the pleasure of plant forms, to the slightly rough tactility suggested by living matter. It also illustrates Le Gall's concern for the beautiful and for current taste. True to his times, which are rife with stylistic encounters and ruled by the myth of individual creativity, Le Gall harks back to eighteenth-century cabinetry, as have a number of French decorators before him, such as Jacques-Émile Ruhlmann, Jules Leleu and André Arbus. The new language he invents ignores fashion but respects the spirit of opulence. D.C.

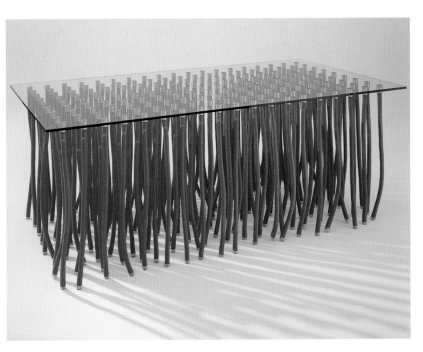

Fabio Novembre
Born in Lecce, Italy, in 1966

Org **Table** (model OG/4)

2001
Glass, polypropylene, steel, cord, brushed stainless steel
73.2 × 100 × 200 cm
Produced by Cappellini International Interiors

Liliane and David M. Stewart Collection
2002.57.1-172

■ Architect Fabio Novembre belongs to the new generation of Italian designers who unabashedly draw inspiration from their country's legendary joie de vivre. Ignoring the trends and fashions of the moment, Novembre focuses on visual concerns that promote innovation and raw emotion. His interior designs – particularly for shops, bars and restaurants – are sumptuous, yet cheerful and sensual. In his quest to foster a total experience, Novembre uses bright colours in tactile surroundings; he designs imaginative spaces that stimulate all the senses, in the manner of an artwork.

The same is true of his furniture. The first piece of furniture he designed was for Cappellini, a manufacturer that relies on the ingenuity of young designers from Italy and elsewhere to revitalize its collections. Favouring seductive charm and luxurious taste, and pursuing new paths that sometimes result in limited editions, Cappellini has succeeded in maintaining a high production quality.

Novembre's very whimsical *Org* table fits in with this approach. Its glass top rests on a base with many legs, not all of them structural, however. Available in a variety of shapes and formats (square, round, rectangular, as a console table), and colours (red, white, black), this intriguing and pleasing table leaves it up to the guest to decide whether to sit down at it . . . or not. D.C.

Index of artists